"*The Pessimist's Son* is a profoundly moving account of the Kimel family's experiences during World War II. Alexander Kimel's narrative spans his childhood in Russian-occupied Poland, his time in the Rohatyn ghetto, and his survival of the ghetto's liquidation. Meanwhile, his wife Eva's remarkable story of perseverance under Nazi occupation, including her hiding in the Ukrainian forests, is equally powerful. Their son Martin thoughtfully edited this history to breathe life into their stories, offering a poignant tribute to the human spirit's capacity for resilience in the face of unimaginable adversity. As the last remaining Holocaust survivors pass away, their stories become increasingly precious, and this account serves as a vital link to the past. The Kimel family's story is a testament to the rich Jewish heritage of Eastern Europe, which the Holocaust and its aftermath tragically ravaged. Through a dialogue between generations, this testimony is a powerful reminder of the importance of preserving the memories of those who lived through this dark period and the enduring legacy of the Holocaust."

— **Prof. Daniel Blatman, The Hebrew University of Jerusalem,
Chief Historian, Warsaw Ghetto Museum, Poland**

"This remarkable book is an account of the lives of two holocaust survivors, Alexander Kimel and Ewa Najnudel.... The book is based on a memoir by Alexander, edited by his son Martin, who has written an account of Ewa's survival and the subsequent history of the couple. It provides a moving analysis of the Nazi mass murder of the Jews of Poland and of the situation of Jews under the Polish communist regime from liberation until 1956. It is essential reading for all interested in the fate of the Jews in East-Central Europe under Nazism and Communism."

— **Antony Polonsky, Emeritus Professor of Holocaust Studies, Brandeis University,
Chief Historian, Global Education Outreach Project, Museum of Polish Jews in Warsaw**

"This manuscript bridges the past and present, weaving a profound dialogue across generations. Authored by the son of Holocaust survivors, it delves into the harrowing experiences of his parents during one of history's darkest periods. The narrative, rich with personal anecdotes and historical context, offers a unique lens into the lives of survivors and the enduring impact of their stories on their descendants. It's a moving testament to resilience and the unbreakable bonds of family, providing invaluable insights into the collective memory of the Holocaust and its lasting legacy."

— **Dr. Daniela Ozacky-Stern, Western Galilee College, Israel**

"A compelling memoir of Jewish life in Russian-occupied Poland in World War 2, the German invasion of Russia, and life underground during the ensuing Holocaust of bullets. Alexander Kimel's story is interwoven at every step with his son Martin's magnificent work of narrative nonfiction to provide a wide-angle view with other first-hand accounts and the larger historical context, including the parallel survivor journey of Alexander's wife, Eva. Beautifully written and deeply researched, *The Pessimist's Son* is a riveting testament to the ingenuity and resilience of the human spirit when faced with impossible circumstances. Everyone should read it."

— **Scott Lenga, author of *The Watchmakers***

"In combining his father Alexander's difficult to comprehend memoir of his harrowing and courageous experience during the Second World War as a teenager, together with the riveting story of his mother, Eva, then a young girl, and her remarkable survival in the Ludwipol ghetto and then in an adjacent forest, Martin Kimel has produced another significant and poignant account of the Holocaust. Demonstrating an extensive knowledge of primary and secondary sources, Kimel knows firsthand the Eastern European setting where these tragic stories unfold. The result is a compelling book that deserves a large audience."

— **Allan Levine, Author of** *Fugitives of the Forest*

"This poignant book is a full-length memoir, meticulously annotated and enriched with research by the son of Holocaust survivors. It offers an inspiring tool for Holocaust education and beyond."

— **Françoise Ouzan, Author of** *How Young Holocaust Survivors Rebuilt Their Lives* **and** *True to My God and Country.*

"Alexander Kimel's Holocaust writings have been widely reprinted, used by educators, and cited by scholars. Indeed, Alex contributed gripping and powerful autobiographical notes for my book on Nazi ghettos, *Life in the Ghetto during the Holocaust.* We are fortunate that we now have his full-length memoir, thoughtfully edited and annotated by his son. In addition, Martin Kimel has extended Alex's story past liberation to include his time in Communist Poland and written his mother's own harrowing story of hiding in the forests of Ukraine. In its excellent 35 chapters, Martin Kimel has done justice to the poignant accounts of Alex and Eva Kimel. Alex and Eva's voices come through distinctly and powerfully as they relate their harrowing experiences before, during, and after the Holocaust. Both are excellent storytellers who relate their accounts in a clear and vivid way. They relate their experiences under both Nazi and Soviet rule and the horrible antisemitism they experienced in post-war Poland. Martin Kimel has done extensive research and has provided very helpful annotations and explanatory notes so that even readers who are not experts on the Holocaust can understand his parents' experiences. This book is a must-read for anyone interested in the Holocaust in Poland."

— **Eric Sterling, Professor of English, Auburn University at Montgomery**

The Pessimist's Son

A Holocaust Memoir of Hope

The Pessimist's Son

A Holocaust Memoir of Hope

Alexander Kimel
and Martin Kimel

CHERRY ORCHARD BOOKS
2025

Library of Congress Cataloging-in-Publication Data

Copyright © 2025, Martin Kimel

ISBN 9798887198002 (hardback)
ISBN 9798887198019 (paperback)
ISBN 9798887198026 (Adobe PDF)
ISBN 9798887198033 (ePub)

Published by Cherry Orchard Books,
an imprint of Academic Studies Press

1007 Chestnut Street
Newton, MA 02464, USA
www.academicstudiespress.com

For Mom and Dad, who did not live to see this book published but whose immense bravery throughout their lives continues to inspire us.

For my grandfather Natan and my grandmother Pesia, as well as all the other relatives I never met who perished during the Shoah.

For David and Sarah, who always make us proud.

For Miriam, who encouraged this labor of love and who put up with my talking about the Holocaust *way* too much at times.

So much was lost . . . , but the final word of Jewish history is not death and destruction, but the remnant that survived, that rebuilt their lives and that dared to face the abyss by remembering.

—Michael Berenbaum, Introduction to *Remembering Rohatyn*

Contents

Foreword	1
Acknowledgments	9
Co-Author's Note on the Use of *Yizkor* Books and Rohatyn Memoirs	11
Zachor—Remember, a Holocaust Prayer, by Alexander Kimel	15
Maps	17
Part 1: Alex's Memoir, Edited and Annotated	21
Chapter 1—The Shtetl	23
Chapter 2—Shtetl Life and the Mystery of the Survival of the Jewish People	35
Chapter 3—My World Collapses	43
Chapter 4—The Russians: Podhajce Becomes a "Workers' Paradise"	49
Chapter 5—Refugees in Rohatyn	57
Chapter 6—The Germans, the Ukrainians, and the Pogrom (Summer 1941)	61
Chapter 7—The Judenrat (Jewish Council)	65
Chapter 8—First, the Ghetto; Then, Awful News	69
Chapter 9—The Labor Camp: Skipping Out on Skalat	75
Chapter 10—The First Action (March 1942)	79
Chapter 11—Building a Bunker, Breaking the Ice (Literally), and My Burning Shame	87
Chapter 12—The Yom Kippur Action (September 1942)	93
Chapter 13—Caught Again: The December Action (1942)	99
Chapter 14—The Baby and the Bunker	103

Chapter 15—My Mother Dies	111
Chapter 16—Luba Goes to Podhajce	113
Chapter 17—An Unpleasant Surprise	117
Chapter 18—The Resistance Group/"The Hope"	121
Chapter 19—Escape and Liquidation (May–June 1943)	125
Chapter 20—In Hiding	133
Chapter 21—The Final Ordeal, Then . . . Liberation!	143
Chapter 22—Our Return to Civilization	147
Photographs	155
Part 2: Eva's Story of Life, Death, and Survival, by Martin Kimel	169
Chapter 23—Fleeing Radom (September 1939)	171
Chapter 24—Ludwipol (Summer 1941)	175
Chapter 25—The Nazis Murder Eva's Father	179
Chapter 26—Into the Woods	183
Chapter 27—Liberation . . . Then Bitter Tears	189
Chapter 28—Some Reunions in Łódź: "Everyone's Been Killed"	191
Chapter 29—The Destruction of Jewish Radom	195
Chapter 30—"Radom-in-Exile" and Motek's Murder	203
Chapter 31—Antisemitism: From Łódź to Legnica	209
Part 3: Alexander and Eva Kimel	211
Chapter 32—1956: Quitting Poland for Israel: A Knife in Eva's Heart	213
Chapter 33—Starting over yet Again in a New Country: Israel to America	217
Chapter 34—1967: Poland Denies Eva's Request to Attend Her Stepfather's Funeral	221
Chapter 35—The "Refugees" Achieve the American Dream—Awe and Gratitude from the Next Generation	223

We Will Never Forget—Auschwitz, by Alexander Kimel   231

Holocaust Lamentations, by Alexander Kimel   233

Relatives Known to Have Perished in the Holocaust   235

Endnotes   237

Bibliography   277

Index   285

About the Authors   291

Foreword

I remember when I discovered that my parents had foreign accents. I was in elementary school in Teaneck, New Jersey, and my best friend, Kenny Greenquist (who was known to tell a tall tale or two), told me.

"No, they don't," I answered immediately.

It turned out Kenny was right. Who knew? Not only did my mom and dad speak with a foreign accent, but it was also a pretty heavy Polish accent, not some faint trace of one. For instance, they had problems pronouncing the "th" sound. When my mother spoke of eating a thick steak, it sounded like, a "tick steak."

It wasn't that I hadn't heard native English speakers. I was one myself. So was my sister, Pam. And so were all my friends, most of their parents, and all my teachers—Mrs. Nagel, Miss Levine, and Mrs. Castro. The way they all spoke unaccented American English sounded normal to me. But the way my parents spoke also sounded normal to me. And virtually all of my relatives of their generation also hailed from Poland, as did nearly all my parents' friends. When they spoke English, they all sounded like my parents. Somehow, I didn't notice the difference in accents between them and American-born speakers.

I don't remember what, specifically, I did with the revelation that my parents spoke with an accent. But I think I already knew that my parents were different from my friends' parents in other ways. My parents occasionally made grammatical mistakes when they spoke English, or they sometimes just phrased things in a way most Americans wouldn't. They didn't tell stories about their American schooling. Unlike my friends' parents, mine were figuring out American culture for the first time, feeling their way as they went, for themselves and for Pam and me. Some adjustments were easier to make than others. For example, Thanksgiving was a new holiday to them but, unlike Christmas, it was a secular one our family could celebrate, and we learned after a while to substitute pumpkin pie (which I liked) for potato kugel (which I never loved).

Another way my family was different was that we couldn't just hop in our car to visit grandma. My mother's mother still lived in Poland, in the same city as my Aunt Regina, Uncle Janusz, and their daughters, Małgosia and Iwona. Poland was a Communist country, under the boot of the Soviet Union. That meant my grandma (*babcia*, in Polish), aunt, and uncle had to ask their government for permission to leave the country, even for short trips. My aunt died young, and I remember seeing her only once: the one time she and Janusz visited us. The Communist regime was more permissive in terms of allowing Babcia (a pensioner) out of the country. We would go several years without seeing her and then she would come for an extended stay with us. Other than that, communication was primarily by post. My mother thought that the mail to and from Poland, which took at least a week in each direction by plane (there was no email then, of course), may have been opened and read by Communist authorities before being delivered.

Children often want to blend in with the crowd. But this was never the case with me. Ethnic pride started becoming popular in America with the 1977 broadcast of Alex Haley's *Roots*, the blockbuster TV series about an African American family and its enslaved ancestor. Even before then, however, I liked that my family was different. We were Americans—my parents were naturalized citizens; my sister and I were born in New York City—but our parents were also Polish Jews. It wasn't that my parents had any great love for Poland. My parents taught my sister and me from an early age that people in Poland used the term "Pole" strictly to mean Polish Catholics. Jews like my parents, who were born and raised in Poland and spoke perfect Polish—with perfect Polish accents—were not Poles. But our *Yiddishkeit*, our Jewish culture and customs, derived from Poland. (My Ashkenazi pronunciation of Hebrew in synagogue drives my wife, who once lived in Israel, crazy.) Our family was also international. In addition to Poland, we had relatives in Canada, France, Belgium, Israel, and Germany (among other places). My parents spoke many languages, as did other Polish-born relatives. At family gatherings, my uncle might tell a joke in Yiddish that my parents' generation would find hilarious. The joke invariably fell flat when translated, usually because it involved a play on words. I felt that my family was special.

Early on, Pam and I knew that we also were special because our parents had survived something called the Holocaust, which had killed a lot of our family. Hitler had tried to erase Jews from the planet, and our parents believed it was imperative that the Jewish people continue. But our parents never let the Holocaust (*Shoah*, in Hebrew) dominate our lives—or theirs. They loved to dance and spend time with their large group of (Polish-speaking) friends.

Foreword | 3

Our parents did speak about the war at times, for which I am very grateful. In researching this book, I was surprised and disappointed to learn that some cousins of my generation know next to nothing about their parents' experiences. Sadly, those stories are lost forever.

This is the story of my parents, Alexander and Eva Kimel. Part 1 is the memoir of the wartime experiences of my dad, taking him from a Polish shtetl to a Nazi ghetto to an eleven-year stint in Communist Poland.[1] He is the Pessimist's Son of the title. Part 2 tells the no-less-extraordinary story of my mother, Eva Kimel (née Ewa Najnudel). Part 3 tells their joined stories. *The Pessimist's Son* is a personal depiction of life in Poland set against two of the most important episodes of the twentieth century: the Nazi and Soviet takeovers of Europe and their cataclysmic aftermaths. In 1946, a Polish commission called the Nazi ghettos "the main instruments whereby the destruction of the Jewish population was carried out."[2] Both of my parents experienced that. This book also discusses the so-called "Holocaust by bullets," which killed my mother's father; and death camps whose mortality rates were far higher than that of Auschwitz. Those camps killed many members of my parents' extended family.

Although English was not my dad's first or even second or third language, somehow this man who was educated as an electrical engineer managed to write in English with a novelist's eye for detail and character. His writing is straightforward, which lends it power and makes the story he recounts all the more moving. My dad even manages some humor, especially in his discussion of prewar Podhajce (pronounced "Pud-HIGH-tse"), his shtetl, in what was then the Polish Ukraine, now western Ukraine.[3] My dad is clear-eyed about his hometown and the colorful people who inhabited it. He writes with some ambivalence, but also obvious affection for the place and a sense of loss. Of course, many events don't lend themselves to humorous treatment, but he uses his wry humor to particularly good effect in mocking the plans of the semi-Fascist regime running Poland before the war, and in discussing the Stalinist "workers' paradise" the Red Army forcibly established in Podhajce when it occupied his town before the German army arrived. My dad doesn't cite Jewish humor as a reason for the survival of the Jewish people, as some others have, but he demonstrates that humor here.

His memoir is important for other reasons as well. My dad read widely, often surprising people with his breadth of knowledge (though you would draw a blank look if you asked him anything about sports teams). This, combined with his deep knowledge of Judaism and European history, allowed him to put his life events—including shtetl life—into interesting cultural and historical contexts. My dad also spoke eight languages—including Yiddish, Polish, Ukrainian, Russian, Hebrew, and German—which enabled him to communicate with all the different people he encountered before, during, and after the Holocaust. Around 1990, my dad wrote a manuscript, *Anatomy of Genocide*, in which he attempted to answer fundamental questions about the Holocaust. I draw on that book here in places.

Like many survivors, my dad felt a strong obligation, even a calling, to bear witness to the Shoah. On his award-winning website (which, alas, is no longer accessible), my dad shared his experiences of the Holocaust and insights on topics such as genocide. He also posted Holocaust-related poetry he wrote. Poems and other writings from his website have been used in schools and colleges, widely reprinted, put to music, and recited by strangers on YouTube. My dad's poetry has even inspired a dance piece. Some of his Shoah-related poems are included here. He also contributed a chapter to *Life in the Ghettos during the Holocaust*.[4] In that book, Prof. Sterling called my dad's autobiographical notes of his life in the Rohatyn Ghetto "powerful and riveting." This book, *The Pessimist's Son*, greatly expands on those notes.

On a related personal note, a few years ago my then-teenage daughter, Sarah, found in our basement a collection of emails my dad had printed out, in which people he didn't know from all over the world had reached out to thank him for his writings and his website. Of course, being a modest man, he never told us about the emails. I was beyond touched (one could say I positively *kvelled*) when my daughter wrote a college-related essay explaining that she wanted to live her life so that, like her "Papa," she too might one day merit receiving a "binderful of gratitude" from strangers.

My father was not even a teenager when the war began. He died at the start of 2018, at the age of ninety-one. Posthumous publishing comes with the challenge that an editor cannot ask the author to expand on or clarify any points. Thanks to Steven Spielberg and the USC Shoah Foundation, however, I have my dad's and mom's detailed video testimonies. While my dad's *Anatomy of Genocide* is not a memoir, it does contain some autobiographical material. I have been able to use it and my dad's video testimony, given in 1996, to help edit and, in places, deepen my dad's manuscript.

My dad essentially ends his story with his liberation and return to Podhajce. His experiences didn't end there, however. For one thing, he and my mother were among the relative handful of Polish Jews who remained in

Communist—and, to a significant extent, antisemitic—Poland after the war. Few Jewish survivors stayed in Poland, largely because survivors frequently weren't welcome, sometimes even meeting with physical violence. My mother's honest discussion in her USC Shoah Foundation testimony of the antisemitism she encountered in Polish public schools following the war—and her resulting efforts to deny her own Jewishness as a teenager—is especially poignant. It provides a concrete and powerful example of the personal emotional toll that antisemitism could, and did, exact even after the Holocaust, and I discuss it in Part 2 of the book.

The testimony of my mother provides a valuable perspective from the point of view of a woman and is an important part of this story. Compared to that of my dad, my mother's upbringing in Radom, a fairly big Polish city, was somewhat more assimilated and more cosmopolitan. (Among other things, Polish was her first language and she had indoor plumbing.) In addition, she was five years younger than my dad. Although both were children of the Shoah, my mother's childhood and her own harrowing story of survival differed in many ways from my dad's. Her story provides another window onto the Holocaust. Fortunately, the interviewer for the USC Shoah Foundation asked both of my parents about their lives before, during, and after the war. I have drawn on these two testimonies and my own knowledge of their lives to complete their story.

Part 2 also draws on other important sources of first-hand information. My grandmother's first cousin and fellow Radomer, Philip Goldstein, survived in Auschwitz-Birkenau as long as pretty much anyone. Philip had a nearly photographic memory and a mind that stayed razor-sharp into his nineties. I benefited from the many stories he told me over the years about our family and his terrible experiences in the Shoah. Philip gave me a copy of his written testimony many years ago, and I have been able to use it in writing about my mother's hometown of Radom. In addition, the superb, unpublished memoir of my mother's cousin, Josefa ("Józia") Steinman, *Lost World*, recently provided to me by Israeli cousins, has been tremendously informative. The *yizkor* (memorial) book of the tiny shtetl of Ludwipol has been helpful with respect to that later part of my mother's Shoah story.[5]

As mentioned, Part 3 of *The Pessimist's Son* tells my parents' intertwined stories beginning after the war, when they met in the Communist Poland of the 1950s. Part 3 also covers my parents' departure for Israel as part of the so-called "Gomułka Aliyah," their emigration from Israel, and their restarting their lives yet again, this time in America. In the book's final part, I also offer my thoughts on the popular notion that most Shoah survivors are "broken" people and that they have passed down their supposed brokenness to their children and grandchildren.

While this book focuses on the stories of my dad and mom, it also touches on the experiences of other family members—some who survived the Holocaust and many who did not. Some were in ghettos, some hid in the forests, some were in Auschwitz and other camps, and some spent the war years in the Soviet labor camps in Siberia.[6] This diversity provides a panorama of the experiences of Jews in Poland taken as a whole. To provide a fuller picture, I have attempted to put these experiences of individuals (including my parents) into a broader historical context by employing the extensive research I have done and discussing the works of historians and other scholars. Frequently, I do this in "Martin's Notes," in Part 1, and in the regular text of Parts 2 and 3. Through this book, my hope is to give readers, including students, a broader and deeper appreciation of what happened to Polish Jewry (including Jews in the Polish Ukraine) before, during, and after the Holocaust.

In editing my dad's original manuscript, I have sometimes shortened and rearranged parts, in addition to adding substantive or explanatory Martin's Notes, bracketed comments, and endnotes. (All endnotes are mine.) On occasion, I use these to offer some thoughts of my own; in this way, this book represents a kind of dialogue across generations. I also have tinkered with some of the chapter titles. In addition, I have changed my dad's original book title, *A Child of the Shoah*. Because my dad is telling his own story, I have tried to edit his writing with a light touch stylistically to keep his voice intact. As a very minor note, I also generally kept my dad's spellings of place names, which tend to use the Polish spelling. I have sometimes changed the Polish spelling of names of individuals so that they would be easier for readers unfamiliar with Polish pronunciation.

I regret that I didn't edit my dad's manuscript and seek to get this published before my dad died. (Around the time my dad wrote it, he asked me to edit it. But I passed because I'd recently gotten married and was busy with my new life—a typical story.) It was after his death, when I was going through his papers, that I came across the manuscript. My dad would have been thrilled to know that his memoir was published, so that the general public could read his story and thoughts about shtetl and ghetto life. He also would have been excited that scholars could use his memoir for their academic research and teaching, as many have already done with his shorter writings. My mother also would have been happy that her family's story was being told. Indeed, during the Shoah, she thought about one day writing a book if she survived. This book can be viewed as a kind of belated fulfillment of that desire.

If there is a heaven, I like to think that my parents are both looking down and beaming. May their memory be a blessing.

—Martin Kimel, September 2024

Acknowledgments

I would like to start by thanking my first-cousin Paula Trief Himmelsbach. Paula knew my dad before I did and has been a great help with this book. In addition to providing encouragement, she read an early draft and provided very helpful comments. She also found and kindly digitized some old family photos for me.

I also wish to thank my Belgian cousin, Mendel Goldstein, for providing me with information about his father, Chilek, as well as my French cousin, Hélène (Goldstein) Sebbon, for doing the same with respect to her father, Henri. To the extent that I now speak French, I also owe the initial suggestion to study it to Hélène. Thanks, too, to my (American) cousin Marc Goldstein, who scanned a photo of Chilek he had for use in this book, and to my Canadian cousin Honey Miller for providing some information about her mother. Also, I thank two of my Israeli cousins, Ami Grynberg and Batami Sadan, for providing me with a copy of the English version of the unpublished memoirs of Batami's mother. Finally, I am grateful to my Polish first-cousin, Iwona Pacułt, and her husband, Grzegorz, for helping me with information about my aunt, as well as context regarding some historical documents of my parents from Poland.

I owe huge thanks also to my good friend, Greg Baruch. Greg is the best-read person I know. He devours serious books, on a wide range of subjects, the way most people breathe. Greg is also a gifted writer and editor. He provided detailed comments and suggestions on an earlier version of the book, including some terrific stylistic improvements. It is he who suggested describing this book as a "dialogue across generations." This book is not the first time that Greg has offered great suggestions to me. In writing articles over the years, I have frequently turned to Greg to get his insightful thoughts and comments. He also provided me with great advice and encouragement regarding this project.

My best friend, Andrés Jaime, also provided me with great encouragement. He provided sage advice as I tried to get the book published and throughout the long, arduous process.

Of course, I have to thank my amazing wife, Miriam. She has encouraged me from the beginning of this long labor of love.

I also made some new friends and acquaintances in the process of editing and writing this book, to whom I owe a good deal of gratitude. Scott Lenga, author of the terrific *The Watchmakers*, about his father's and uncles' experiences in the Shoah, was very generous with his time. He provided me with a lot of good advice about the publishing process. In addition, he took the time to read the manuscript and give me useful feedback. Scott made *aliyah* many years ago and lives in Israel.

Alexander Feller of Chicago founded and has led the Rohatyn District Research Group since 2009. Alex, an anesthesiologist, is an amazing genealogist and when he heard my paternal grandfather was from Bursztyn (which is within the Rohatyn district) he immediately took it upon himself to research that part of my family tree. Thanks to him, I now have a family tree going back to my great grandparents, as well as birth records, photos, and other documents from Poland (then Austria-Hungary).

Yisrael Schnytzer of Israel and his father kindly gave me permission to reprint the photo of the Rohatyn Ghetto's Judenrat. I am further grateful that Yisrael took time to scan and email the photo to me during a very busy time for him. Thanks also to Jay Osborn and Marla Raucher Osborn, who were living in Lviv, Ukraine, for sending me a copy of their Rohatyn Ghetto overlay map and for all their great work with the Ukrainian NGO they founded, Rohatyn Jewish Heritage. Among their many important projects, their website contains a wealth of information about Rohatyn during the Shoah. They also have cleared old Jewish cemeteries and burial sites in addition to installing signs, in three languages, at the two Jewish mass grave sites in Rohatyn informing visitors of what transpired there.

In addition, I would like to thank my book's international team at Academic Studies Press for all their hard work: Alessandra Anzani, Matthew Charlton, Alana Goldberg, Maurice Iglesias, Diana Kim, Kira Nemirovsky, Ilya Nikolaev, Evelyn Petrova, and Ekaterina ("Kate") Yanduganova.

Finally, many thanks to my blurb providers, who took the time to read the work of a stranger and write a few words afterward. I greatly appreciate their kindness.

Naturally, I alone am responsible for any mistakes in the book.

Co-Author's Note on the Use of *Yizkor* Books and Rohatyn Memoirs

A challenge of posthumous publishing is that human memory is, of course, imperfect. In discussing the testimony of survivors of a Nazi labor camp in Poland, the Holocaust scholar Christopher Browning wrote that each witness experienced the camp from a different perspective and "each has remembered, refashioned, forgotten and repressed aspects of this experience in his or her own way."[1] One way to view this is that every survivor has a unique and important account. Indeed, in arguing that "testimonies are . . . historical documents of invaluable importance that have been grossly underused by historians, especially in the case of the Holocaust . . . ," Shoah scholar Omer Bartov notes that "no two individuals can see the same event with precisely the same eyes."[2] But I take Browning's general point, and I have checked my dad's story of the Rohatyn Ghetto against other sources to the extent possible. The memoirs of two fellow Rohatyn Ghetto survivors, Sylvia Lederman (*Sheva's Promise*), and Jack Glotzer (*I Survived the German Holocaust against All Odds: A Unique and Unforgettable Story of a Struggle for Life* [published online]), have both proved very valuable in this regard, and they are well worth reading on their own merits. To those authors, I owe a debt of gratitude.

I also am deeply indebted to the survivors of Podhajce, Radom, Rohatyn, and Ludwipol (among other Polish-Jewish towns) who had the foresight—and undertook the tremendous effort—to create *yizkor*, or memorial, books for their hometowns. These books, *Sefer Podhajce*, *Remembering Rohatyn*, *Sefer Ludwipol*, and *Sefer Radom* (*sefer* means "book" in Hebrew) were originally written mostly in Yiddish or Hebrew and sometimes partly in Polish, and have now been partly or fully translated into English. In these collections, survivors contributed essays, poems, and photos about their communities and life there before, during, and after the Shoah. *Yizkor* books are not contemporaneous documents, though many were started soon after

The Pessimist's Son

the war by survivors in Displaced Persons camps. As discussed in Part 2, *Sefer Radom* is an example. Regardless of when they were begun or completed, however, they are "unique historical documents" that are a "storehouse of information on the traditions and transformations that marked everyday life . . ." in Polish shtetls and cities.[3] This effort to preserve memory strikes me as a quintessentially Jewish—and human—endeavor. These *yizkor* books have been invaluable to me by providing additional perspectives on those towns and additional first-person accounts of what happened there during the Holocaust. Where there are differences in recollections among survivors on important points, I have pointed this out to show the many-faceted nature of the events and people's reactions to them. Often, the inhabitants of different ghettos had similar experiences, reflecting the uniformity of Nazi barbarism (such as Germans casually shooting Jewish patients in their hospital beds), and I have noted such practices when I came across them.

Sometimes, the *yizkor* books have contained personal surprises for me. To my astonishment, the *yizkor* book for the tiny town of Mikulince provides information about the murder of my dad's aunt. And *Sefer Radom* recounts one of my mother's uncles arriving in Auschwitz. I briefly discuss these in this book. From *Sefer Ludwipol*, I learned that it is probable the Nazis murdered my maternal grandfather on August 26, 1942. Eighteen is a special number in Judaism because it signifies *chai*, or life, in Hebrew; and, exactly eighteen years later to the day, Natan's grandson was born and was named after him. That grandson was me, though I believe my parents never knew the dual significance of the date. It is fitting that I am now telling my grandfather Natan's story. Another *yizkor*-book surprise for me is that *Sefer Podhajce* mentions my dad's family being in Wrocław, Poland, after the war. Finally, the Bursztyn *yizkor* book, just recently translated to English, has a *yizkor* commemoration item written in Yiddish by my grandfather Leon and/or his then-surviving siblings. It is a strange experience to read a book for research and find it, in a way, directly speaking to you.

Importantly, the *yizkor* books are not limited to the destruction of their communities—they are not just a commemoration of death and loss. The foreword to *Sefer Radom* explains this eloquently:

> The Yizkor Books tell about a variegated, impulsive, ebullient life throughout centuries. They tell about tradition and ways of life, about struggles and conflicts, about the unique Jewish fate [*faith?—MK*] that carried us through all our generations, until the terrible destruction of the settlement.[4]

Indeed, in addition to presenting portraits and vignettes of pre-war life and lives, in recognition of the centrality of life and community to Judaism, these books celebrate the post-war communities that survivors of their respective towns created in Israel, the United States, Canada, and other countries to which they emigrated. I like to think that those survivors no longer with us would have been pleased that their work is being read and cited—in many cases, many years after their departure.

—Martin Kimel

Zachor—Remember, a Holocaust Prayer

By Alexander Kimel

A Prayer for the Children:

Almighty God, full of Mercy, remember the generation of Jewish children reared for slaughter. Reared for slaughter. Remember the multitudes of children, who in their short lives never experienced joy, knowing only hunger, deprivation, and fear.

A Prayer for the Mothers:

Almighty God, full of Love, remember the Jewish mothers, who carried their babies to their execution, led their children to the gas chambers, witnessed their burning, poisoned them with cyanide, or killed them with their own hands. Let their anguish, pain and torture never be forgotten. Never be forgotten. In our memory they will live forever and ever. Amen.

A Prayer for the Orphans:

Almighty God, full of Compassion, remember the orphans of the ghetto, children who had their parents torn away. Orphans who waited in misery and hunger for their turn to be gassed, to be reunited with their parents in the heaps of human ashes.

A Prayer for the Fathers:

Merciful God that Dwells in Heaven, remember the pain of the Jewish fathers who helplessly witnessed the starvation of their daughters, watched their sons drowning in blood of the mass graves, scraped from walls the smashed brains of their babies. Almighty God, remember their torturous walk through the Valley of Death, a valley saturated with the blood of their children and engulfed in smoke from their burned flesh.

A Prayer for the Fighters:

Almighty God, remember the fighters of the ghettos, Jewish partisans and members of the resistance. They fought without weapons, without ammunition, without hope. Their heroism paved the way for the rebirth of our people. Without the Warsaw Ghetto Uprising, the Six-Day War would have been impossible.

A Prayer for Families:

Merciful God, full of Compassion, remember the plight of the Jewish families who, packed tightly into cattle cars, traveled for weeks to the gas chambers. They traveled without food, without water, without air to breathe knowing that at the end of journey, within hours, they would be converted into smoke and ashes.

A Prayer for the Six Million Victims:

Almighty God, remember the six million people who were gassed, killed, drowned, burned alive, tortured, beaten or frozen to death. For the sake of one man, a whole nation was persecuted, while the world looked on in silence. In our hearts, their sacred memory will last forever and ever. Amen.

God of our Fathers, let the ashes of the children incinerated in Auschwitz, the rivers of blood spilled at Babi Yar or Majdanek be a warning to mankind that hatred is destructive, violence is contagious, while man has an unlimited capacity for cruelty. For our own sake and the sake of our children, we have to be our brother's keeper.

Maps

1. Map of Poland, 1933. (Courtesy of United States Holocaust Memorial Museum.)

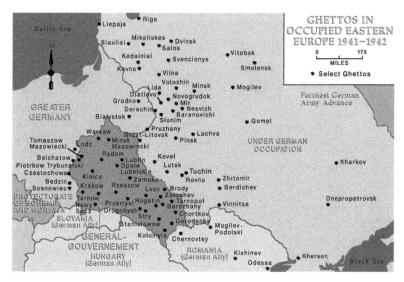

2. Map of Ghettos in Eastern Europe. (Courtesy of United States Holocaust Memorial Museum.)

18 | The Pessimist's Son

3. Map of Poland Territorial Changes. (Courtesy of United States Holocaust Memorial Museum.)

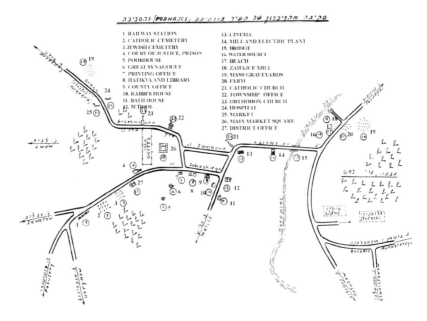

4. Podhajce Map from Yizkor Book. (Courtesy of JewishGen.)

Maps | 19

5. Rohatyn Ghetto Overlay Map. (Map courtesy of Rohatyn Jewish Heritage, created from a June 1944 aerial photograph taken by the German Luftwaffe, sourced from NARA by Dr. Alexander Feller.)

PART 1

ALEX'S MEMOIR, EDITED AND ANNOTATED

CHAPTER 1

The Shtetl

Podhajce was a town forgotten by time, tucked between a high mountain and a large lake, with a horse-drawn fire engine, a half-blind town crier, and one automobile. The huge market square—*rynek*, in Polish—was the soul of the town. Here, every Thursday, hundreds of peasants sold their eggs, chickens, and butter and bought their dry goods. At the same time, their horses deposited in the market a huge supply of manure, the sole source of pollution in town.

The only car in the shtetl—when it ran—was a reason for excitement and the pride of the town. When it appeared running at a top speed of fifteen miles per hour, children tried to outrun it and touch this huffing and puffing symbol of modernity.

A mix of Poles, Jews, and Ukrainians, living in a hateful harmony, inhabited the town; they needed and hated each other. They lived in dilapidated, whitewashed clay huts with flickering kerosene lamps. The few rich people lived in high, two-story stucco buildings with electric lights and hand-cranked telephones.

The town had an assortment of "celebrities" from all walks of life: B., the half-witted town fool, master of profanity; E., the town's crazy man; W., the one-handed invalid peddling an antisemitic newspaper; the Burstiner Rebbe, the religious leader, and his *gabbai*, or business manager, Joel.[1]

What did the town's people live on? The Poles owned the land; the Ukrainians toiled on their small lots and on the big estates of the Polish landowners; and the Jews traded. They traded everything and with everybody and even among themselves. A bushel of wheat worth ten zlotys went through many hands, increasing the price by a whole fifty groshen (half a zloty).

The Jews lived in a close-knit, diverse society. It was comprised of the *gevirim*—the rich men; the *balabatim*—the well-to-do citizens; the *balmelochis*—the tradesmen, the butchers, the shoemakers, the tailors; the *shnorrers* ("beggars," in Yiddish)—the market women and the middlemen living from day to day. Most of the Jews were poor. Even the successful merchants were not millionaires. How much money can you make selling five cents worth of sugar?

Despite the general poverty, life was passable. Entertainment was plentiful, and food was cheap. For fifty groschen, you could buy a pail of fresh cherries; a sack of potatoes was seventy-five groschen; and a live chicken also cost seventy-five groschen. The only problem was how to earn the needed money.

People were known by their trades, which were passed down from generation to generation: "Velve the *katzif*"—Velve the butcher; "Meir the *schnader*"—Meir the tailor; "Shloyme the *balagule*"—Shloyme the coachman. There also was no generation gap. There is less room for generations not to understand each other when each generation has the same livelihood.

<u>Martin's Note</u>: *Many people had nicknames unrelated to their professions. Nicknames in shtetls could be brutal,[2] and Podhajce was no exception. It seems that many people there got nicknames relating to their worst personal traits. For example, writing in* Sefer Podhajce, *the yizkor* book *of Podhajce, Baruch Milch mentions Yehuda the* Lo *(Judah the "no"), who was referred to as such because he always expressed a negative opinion and stressed the vowel in* lo *("no," in Hebrew). Milch also tells the story of a shoe wholesaler from Lwów (now Lviv, Ukraine) who was dunning a Mr. Leon Weiss, a leather and shoe merchant, for late payments. He asked many people in Podhajce where Leon Weiss lived, but nobody recognized the name. Eventually, he discovered that Weiss was known in the town by his nickname, Leibele* Trask*—"Leibele the Smack," because he got upset easily and threatened to "smack" people.[3] Apparently, my dad got off easy: he had a nickname related to his Hebrew name, "Shiko" (derived from Joshua). I believe that my grandfather, who was born Leib Hersh, was referred to in Podhajce as Hersh.*

* * *

There was no television to isolate people from one other, to make them lonely. At six o'clock, the youth of the town provided the shtetl with an unstaged show. The "Corso," as the sidewalk area around the *rynek* was called, was full of young couples walking hand in hand. It was a colorful pageant. The Corso served many purposes. It was a mating place for young people. Here, the town beauties would select their boyfriends. It was a non-stop fashion show, too; here, a girl named Dziunia would show off her mother's creative talent in copying the latest fashion journals. Because of this show, some people called Podhajce "the Paris of Galicia."[4]

The Jews in the town lived from week to week, and the most important days in the week were Thursdays and Saturdays. Saturday (the Jewish Sabbath, known as Shabbat) was the holy day. Thursday was the day that you earned the money needed to celebrate the Sabbath. Each Jew, regardless how poor he was, had to observe the Sabbath with a good meal. So, Thursday was a hustling day; the poor men ran around the horse-driven peasant's carts, trying to trade, buy, or sell while the merchant stood in front of the meager stores hawking brown leather shoes or colorful cottons for dresses.

The women had a field day. They were doing the shopping for Saturday's treats, bargaining with the peasant women selling loaves of yellow butter wrapped in green leaves, or buying noisy chickens, geese, or ducks.

Buying a chicken was a ritual, an art passed down from mother to daughter. First, you had to weigh the chicken, holding it with your right hand, trying to guess its weight. Then you had to turn the chicken around, take it under your arm, blow off the feathers around the rear and see how much fat the chicken had. After determining that the chicken had a fat rear end, the bargaining process started in earnest. The trick was to offer a low price and never let the chicken out of your hand. It was a loud ritual: the peasant woman cursing, trying to get the chicken back, the buyer arguing loudly that the chicken had not even one ounce of fat—and the surprised chicken cackling loudly.

My Schooling

Like other Jewish boys, I started my schooling at the age of three. I attended a *cheder*—a one-room school in which children got religious training. The *cheder* was really a combination religious school and nursery. Our teacher, Nusen the *Melamed* (Nusen the Teacher), taught groups of children, ages three to twelve. When one group of children was taught, the other group played outside, in the small yard. The *melamed* used proven, ancient methods of instruction. We repeated in unison the Hebrew words and the Yiddish translation. For example: *"Vaydaber Adonai l'Moishe"* ("And God spoke to Moses").[5]

In most *cheders*, attention and discipline were reinforced with a *shteken*, a stick. But Nusen the *Melamed* used a belt. "When you hit a child with a belt in the rear end, wisdom flows directly to his head," he used to say.

At age seven, I started to attend public school and religious school. From 8 o'clock in the morning to 6 o'clock at night I attended classes. It was not a real childhood; instead, it was an intensive preparation for adulthood. When I reached eleven, I graduated to studying the Talmud, the ancient laws of the Jews in Babylon. I really didn't have any interest in knowing what the responsibilities of the owner of a bull that gored a pregnant woman were. I had never seen a bull and couldn't tell a bull from an ox or a cow. It was much later in life that I recognized the benefits of this early intensive intellectual training. Some famous lawyers or physicians started their development in *cheder* at the age of three. This was their head start.

The Fire

One of my earliest memorable events was the great fire that almost burned down our house. Behind our house, there was a small soap factory operated by our neighbor, Jupiter. In a small-unheated shed Jupiter produced coarse soap that he sold on an open market stand. Rain or shine, the stand was packed with piles of yellow soap.

One night, the factory caught fire, and the drums of the chemicals made it dangerous to try to extinguish the fire. Soon the whole sky was painted with reddish flames and dark fumes covered the whole street.

I was awakened by the loud sound of a trumpet and when I looked out through the window, I saw a strange spectacle. Tomaszewski, the head of the Volunteer Fire Department, was blowing a trumpet. Dressed in a golden helmet, he was driving the horse-drawn red-and-gold fire wagon. The funny part was that he was driving in circles.

Tomaszewski blared the trumpet with such fervor and virtuosity that the walls of Jericho would have collapsed. The sound of the trumpet did not collapse any walls, but it did scare the horses. One scared horse was pulling to the right, while the other pulled to the left. The outcome was that the fire wagon was running full speed around the marketplace, but in big circles. It was a sight to behold: Tomaszewski riding high on the red fire wagon trying to control the scared beasts, and the Volunteer Firemen running behind him. The Volunteer Fire Department was a very selective and discriminating institution, but it selected more for musical ability than for firefighting skills. Besides fighting fires, it also maintained the only marching band in the county. To be accepted to the Fire Department, one had to play at least one wind instrument. In reality, the volunteers had strong lungs, but they were poor runners.

When the wagon and the firemen finally arrived at scene of the disaster, the building had already burned down. To show off their skills and to make up for lost time, though, the whole fire department worked feverishly, flooding the adjacent houses. As a result, the soap factory's neighbors were more afraid of the fire brigade's flood than of the fire.

Matchmakers and Private Armies

Besides the Fire Department/marching band, the shtetl developed many interesting institutions that provided distraction and entertainment. One such institution was Tunis the Matchmaker. Mr. Tunis was the only matchmaker in Podhajce; he knew everybody, and everybody knew him. They said that Mr. Tunis with his ingenuity single-handedly changed Podhajce from a small town into a metropolis with 10,000 inhabitants. Rain or shine, the matchmaker moved around the town with his big black umbrella, the sign of his profession. Meir, the town joker, used to tease him. "Why don't you throw away the umbrella and marry off your own four daughters? Charity begins at home." The matchmaker used to get angry, punching the air with the black umbrella as if fencing. Then he turned around, grabbed the elbow of a young passerby, and launched into his well-worn spiel.

Another institution of my shtetl was Semelke with the *Gule* and his private army. "Semelke with the *Gule*"—Semelke with the Boil—was a third-grade teacher, who had been rejected by the Polish army. To compensate for his rejection, he developed an army of his own—a military made up of third graders.

Semelke's "army" was equipped with wooden carbines and toy sabers and exercised diligently during school recess. The hapless boys presented their wooden sticks during the roll calls, while the boy officers saluted as reporting to the army chief, Semelke. Semelke had his laughingstock army, and nothing could be done about it.

Names and Dates

The Jews in Podhajce had problems with names and dates—specifically, last names and dates of birth. For example, my sister Luba, in first grade, was known as Luba Lehrer. In second grade, she went under the name Luba Treiser. In third grade, she was known as Luba Kimel. When she started fourth grade, the teacher asked her, "Luba, what's your name *this* year?"

It sounds complicated, but it really wasn't. Most married Jewish couples exchanged religious vows only. They did not have a civil wedding because a civil marriage was cumbersome and expensive. When my parents were married, my father's last name was Treiser, which was his mother's maiden name, and Luba carried our mother's maiden name, Lehrer. When my parents legitimized their union, Luba became a Treiser. The next year, my father retroactively legitimized the marriage of his parents, and Luba (along with the rest of the family) became a Kimel.

The Jews had also trouble registering the births of their children. As the old joke goes, when a son is born, his father asked how he should register the baby's birth: "Shall I register him as born a year later? No good! He will start his schooling late. Shall I register him as born a year earlier? No good, he will face the draft sooner. What is better?"

"Why don't you register him on his real birthday?" asks his wife.

"Real birthday?" replied the husband. "It's a fantastic idea! Why didn't I think of it?"

A Harsh Life

Life in the shtetl was very harsh. It was difficult to make a living, difficult to get an education, difficult to get a job. The youth had no future, no prospects of getting married. In addition to the bleak economic future, Jews faced heavy taxation, the chicanery of the Polish authorities, and rampant antisemitism.

In the years before World War I, Poland did not exist. All its territories were occupied by Germany, Russia, and Austria. All annexed areas were integrated economically with the main territories. After World War I, Poland became independent, but lost all of its markets and became a strictly agricultural country in which the Polish aristocracy owned most of the land. The Polish peasants lived in dire poverty and could not support the craftsmen, artisans and small-time brokers of the shtetl.

The conditions were deplorable: limited economic opportunities and high unemployment. *Parnussy,* "profit," or making a living, was a source of constant worry. The most burning issue was the lack of opportunities for young people. For them, it was impossible to get an education—even a high school diploma was unattainable. The Jewish enrollment in state-run schools were limited to about ten percent. The Jews constituted ten percent of the total population, and the Polish authorities tried to limit the number of Jewish students in schools and universities to the same percentage.

Even the few lucky students had a difficult time. The nearest high school was about twenty-seven kilometers—sixteen miles—from the shtetl. The students had to rise at 5 o'clock in the morning, walk two kilometers to the railroad station, and take an hour's ride on the train, to be at school by 8:00 in the morning. They came home at night, to do their homework and prepare to get up early the next morning.

Worst of all was that, even if you could get a place in school, education was useless for making a living. A Jew could not get a government position, and there was no private industry to provide employment. I remember that our neighbor, Moshe Orenstein, spent his life serving vodka and beer in his noisy smoke-filled inn and living frugally to save his pennies. As a result, he was able to educate all his children. His daughter Zusia was an unemployed pharmacist and his sons, Munio and Dudzic, were unemployed intelligentsia. They always dressed immaculately and walked around reading books, ashamed to help their parents serve vodka, afraid to lose their status. Their education was useless and even a hindrance in life.

Most of the young people were employed as tradesmen apprentices or as store helpers. A store helper worked about seventy hours a week and earned ten zlotys a month, the equivalent of two dollars. Our neighbor's son, Srulek, held such a job for about fifteen years. It was a big store, and he reached a monthly salary of thirty-five zlotys. At the age of thirty, he had reached his peak earning power and he couldn't even dream of getting married and starting a family.

The best indicators of the harshness of life were the odd, low-income professions that proliferated in the shtetl. For example, the *jajęcznik* [pronounced "yigh-yench-neek"] or "Egg Man." Our area exported eggs, a very perishable product. The Egg Men traveled each morning to the outlying villages to buy fresh eggs. It was difficult to get up at 5 o'clock in the morning, rain or shine, to harness the horses and ride the squeaking wagon on dirt roads, full of mud in the summer and snow in the winter. It was a dangerous and difficult job, but it brought *parnussy.*

Our Store

Our family owned a big store located in the middle of the town, next to the *rynek*. We owned a two-story building, one of the few two-story buildings in Podhajce. (See photo.) The retail and wholesale store sections took up the first floor, and our living quarters were on the second floor.

My father was a very ambitious, competitive man. Each morning, he used to wake up my mother at 6:00 in the morning. "Look, your sister Ethel opened her store half an hour ago. Let's get up! Enough sleeping!" The competition and dealing with capricious customers weighed on him, but his greatest stress came from worrying about taxes.

To avoid the burden of the heavy-handed and discriminatory Polish taxation system, my father had maintained a double set of books—one for the government and the other with the real figures. Under the rules, he was obliged to make an inventory account annually. It was impossible to reconcile the official books with the current inventory. Even a spot check of the inventory could have sent my father to prison. So, he worried endlessly—and had illnesses to prove it. Every year, Father left for resort places like Niemirów or Truskawiec, to cure the ulcer with waters and treat his rheumatism with a mud bath called *borowina*.

My Grandmother

At a young age, I helped my grandmother in her store and there I had my first encounter with the poverty of the shtetl. My grandfather managed the wholesale section of the store while grandmother was in charge of the retail part.

My grandmother, Roncia [pronounced "Roncha"] Lehrer, was an exceptional woman who loved music. Whenever there was a wedding in town, she went to listen to the music, clapping her hands to the joyous klezmer tunes. Despite her love of music, she never owned a radio. She preferred spending her money helping the poor. Grandmother never cared about money. Whatever money she made, she used to "lend" it away or, rather, give it away to her customers.

The town was inhabited by poor people who struggled the entire week to save money for their Sabbath dinner. During the weekdays, one could eat potatoes but, on the Sabbath, a full feast with boiled chicken was obligatory, for rich and poor alike. If you didn't have money, you borrowed it from the rich. Nobody would dare refuse to make a loan for a festive Sabbath meal.

My grandmother had a retinue of poor market women who on Fridays borrowed a zloty or two for the Sabbath, promising to pay it back next week. By Thursday, they had paid back half of the loan, so they could again borrow on Friday. The poor market women labored day and night, rain or shine, to make a living. When I was older, I realized that my grandmother was literally giving away the store and that she enjoyed doing so.

At age six, I was a full-fledged store helper, and I managed quite well. When a customer asked for five groshen worth of sugar, I tore a piece of wrapping paper, counted five pieces of sugar, squashed the package and handed it over to the customer. Selling salt was a little more complicated. For a ten-groshen transaction I had to tear up a piece of wrapping paper, always lying on the counter, roll it into a cone, tighten up the end of the cone, and fill it with salt.

Antisemitism

A Jew in Poland was constantly reminded that he was an outsider. At school, we had fist fights every day with our Ukrainian or Polish classmates. The Boy Scouts did not accept Jewish kids. The streets reverberated with the cries of Wroblewski, peddling his hate-mongering paper, *Polska bez Żydow* (Poland without Jews).[6]

The *Ofkejferin*

Only in Podhajce could one find an array of *ofkejferin*—"Chicken-Women" who bought chickens from the peasants, killed them, cleaned them, removed the fat, and sold pieces of meat in the market stalls. In the winter, they used coal ovens to keep their hands from freezing. It was a hard life, full of sacrifice, and done to keep their husbands in warm houses studying the Torah. All the Jewish market women had learned husbands.

The Water Carrier

The shtetl didn't have running water. The town maintained a few hand pumps scattered over the town. If you needed water, you had to carry it from the pump or pay Moshe the Water Carrier. Moshe charged ten groshen to deliver two pails of fresh, crystal-clear water. He cornered and maintained the water distribution system of Podhajce. With his two pails and a wooden yoke, Moshe delivered cold clear water, no matter the weather. Perrier could not have delivered better-tasting water.

Meir Shapse

Meir Shapse was another celebrity of the shtetl. He was a small man, heavy-set, with a white beard covering his open fly. And what a booming voice he had! The *rynek* was the center of the shtetl, and Meir was the epicenter of the *rynek*. Here, Meir yelled a whole day:

"Ten groshen a pound, women. Ten groshen a pound, women."

Meir wasn't selling human flesh. He was just advertising his cherries at a low, low price. Pavarotti could not have done a better job.

Shloyme the *Balagule*

In the shtetl, Shloyme was an institution. Shloyme was not a *gevir*, as the rich men were called. He did not have an honored seat at the eastern wall of the synagogue. He wasn't called to the Torah every second Saturday. Nevertheless, he was liked and even admired.

Shloyme earned his living as a *balagule*, or a coachman. He owned a squeaking buggy drawn by an old, beaten-up horse resembling a dried California prune. The living he made was very precarious. For a few pennies, Shloyme would hire himself out to deliver a sack of potatoes, a pile of wood, or a sack of salt.

Although Shloyme cornered about half of the transportation market of the shtetl, his outward appearance did not indicate great success. Summer or winter, rain or shine, Shloyme was dressed in the same old, black coat, ripped in the seams and that looked like a quilt with multiple patches. In the winter, he stuffed his boots with straw to keep his feet warm. His competition tried to undermine him with the claim that he gained his competitive edge by starving his horse.

In the shtetl, Shloyme was known for his multitude of children, his good nature and unorthodox approach to life. Some envious souls claimed that

Shloyme didn't believe in God and that, although he dutifully attended religious services, he didn't pray as God had commanded.

The truth is that each day Shloyme joyfully attended services. But during the Amidah, the silent prayer when the congregation silently recited the Eighteen Blessings and asks God for forgiveness for its sins and transgressions, Shloyme was engaged in a one-sided conversation, in Yiddish, with his personal God.

Shloyme did the talking, and God—and the congregation—listened.

"God, You know that for myself I ask little, a bowl of soup and a piece of herring and I am happy. I am grateful to you for my devoted wife, Pearl, for my growing family. But . . . for the horse, I beg you for help. This poor creature of yours doesn't know the taste of oats—even a bale of hay is luxury. How long can he survive? What will happen to us if the horse dies? How are you going to support us?"

Shloyme was often chastised for his loose praying habits. To his critics, Shloyme used to answer, "Do you think that God enjoys your mindless repetition of two-thousand-year-old prayers? He knows them by heart and is bored with them. Do you think that God of Abraham, Isaac, and Jacob speaks only the Holy language—Hebrew? Our God speaks Yiddish also, and believe you me, it is a lot easier to communicate with the Blessed One in your own language."

People liked to deal with Shloyme; he never haggled over a few pennies, and always told beautiful stories about rich princesses, poor beggars, and smart horses. Despite the hardships and deprivations, he never complained, and his eyes always shone.

"God blessed me with full house of children and no money. Mendel the *Gevir* is blessed with full coffers of money and no children. My wife nurses a new baby each year, and his wife nurses the same ulcer year after year. Which is better?" He used to ask half-jokingly.

The Jewish "Mafia"

Podhajce had its own "mafia"—the band of porters headed by M. The porters cornered the market for loading and unloading goods delivered to wholesale merchants. M. set the price of twenty-five groshen per sack. It was an exorbitant fee that merchants had to pay if they wanted the goods delivered undamaged.

As the saga goes, M. never paid taxes. Each time a tax official visited his house to collect money, he would line up the ample Mrs. M. and all six of his children, by age, alongside the old commode. He would say: "Money I don't have, but you can take my wife, my children, or the old commode. The choice is yours."

Of course, his generous offer was always rejected. Later, when the Russians took over the town, M. became the director of the flour mill. When he started to steal, he was sentenced to five years in prison. The Russians did not play Jewish-mafia games.

Martin's Note: In her long essay in Sefer Podhajce, *Henia Schourz notes that, after the war, Yisrael M., whom she calls "an avowed Communist," was appointed by the Soviets to be the chief overseer of the entire economic life of Podhajce, especially over the town's flour mill. The spelling/transliteration of his name in the translated essay is different from the spelling in my dad's manuscript, but Schourz is clearly referring to the same person as my dad. She writes sarcastically that "it was not easy to approach the great M., who used to be a porter and now had reached the rank of commissar."[7]*

CHAPTER 2

Shtetl Life and the Mystery of the Survival of the Jewish People

One of the great mysteries that has puzzled sociologists for ages is the mystery of Jewish survival. For two thousand years, Jews survived the diaspora, despite their powerlessness, persecution and dispersion. Many powerful nations appeared on the historic scene, dominated the landscape for a while and vanished. Who today knows what happened to the Vikings, Goths, Visigoths, Celts, and Mayans? For example, the Mayans developed a mighty civilization and suddenly they disappeared without leaving the slightest trace—disappeared without giving a forwarding address.

In the seventeenth century, during the Uprising of Bogdan Khmelnytskyi, about sixty percent of the Jews in Podhajce were killed. Despite that, the Jews had maintained their presence in Podhajce for the previous 500 years. They survived the killing by hordes of Ukrainians during the Uprising of Khmelnytskyi, persecution by the Turkish Ottoman Army, the rapes and killing by the Cossacks. The Jews mastered the art of survival. How did they do it?

A Life-Oriented Religion

The shtetl survived as long as it did because the Jewish religion is life-oriented. It was designed to protect and support life, individual and communal. *L'Chaim*—"To Life!" This was not only a toast; it was a philosophy. Judaism is not preoccupied with the afterlife: The notion of the Messiah, the Redeemer, is only loosely defined in the Jewish religion. The Messiah is not a

36 | The Pessimist's Son

divine figure, but, rather, the leader who will redeem the world, and bring all the Jews, living and dead, to the Promised Land. The Jewish Messiah is more a mythical and folkloric figure than a theological one.

For the Jews, facing continuous persecution and hatred, the preservation and propagation of Jewish life and culture were the highest priorities. They were facilitated by the high, almost universal literacy of the Jewish masses. A Jew was required to pray for himself and establish his own connection with God, so one had to be able to read the Hebrew prayer books. Moreover, Jewish learning was prized. For example, my grandfather had only a fourth-grade education, but he was well versed in the psychological and philosophical concepts expounded in the Jewish religious writings like the *Ethics of Our Fathers* (The *Pirkei Avot*), which he often quoted verbatim:

> Who is a rich man? A man who is satisfied with his lot.
> Who is a respected man? A man who respects others.
> Who is a learned man? A man who learns from others.
> Who is an esteemed man? A man who holds others in a high esteem.
> Who is a strong man? A man who conquers his temper.

Because people in the shtetl valued communal life, shtetl life was organized to help those in the community in greatest need. A powerful Polish king had granted the Jews the right to maintain separate communities with the right of self-taxation. The community raised taxes according to its needs, paid by each member according to his means. Who determined the means? A committee, of course. Every year, at taxation time, the whole town was in an uproar. "Why will Moshe pay only 300 zlotys, while I have to pay 500 zlotys? This is injustice that calls for heavenly intervention!" Most of the time, however, the heavens did not intervene. People paid a lot, but nobody left the *kehilla*, the Jewish community.

The politicians of the *kehilla* prudently invested the money in "mutual funds." But because there was no Dreyfus Jewish Fund or Jewish Fidelity Fund, they invested in funds with low capitalization but high social returns, like the Torah Education Fund, the Orphans' Fund, the Poor-Girl Dowery Fund, the Burial Society Fund, etc. These funds, administered by honest people of means, supported poor orphans, paid for their education, provided dowries for poor girls and loans for merchants in trouble. The Jews were their brothers' keepers. This cohesiveness created a feeling of security that gave each member of the community the assurance that his family would not die of starvation. It also contributed to keeping people in the community.[1]

Some Other Ways that Judaism Adapted

To survive in the diaspora, the Jews developed a new national structure, adaptable to various environments, that was suitable for future generations. With the passing of time, symbolism substituted for the physical existence of the ancient Temple. In place of the national structure, the priesthood, the aristocracy, the Jews placed the veneration for the Torah and the esteem for men of learning. "The Torah is a higher state than the priesthood or royalty" (*Ethics of Our Fathers* 6:6).

Even today, it is possible to observe the veneration given to the Torah. The Torah is a symbol of royalty, and when the Ark [holding Torahs] is opened during prayers, the entire congregation rises out of respect. During the services, the Torah is carried around the synagogue, wearing a crown of silver and a mantle of velvet. Worshippers reach out with a prayer book or a prayer shawl and kiss the spot where it touched the Torah. The Torah personifies, and substitutes for, the royalty lost by the Jewish people two thousand years ago.

Martyrdom—*Kiddush Hashem*[2]

To survive in dispersion, the Jews had to abandon their military traditions. They had to learn humility and to accept the harassment meted out by their rulers. The idea of martyrdom helped the Jews face persecution without fighting back; it gave the individual a rationale to sacrifice his life for the community in the name of God, for the honor of Israel. The idea of martyrdom was incorporated into the liturgy.

Jewish Traditions that Discouraged Assimilation

Martin's Note: My father understood well that racial antisemitism and persecution against Jews often made assimilation extremely difficult, if not impossible, in that even Jews who converted to Christianity and wanted to assimilate often were not truly accepted by non-Jewish society. Here, however, he is discussing Jewish traditions that were designed by Jews, in his view, to discourage a desire to assimilate.

The Jews were master interpreters of their religious laws, creating a set of injunctions that maintained a strong cultural identity by creating an invisible gulf that separated Jews from Gentiles. To keep Jews as a separate group, the rabbis came up with many injunctions and prohibitions that, over time, morphed into traditions. For example, take Judaism's dietary laws. The innocent injunction of the Torah: "Thou shall not seethe a kid in his mother's milk" (Exodus 23:19) was developed as part of a complex set of rules that made it impossible for a Jew to share a meal with a Gentile. In all my childhood years, I don't remember even once eating in a non-Jewish home. How can you share a meal with a Gentile when you must have two sets of dishes, can't mix meat with dairy foods, and must wait four hours, after eating a meat dish, before you can have any dairy?

Another example is wearing a skullcap. Nowhere in the Torah is there a requirement that a Jewish male cover his head at all times. However, because Christian men took off their hats as a sign of respect, the Jewish tradition developed that men kept their heads covered. The skullcap brilliantly enabled Jews to remove their hats when meeting a Gentile but to still keep their heads covered.

The observance of the Sabbath also powerfully guarded the people of Israel against assimilation. It is a day of rest from work, but it has been interpreted to prohibit Jews from engaging in most goal-oriented activities. You can't cook—you can't even walk even to synagogue carrying your prayer shawl. To cope with those pervasive prohibitions, some creative circumventions were necessary.

Let's take cooking. The preparation of any food was considered work, so you couldn't cook on Saturday. But how could you observe a holiday without a hot meal? The Jews invented *chulent*. It is a mixture of barley, chunks of meat, beans, and potato left to simmer in a hot oven for twenty-four hours before the start of the Sabbath. The fat from the meat penetrated the beans and browned the potatoes into a succulent, delicious, amorphous mass. There are many other examples in other areas, including the *eruv*, which enables religious Jews to carry items on Shabbat within defined areas.

Religious Life in the Shtetl

There was complete decentralization and autonomy in religious life. There were about twelve synagogues in Podhajce, each with a different ambience. For instance, there was the Alte Shul, the old synagogue. It was a tall structure that had once served as a Turkish mosque, and it had very bad acoustics. Adjacent to the Old Shul was the Braite Shul, a more modern structure with one big *shul* and two small independent synagogues. The Braite Shul was the most prestigious synagogue and attended by the richest people.

What do you do during the services when the prayers, repeated a thousand times, you know by heart? You talk. You talk about business deals or family affairs. At times the noise of the conversations drowned out the prayers. At such times, the *shamis*, or beadle, banged his fist on the prayer book. My guess is that he was afraid of competition. God might be more interested in listening to the creative business deals being discussed than in paying attention to the familiar, thousand-year-old prayers.

The Jews in the shtetl were good businessmen and they realized that congregants with money were looking for recognition: *kavod*. In Hebrew, it means honor and respect. The community decided to raise money for the synagogues by auctioning off the *kavod* and letting market forces determine the value of the recognition. To be called to the Torah, especially on the high holidays of Rosh Hashanah and Yom Kippur, was a mark of honor. So, on the last Saturday before the holidays, an auction was held during the services and the highest bidder got the most honorable *aliyah* (that is, being called to the Torah). It is amazing that a prestigious *Maftir aliyah* could garner up to 200 zlotys—more than a year's income for half of the families of Podhajce.[3]

It is also amazing how much joy and pleasure religion provided to the Jewish children.[4] Each holiday—and the Jews had many holidays—had a special flavor for them.

Passover was a joyous holiday. Most children got new suits or new shoes and helped bake matzos. The matzo requires perforations, which today are usually made by machine. We made the perforations by hand, using small clock gears. Then came the seders with the "four questions." On Passover, we got to drink real wine, not the boiled syrup from dried grapes we drank every Shabbat.

40 | The Pessimist's Son

Purim was another joyous holiday, a carnival-type holiday. Older children made masks for themselves and collected small change. On Purim, the whole town looked spooky, with many Hamans hanged in effigy. At Hanukkah, the festival of lights, we enjoyed playing dreidel, eating potato pancakes and lighting the menorah.

Even Yom Kippur, the Day of Atonement, the day of fasting, brought lots of happiness to children. Older people kept small bottles of ammonia to revive themselves and fight off exhaustion. So, we children also carried small bottles of ammonia, smelling each other's bottles, and bragging that only ours was the real McCoy.

Tish'a B'av, the lamentations holiday that marks the destruction of the ancient Temple, was a time for mourning for the adults congregating in the synagogue. The children, on the other hand, enjoyed collecting tickets and throwing them at each other's hair. All the other Jewish holidays like Simchat Torah and Sukkoth had different flavors and brought much joy to the children.

Conclusion

All these methods of survival developed over centuries: a separate culture, diffuse religious authorities, a lack of military training, and the doctrine of *Kiddush Hashem* worked for the Jewish people for 2,000 years—until Hitler came. Then these methods proved disastrous. And now this world is gone, never to be seen again.

Martin's Note: Bogdan Khmelnytskyi was the leader of the Cossack and peasant uprising against Polish rule in the Ukraine in 1648–1657, which resulted in the destruction of hundreds of Jewish communities. He was bent on eradicating the Jews from the Ukraine. At the time, colonization of Ukrainian land by the Polish nobility inflamed Ukrainian resentment and Jews were closely associated with the Polish nobles, who had leased their estates to them and granted them protection and monopolies for the manufacture and sale of products like flour and alcohol.[5] Jews were regularly depicted as "bloodsuckers living off the wretched peasants as well as representing the age-old 'enemies of Christ.'"[6] Hence, violent Ukrainian nationalism and antisemitism had a long history when the war began. Today, Khmelnytskyi is a symbol of Ukrainian political independence. A city and region of Ukraine are named after him, and his image is on some Ukrainian banknotes. Bartov argues that stereotypes of Ukrainians as barbaric murderers resulting from Khmelnytskyi's 1648 uprising became part of the Jewish collective memory while "anti-Jewish stereotypes merging religious prejudice and popular superstitions with economic resentment . . . became part and parcel of the emerging Ukrainian national literature."[7]

Regarding Jewish survival in twentieth-century Nazi ghettos, historian Lucy Dawidowicz writes that Jews had developed "a strategy of accommodation, a tactic of adaptability, which centuries of powerlessness under oppressors had fashioned into a serviceable tradition." She argues that this tradition of accommodation "stood [Jews in the ghettos] in good stead":

> *Lacking weapons and military organization, they learned to use tricks of intelligence and manipulation to prevail against their persecutors. They learned not only to invent, but to circumvent; not only to obey but to evade; not only to submit but to outwit. Their tradition of defiance was devious rather than direct, employing nerve instead of force.[8]*

While these skills no doubt helped a tiny fraction of Jews survive (and may have helped some others survive a little longer than they would have otherwise), Jews in ghettos and as a whole in the Shoah, did not "prevail against their persecutors"—unless one sets the bar very low as to what constitutes "prevailing." Over 600,000 Jews died in large and small ghettos scattered throughout German-occupied Eastern Europe.[9] Two-thirds of European Jewry was wiped out by Hitler and his henchmen. Indeed, only about one or two percent of Polish Jews who hadn't fled to the USSR proper, and thus escaped German occupation, survived.[10] In the words of one writer, "The Nazis lost their war against the Allies, but they won their war against the Jews."[11]

Heller shares my father's views on this point:

> *The traditional mode of coping, developed during centuries of oppression, proved impotent under the conditions of modern anti-Semitism. Nevertheless, numerous [religious] Jews could not shed it, since it had become deeply imprinted in their psyche and intertwined with their religious Orthodoxy and traditional culture.[12]*

Jacob Sloan, the editor and translator of Ringelblum's Notes from the Warsaw Ghetto, *also is much closer my father's view and mine than to Dawidowicz's:*

> The Ghetto was actually a milder form of . . . a concentration camp. The Jews had actually developed a special technique for dealing with hostile authorities over the centuries—bribing them, making themselves economically indispensable to them. . . . For a long time, the Jewish will to live supported them psychologically. . . . But the Nazis, though human and hence corruptible, were not to be conciliated in the long run.[13]

Christopher Browning puts this well (note: he uses the Nazi term "work Jews" for Jews doing slave labor):

> Until the spring of 1943, the Jews of Poland had clung to the all too understandable but mistaken assumption that even the Nazis could not be so irrational by utilitarian standards as to kill work Jews making essential contributions to the German war economy. They had therefore pursued the desperate strategy of "salvation through labor" as the only hope that a remnant of Jews would survive. But the Jews were gradually being stripped of their illusions. The Germans encountered resistance when they tried to carry out the final liquidation of the Warsaw and Białystok ghettos, and revolts broke out in the death camps of Treblinka and Sobibór when the work Jews there realized that the camps were about to be closed [and the remaining Jews exterminated].[14]

CHAPTER 3

My World Collapses

In the 1930s, startling new developments took place in the world arena. In Germany, Hitler rose to power and the persecution of the Jews began. Soon afterward, the first wave of German refugees hit the shores of Poland and my town felt deep anxiety because of the approaching war.[1]

In Poland, after the death of Marshal Jozef Piłsudski in 1935, a clique of incompetent colonels grabbed power and created a semi-Fascist government, modeled on the Fascist regimes. They began inept efforts to modernize the backward country. Poland created its own concentration camp: Bereza Kartuska, where Communists and members of other opposition groups, were interned without a court order.[2]

Next, the colonels turned to the "Jewish Question." Poland had too many Jews, the colonels declared. Ten percent of the population was much too much, in their eyes. Small-scale pogroms, like the one in Przytyk, were organized to push Jews to emigrate.[3]

Soon, a total ban on the kosher slaying of animals was hotly debated in the Polish Parliament. The ruling clique accepted the dire poverty of the nation, but the welfare of the slaughtered animals suddenly became the most important issue facing the colonels. Their line of thinking was simple and clear: You deny the Jews kosher meat and they will have to leave the country.

In Poland, ninety percent of the population owned only ten percent of the land; the Polish gentry owned the other ninety percent. The society needed land reform, not pogroms or antisemitic hysteria. The Jews were used as a scapegoat to divert attention from the country's dire poverty.[4]

A few years before the war, hate-spreading antisemitic newspapers became popular. The most hateful was the paper *Polska bez żydow* (Poland without Jews). It was modeled on the Nazi paper the *Stürmer*, and featured caricatures of Jews with hooked noses and blood-dripping hands. The Jews were blamed for all the ills of the world going back 2,000 years, starting with the crucifixion. Another well-known antisemitic newspaper was the *Kurier*,[5] edited by Father Maximilian Kolbe, who later became a saint.

Next, the regime called Sanacja, or "Cleaners," turned its attention to the exterior looks of the towns. Again, their thinking was simple and clear: To *be* prosperous, a country had to *look* prosperous. The prime minister, Sławoj Składkowski, decreed that all that all storefronts were to be painted gray, all fences whitewashed, and the outhouses painted a deep-camouflage green. "My green outhouse with the round opening in the door looks like a bunker. I think that the minister wants to the Germans to think that Podhajce is a fortress defended by a network of green painted bunkers—a new Maginot line," quipped Reb Meir, the town joker.

In one week, Poland had consumed more paint than in all its history. Even the peasants had to drop their harvesting to paint the outhouses. Soon, a uniform coat of paint covered all the economic ills of the country.

Having achieved a high prosperity level by painting the outhouses, the colonels started a campaign to get colonies: "Yes, Poland being a first-rate military power deserves colonies. England has colonies, France has colonies, and even Italy had Ethiopia. Why not Poland?" the regime said. How do you get colonies? Simple: organize rallies. Podhajce saw its biggest political rally ever. A thousand people marched around the market square with big red and white banners. "We want colonies! We deserve colonies!" chanted the Polish patriots.

A "Polish Colonial League" was organized to impress the world with the injustice done to the Polish people. As Tomasiewicz, the town crier, put it, "Poland was the bulwark of Christianity for ages. We deserve colonies!" His nephew, the commander of the horse-driven fire engine, was with him. "We Poles are ferocious fighters," the younger Tomasiewicz growled. "If France and England want our help in stopping Fascism and Communism, they have to cede us some colonies."

The Polish Army was projecting an image of might. Each officer, with his hand-tailored suit, shining boots, and silver braids could easily have walked onto any stage to play the role of a prince in Lehar's operettas. The soldiers were tough and rugged; they did not use socks, just long green bandages called *onuce* that were easy to wash but hard to put on.

Then the military clique started an intensive program to make and buy armaments. School children had to do without lunches and contribute to the arms race. For each 150 zlotys collected, a new rifle was purchased and presented to the Polish Army. A special Army detachment from the Fifty-fifth Infantry Brigade of Brzeżany was sent to accept the rifle, and a big ceremony was held in the *rynek*. In his acceptance speech, a brave lieutenant held out to the children the vision of a Poland as a great power with borders extending from sea to sea, from the Baltic to the Black Sea—*Polska od morza do morza*. "Yes, we Poles should rule the Ukraine, not Russia," echoed Tomaszewski, the fire chief.

Poland did not get Madagascar as a colony, but the drive to buy armaments paid off.[6] In 1938, Poland helped Hitler dismember Czechoslovakia and was rewarded with a small strip of Czech territory called Zaolzie. The Polish cavalry proudly marched into Czechoslovakian territory and linked up with the German tank columns. The colonels made their first kill, and B. the town fool had a chance to welcome the return of Zaolzie to the motherland. Poland was on her way to becoming a first-rate military power. But the nation's anxiety level spiked. Even our forlorn town felt the disquiet caused by the gathering dark clouds, the war-like threats of Nazi Germany. The Jews were afraid and uneasy. By contrast, the romantic Poles eagerly anticipated repeating the glory of World War I. Meanwhile, the Ukrainians, stirred by German emissaries, looked forward to future looting and settling accounts with both Jews and Poles, and talked loudly about an independent Ukraine.

A month before the outbreak of World War II, the pace of life changed rapidly: A complete blackout was enforced. Windows were taped to protect them against bomb blasts. Cellars that always had been used for storing cheese and pickles were now converted into bomb shelters. Podhajce's leisurely pace of life was interrupted by countless air raid alarms that sent people scrambling into their flimsy, pickle-filled "bomb shelters."

The summer of 1939 was exceptionally beautiful, and the harvest was plentiful, but everybody was talking about war. On such a warm sunny day, the town crier started to deliver the ominous white call-up slips. Mothers of young boys fainted at their sight.

The white slip instructed them to come the next day to the City Hall with a three-day supply of food. At City Hall, a sergeant sitting behind a small desk checked off their names and they joined the group of inductees. The group consisted mostly of peasant boys, who came with their home-made wooden suitcases, tied with rough flax string.

After a while, a marching group was formed and left standing for two hours in the hot sun, waiting for the marching band. Soon, the band of the Volunteer Fire Department arrived playing a World War I march glorifying the Polish Cavalry. In front of us, a group of urchins was running, trying to imitate their martial pace.

Soon, the shtetl experienced its first war panic. A loudspeaker announced a coded message, "*Nadchodzi Rzym*"—Rome is coming. The piercing whine of sirens created unbelievable havoc. Stores were hastily shut, children cried, mothers desperately searched for their children, and Podhajce took on the appearance of a ghost town. It was an ingenious code that sent people racing to improvised shelters in a 200-mile radius because of a single German plane. The so-called LOPP, the civil defense league, did more damage to the country than the German planes did.

A week later, another German plane arrived to face fire from an improvised machine gun. A Polish lieutenant came up with the idea. Wanting to impress the German pilots with modern Polish technology, he collected his platoon and ordered them to shoot in sequence to mimic the firing of a machine gun. When for whatever reason the German plane flew away, the lieutenant declared himself a military genius. "My ingenuity saved Podhajce from destruction," he proudly declared.

Soon, however, the town was flooded with the masses of the disorganized units of the Polish Army, retreating toward the Romanian border. The narrow streets and dirt roads were clogged with people, horse-drawn wagons, artillery pieces, and field kitchens.

The Polish Army had few motorized vehicles. The infantry was self-propelled, but the transport units used horses for drawing the supply wagons, field kitchens and artillery pieces. The higher army echelon had its own private cars, but there was a shortage of gasoline, so the inventive Polish officers used real horsepower to pull their small cars. It was quite a sight to see a husky orderly sitting on the hood of a small car trying to steer two scared white horses. He was driving the colonel to the safety of the Romanian border.

That day, I witnessed my first execution, and it shook me. A lieutenant saw a civilian in military boots walking in the opposite direction from the disorganized army. Suspecting that the man was a deserter, he approached him swiftly and pulled off his hat. Recognizing the military crew cut, he pulled out his revolver and simply shot the hapless deserter. I was shocked. Human life was so cheap—no court martial, no inquiry, and a young life was terminated so needlessly. A few days later, when the collapse of Poland became obvious, the town's people started to supply civilian clothes to deserters, and their green uniforms and weapons were stored in the synagogue, beneath the platform used for reading the Torah, the *bimah*.

My father bought a pair of horses and a buggy, loaded the whole family, and left for the Romanian border, only to get stuck about ten miles from our town.[7] The main road was clogged with retreating Polish Army units, so we took dirt roads. The first stop we made was in a minuscule town named Wisniowczyk.

The town had a post office, four stores—and an unbelievable swarm of flies. They used to say that Wisniowczyk was the "Fly Capital of the World." There wasn't even a single radio in the town, no newspapers, and the people were completely oblivious to the war.

The appearance of refugees on the eve of the High Holidays stirred panic. Jews dressed in holiday garb, black caftans, and hats with dangling fox tails were congregating in the synagogue. "You can't desecrate the holidays. Wait two days, and later you will proceed," they argued. My mother felt guilty that she had left her parents behind and influenced father to wait a few days in Wisniowczyk.

Two days later . . . it was too late. The Russians were already on the move, the escape route was blocked, and the family returned to Podhajce. Soon, I witnessed the entrance of the Red Army. A horse-mounted Russian disarmed the last Polish policeman, Schmidt. I felt that my childhood had come to an abrupt end. I was full of apprehension and very sad.

Martin's Note: *In June 1936, Składkowski backed an economic boycott of Jewish businesses,[8] which the Polish Catholic Church also supported.[9] Indeed, the Catholic press in Poland spewed anti-Jewish hatred.[10] Virulent antisemitism predated the Sanacja regime established by Pilsudski's 1926 coup too. In 1912, antisemitic hatred erupted following Polish-Jewish support for a candidate to the Russian Duma. According to Celia Heller, "resentment and hate raged against Jews in the remaining years before Poland gained its independence . . ." and "[a]nti-Jewish attitudes, feelings, and activities constituted a strong link between diverse elements of the Polish nation."[11] On November 11, 1918, Poland's independence day, masses of Poles, including armed soldiers on leave, burst into a Jewish assembly in the city of Kielce, beat the Jews inside and then looted and pillaged Jewish stores for three hours, killing two Jewish men and injuring others.[12] Pogroms erupted elsewhere in Poland that month, including in Lwów.[13] Poles worried about their international image and, in June 1919, President Wilson set up an independent inquiry headed by Henry Morgenthau to investigate the pogroms.*

In 1919, post-Polish independence, the right-wing Endecja (National Democratic) party won the most seats in the Polish parliament.[14] And from the early days of the Second Polish Republic, Poland's political, Church and military authorities, at every level of the various hierarchies, demonstrated "generally mindless hostility . . . toward the Jewish inhabitants now under their rule."[15] *Polish politician and Endecja founder Roman Dmowski wanted to "de-Judaize" Poland and drive Jews from the economic life of the country. (In June 1919, Dmowski unabashedly told Morgenthau, who was chairing the American-led investigation into Polish pogroms, that Dmowski didn't object to Jews so long as they weren't in Poland.*[16]*) Endecja supported economic boycotts and a quota system at Polish universities. Jewish enrollment in Polish universities dropped from 24% of students in 1923–1924 to 17% by 1933 to just 8% in 1938.*[17] *In addition, most universities "did nothing as Jewish students were beaten and intimidated until they sat in the last rows of the lecture halls, called 'ghetto benches.'"*[18] *Like the Roman Catholic Church in Poland, Endecja tended to associate Jews with Bolshevism.*[19]

As for Father Kolbe, he was canonized by Poland's Pope John Paul II for taking the place of a condemned Polish Catholic prisoner. There is a prominent display venerating Kolbe in Auschwitz today which, as historian Mary Fulbrook noted, "might be seen as an affront by anyone aware of Kolbe's prewar editorship of a journal that gave space to antisemitic articles."[20] *While the Pope was well intentioned with respect to Polish-Jewish relations, his visit to Auschwitz in 1979 rankled Jewish sensibilities. Tens of thousands of Catholics gathered on the hallowed grounds of Birkenau, the camp primarily dedicated to the extermination of Jews, for an open-air papal mass beneath a gigantic cross, thus appropriating a site of Jewish martyrdom. John Paul then suggested Kolbe was a stand-in for all who were martyred there. The Pope also praised Edith Stein, a convert to Catholicism then known as Sister Benedicta (later canonized as St. Teresa Benedicta of the Cross), as another Catholic martyr killed at Auschwitz. From a Jewish perspective, this was problematic as Benedicta was murdered because she had been born Jewish. To the Nazis, it mattered not that she had converted to Catholicism, become a nun, and taken a new name.*[21]

CHAPTER 4

The Russians: Podhajce Becomes a "Workers' Paradise"

In two short weeks, Hitler conquered Poland and ceded half of it to Stalin, although for a short time only.[1] Our town was annexed to Russia and overnight it changed dramatically. Gone were the blue uniforms of the Polish police; gone was Tomaszewski with his Volunteer Fire Department; gone was the town crier reading in halting voice the proclamations of the mayor. Even the Polish mayor was gone.

Red became the prevailing color: Red flags were fluttering in the wind; red banners were strung over the streets; and the militia patrolling the streets wore red armbands. A "Red Paradise" was swiftly established.

People were glad that they had avoided German occupation, and expectations ran high. The poor expected that the Communists would take resources away from the rich and distribute them to the poor— an equalization of wealth. Instead, the Russian took from the rich and poor alike, and an equalization of *poverty* took place. In some respects, life improved for many people. The establishment of an extensive bureaucracy created employment, and free education created a cultural boom. Only after the Communists started to drain the meager resources of the poor society, did our "Workers' Paradise" turn sour.[2]

The ruble, the Russian currency with little buying power, was declared on par with the Polish currency, the zloty, and the town was flooded with Russian soldiers on a buying spree. A Russian soldier walked into a watchmaker's store, asked for the price of watch and bought a dozen. A Russian officer who walked into a store to buy a piece of chocolate, walked out with half the store.

After a while, it dawned on the merchants that there must be a shortage of goods in Russia, and that the inventory sold was not replaceable. Suddenly, shortages developed. Merchants hid their goods, and a black market was created. The Russians clamped down. A neighbor of ours was sentenced to five years of prison for hiding ten lemons. Stalin believed that all the economic and social problems of a society could be solved with the proper dose of terror.

The "Workers' Paradise" soon featured stores with empty shelves and long bread lines—but ample fear. Stalin was a genius in the revolutionary changing of reality. All problems were easily solved by changing the meaning of words: "tyranny" was called "democracy," "servitude" was called "freedom," and a "lack of merchandise" became "abundance."

At schools, teachers asked their first graders to pray and ask God for candy, and when that didn't work, they prayed to Stalin—and got the much-desired candy. When you pray to "Batko Stalin"—Father Stalin—your wishes come true, the terrified teachers told the trusting kids.[3]

The dictionary changes were reinforced with a few five-year prison sentences. The Russians introduced a modular justice system. A five-year prison sentence was the minimum base sentence, followed by ten, fifteen or twenty years. People learned to keep their mouths shut.

The ongoing revolution was accomplished by pervasive terror, coupled with relentless propaganda and helped by taxation. In an ingenious way, the Communists used taxation to change society. The so-called rich people were simply "nationalized," which means that their businesses were taken away and they were driven from their houses. The poor merchants were taxed to death and forced to abandon their "evil" ways of making a living by trading.

Taxation without mercy sealed the revolution. The Communist authorities used Polish tax records to mete out tax adjustments going back ten years. "You cheated the Polish authorities by underpaying taxes. The Proletarian state you can't cheat. We are too smart," they would say. The Communists then doubled, tripled and even quadrupled the back-taxes they demanded, and the small storekeepers went out of business.

Afterwards, the Communists clamped down on the religious life of the populations by putting a heavy tax burden on the churches and synagogues. Many small synagogues closed.

Soon, serious shortages developed, and Meir, the town joker, used to say that we were going to live as if on permanent holiday: We would dress like we would for the Purim Carnival and eat like we did during the Yom Kippur

The Russians: Podhajce Becomes a "Workers' Paradise" | 51

fast. The relentless Communist propaganda declared that people were living a happy life. I, myself, discovered, by coincidence, that there was a grain of truth in this statement.

When shortages developed, people started to panic-buy whatever goods appeared on the empty shelves. One day, I was passing in front of a store when a shipment of salt arrived. A long line of people immediately formed, with me at the head. When I was finally admitted to the store, the salesman asked me for the bag. "You have to bring your own bag. We don't have any bags," he said.

After a moment of hesitation, I pulled down my shirt, and using the sleeves, tied a knot around the collar, and presented my improvised bag to the salesman. Then, I watched with pride how my shirt filled up with tasty salt. Elated, I brought home a full shirt of salt. I was proud and happy. It looked like shortages of good and foods *do* create happiness.

Soon, shortages of bread developed. It was unbelievable that in the Ukraine, with its rich black soil, the breadbasket of Europe, there could be a bread shortage. But the shortages were real. Lines in front of the stores started forming at 5 o'clock in the morning. Before going to school, I had to stand in line, to pick up a half loaf of bread. Fortunately, my father taught me a trick that cut my early rising down to every second day.

There were two bread lines: one in front of the bakery and the other inside the store. My trick was to get a half loaf of bread at the counter, hide it under the arm, and get back to the end of the line, to get another half loaf. The next day, I could sleep longer, and I was happy.

Later, Stalin increased the dosage of the senseless, unpredictable terror, through "resettlements" to Siberia. At night, victims got a knock at the door and a half an hour later they were on the way to the railroad cars with smoke-stacks, taking them on a thousand-mile journey to Siberia. [*Entire families—men, women, children, and the aged—were jammed into unheated cattle cars and were given food and water irregularly. Many people died en route. Those who survived were placed in forced-labor zones in Soviet labor camps. Aryeh and Cyla Blech of Rohatyn also speak of the Soviets dragging "enemy elements" from their beds and loading them onto freight cars to Siberia and other regions deep in Russia.[4]—MK*]

First, the Russians took all the families of the Polish officers. Ironically, they also took Jews. One of the victims was the Fink family. The Finks owned a small dry-goods store, and barely scratched out a living. One of their sons, Lonek Fink, was an extremely bright young man. Without attending high school, he had passed all the required exams and earned a high school diploma. Because of his education, he reached the rank of a lieutenant in the reserves of the Polish Army. He was the only Jewish officer in his brigade and the only unemployed officer in the reserve. All his Polish counterparts held government positions. Because of their son's military position, the family was resettled to Siberia, where they survived the war, while their son was killed in Katyn.[5]

In the next resettlements, the Russian took all the Polish settlers who had received land allotments during the agrarian reforms. The paranoid Stalin did not trust them. With this transport also went the father and the family of our Communist mayor, Moses Erde.

The father of our mayor had an unusual profession for a Jew—he was a beekeeper. A few years earlier, he had bought a parcel of land from a Polish settler. This land deed qualified him as a Polish settler, an "unreliable element," to be frozen to death in Siberia.

Our mayor was a Communist who had served time in the Polish concentration camp, Bereza Kartuska. He valiantly tried to get his family released, but to no avail. The whole town watched how he dejectedly accompanied his father on the ride to the smokestack wagons. One thing I have to say about the Russian bureaucracy: It was orderly and without imagination. All resettlements took place only on Friday night, and, if they didn't find the designated victims at home, they were safe. They could resume their regular life on Saturday morning, no questions asked.

The "resettled" people were given half an hour to pack their belongings and driven by wagon to the railroad station, to the train called "Echelon." The train was comprised of red freight cars equipped with black iron wood stoves. The people called them "Chimney cars."

The "Chimney cars" arrived usually on Friday afternoons and soon it became a habit for people to sneak into the railroad station to check if the "cars with the chimneys" had arrived. One Friday morning, my father asked me to go to the railroad station to look for the chimneys. I found them. I saw a long row of brown cars with the round metal chimneys sticking out from the small windows. The "Echelon" train was ready for its next victims. That night we did not sleep at home.

During the third wave of resettlements, the largest of all, only Jews were taken. After the outbreak of the war, Jews from the western part of Poland had escaped the advancing German army. Mostly men had escaped, leaving behind their families.[6] Now, they wanted to return to reunite with their wives. In Stalin's eyes, this was a criminal offense. At night the NKVD struck and about 350,000 Jews were resettled.

Soon our turn came. One day a group of Communist officials forced their way through the closed store and declared that they were the "Nationalization Committee." A neighbor, Yossel S., headed the group. He assembled the entire family in the bedroom and informed us that we were being nationalized, meaning that all business and personal property were to be taken over by the state. Each member of the family was allowed to take two pairs of shoes, two suits, two shirts, and so on. All other personal belongings, all furniture, and the store itself were nationalized and were to belong from then on to the Socialist state.

My mother broke down and started to cry. "For twenty years we worked day and night, now we are thrown out on the street like dogs. Why? I ask you. Why? Aren't we human beings?"

Yossel S. was our neighbor's son and my mother's schoolmate.[7] He had never married and was supported by his old father. He had never worked a day in all his life. Now, he was a big shot, advising the Russians on how to exploit the newly conquered territories.

My mother turned to her old schoolmate. "Yossel, you know how hard we worked. We worked from 5 o'clock in the morning to 12 o'clock at night. Aren't we entitled to something for our labors?"

"You are bourgeois and you are being nationalized," came the stiff answer from Yossel. "And besides, you are slandering the Proletarian state with your insinuations of injustice done to you."

"Yossel, I am asking only for my personal belongings, some dresses, underwear, and stockings. That's all that I am asking for," cried my mother.

We started to collect the meager belongings allowed us, when Yossel observed that my father picked up a wedding ring from the night table and put it on his finger.

"Put the ring back. You aren't allowed to take any jewelry," Yossel barked.

"But this is my wedding band. Am I not allowed to keep my wedding band?" objected my father.

"You didn't have it on your finger, and you can't take it now. That's the rule."

"Yossel, you know that we were married for twenty years. Your father attended our wedding. This is really his wedding ring. Let him keep it," my mother pleaded.

"Nothing doing," Yossel replied. "I have to stick to my instructions. Please hurry up. We still have other stops to make." Crying, my mother pulled off her own wedding band and threw it into the drawer. "We were married for twenty years. We don't need gold rings to prove it."

In the middle of the winter, we were thrown out of our house without a place to live.

"Tough luck," commented "Chairman" S. "For twenty years, you exploited the poor. I feel no mercy for you." My hard-working parents had suddenly become "exploiters," while freeloaders like Yossel became "exploited workers." Another adjustment by the Communist-dictionary writers.

Luckily, the Russian officer that took over the apartment had more heart than this Jewish neighbor. He let us live in an unheated, empty back store-room, until we could find a place to live. In a few weeks, the whole family left Podhajce and moved to another city—Rohatyn.

"There, nobody knows us and we will get rid of the stigma 'bourgeois' that is haunting us here," Father declared.

Martin's Note: With respect to the third wave of resettlement, that of Jews, Podhajce survivor Leah Feldberg writes that the Soviets told refugees in Podhajce they could register and go home, but that this was a trick and that those who registered were sent to Siberia or other far-off places in the USSR.[8] In the mass deportation of June and July of 1940, refugees in Soviet-occupied Poland who declined to become Soviet citizens (because they hoped to go back to their homes after the war or were afraid of being drafted into the Red Army) were sent to the Soviet labor camps. This happened to Yechiel Goldstein, a cousin on my mother's side, and is discussed in Part 2. A small fraction of Jewish refugees turned down Soviet citizenship and returned to German-occupied Poland in the hope of reuniting with their families. Nearly all of them would perish in the Holocaust, some without ever seeing their loved ones.

Polish Jews suffered as much or more than any other group under Soviet rule.[9] That Polish Jews preferred to be occupied by the Soviets rather than the Nazis (because they viewed the Russians as the lesser of two evils), that some Jews were Communists (as indeed were some Poles) and that some Polish Jews like Yossel S. took local governmental positions under the Soviets (which they generally weren't permitted to do in antisemitic pre-war Poland), are facts that have often been used to label all Polish Jews as Communist, pro-Soviet enemies of Polish sovereignty and to justify or excuse Polish antisemitism.[10] Of course, this ignores the fact that Jews like S. also collaborated with the Soviets against their fellow Jews. Indeed, while Soviet *nationalization policy was not aimed at Jews as Jews, the policy had a greater impact on Jews than other ethnic groups in Poland (including in the Polish Ukraine) because Jews disproportionately were traders and business owners like my father's family.*

In his 1940 report on occupied Poland for the Polish government-in-exile in London, the Polish diplomat, courier and resistance fighter Jan Karski, warned that Nazi policies toward Jews found support in "a broad segment of Polish society":[11]

> *It is generally believed that the Jews betrayed Poland and Poles, that they are basically communists. . . . The Jews have created a situation in which the Poles regard them as devoted to the Bolsheviks and—one can safely say—wait for the moment when they will be able simply to take revenge upon the Jews. Virtually all Poles are bitter and disappointed in relation to the Jews; the overwhelming majority . . . literally look forward to an opportunity for "repayment in blood."[12]*

Nazi ideology also associated the Jews with the theories of the Jewish Karl Marx. The Judeo-Bolshevik myth—the canard that Communism was a Jewish plot to destroy the nations of Europe—was of "crucial importance to Nazi Germany, and ultimately to Nazi genocide. . . ."[13] (Even today, Neo-Nazis and their ilk make Judeo-Bolshevism a prominent part of their worldview.) Snyder argues that the Judeo-Bolshevik myth confirmed for the Nazis that their invasion of the Soviet Union in June 1941 was justified because one blow to the Soviet Union would begin the undoing of the world Jewish conspiracy Hitler saw, and that one blow to the Jews in Soviet territory could bring down the Soviet Union, which Hitler believed they controlled.[14] And the Germans used the Judeo-Bolshevik myth to stoke hatred of the Jews, especially in countries and areas where the Soviets had been occupiers and had killed or deported thousands of locals, including Poles, Ukrainians Lithuanians and Latvians.[15] The myth is often also referred to as the Judeo-Communism myth. It has a long history in Poland and other European countries. For example, in 1919, Polish soldiers killed thirty-eight Jews in Pinsk and at least sixty Jews in Wilno (Vilnius) based on unfounded suspicions they were aiding the Bolsheviks in their war with Poland.[16] In addition, in August 1919, the Polish takeover of Minsk saw 31 Jews killed in a pogrom.[17] In the wake of the furor over the killings in Pinsk, the Polish government was compelled to sign a Minorities Treaty, to be guaranteed by the League of Nations, granting certain collective rights in matters of religion, culture and education to minorities such as Jews, which was bitterly opposed by the Polish right.[18] On August 16, 1920, the day Pilsudski launched a counteroffensive in the Polish-Soviet War of that year, Poland's Minister of War ordered the internment of Jewish soldiers, officers, and volunteers at a camp in the town of Jabłonna, north of Warsaw, based on unsubstantiated reports of Jewish soldiers deserting the Polish army and joining the Red Army.[19] Also, in 1920, Poland's bishops wrote to their fellow bishops around the world claiming Judeo-Bolshevism to be the manifestation of the Antichrist.[20]

The notion that Poland's Jews were to blame for the "Sovietization" of Poland has been thoroughly discredited,[21] but the Judeo-Bolshevist myth continues to this day as an excuse for past Polish antisemitism and even underlies some antisemitism there currently.[22] The Polish-born Princeton historian Jan Gross suggests, however, that this was not the primary reason for Polish antisemitic conduct: "In the Polish Catholic imagination," he writes, "Jews are God-killers, they use the blood of Christian children for matzo, and they are also Communist."[23] For centuries before 1939, the Roman Catholic and Catholic church in Poland condemned Jews as Christ-killers. As part of its classic antisemitism, the Polish Catholic Church also viewed Jews as leeches who spread depravity throughout the Polish nation.[24]

That said, as can be seen from my earlier discussion about commemoration at Auschwitz, the subject of Polish-Jewish relations is a thorny one, with some shades of grey. Many Poles—themselves under great oppression from the occupying Germans—risked their lives to help their Jewish countrymen. Over 7,170 Poles have been honored by Israel's Yad Vashem as the Righteous Among the Nations, non-Jews who took great risks to save Jews during the Holocaust. As discussed later, individual Poles helped each of my parents survive. In addition, after the Warsaw Ghetto was liquidated in the spring of 1943, about 20,000 Jews lived in hiding in the "Aryan" side of Warsaw. Żegota, the underground Polish Council to Aid Jews, which was sponsored by the Polish government-in-exile, distributed financial help to Jews (with money provided by the American Jewish Joint Distribution Committee) and provided Jews there with fake Aryan papers.[25] Albeit a small percentage, many Poles risked everything hiding Jews. Ringelblum calls them "heroes who have fought against the greatest enemy of mankind and saved thousands from certain death."[26] Unfortunately, however, "[s]izable parts of Polish populations participated in liquidation actions and, later, during the period between 1942 and 1945, contributed directly or indirectly to the death of thousands of Jews who were seeking refuge among them."[27] Of course, in the final analysis, it is the Germans who bore primary responsibility for the Holocaust. They planned and executed it. They committed mass murder on an untold scale. The Germans also incited other nationalities to murder Jews, created conditions and incentives for them to do so, and threatened to kill anyone who helped Jews.[28]

CHAPTER 5

Refugees in Rohatyn

All of our family, including my grandfather, my uncle Zysio, and Aunt Regina, as well and my Aunt Ethel and her husband, Avraham, were "nationalized"— thrown out of their houses.[1] My immediate family moved to a small town called Rohatyn.[2] In the Soviet Union, after the annexation, everybody received a Russian passport. My father had received a passport with the notation "paragraph 861." Being a very suspicious man, he perceived that this paragraph 861 indicated resettlement to Siberia.

Somehow, he found in Rohatyn a connection to the Communist authorities and, upon payment of a big bribe, received a "clean" passport. Soon after we moved to Rohatyn, we settled down in a one-bedroom apartment. My father tried to get a job, but jobs were scarce, especially for nonpolitical people. So, my father joined a cooperative producing woolen blankets. The whole cooperative consisted of dispossessed merchants who diligently cleaned coarse wool, spun it, and wove primitive blankets to be bought by the Russian army. Selling the blankets to the Red Army was a money-losing proposition but was perceived as probation from resettlement to Siberia.

Rohatyn is an ancient town that received his name from the Ukrainian word *roh*, which means a horn. And indeed, an elk horn was the official emblem of the town. It was a beautiful town with a *rynek* consisting of many colorful multi-story buildings. Two monumental churches, the Roman Catholic church and the Greek Catholic church, adorned the square. Linden-lined streets crisscrossed the town.

Rohatyn had a rich Jewish history. In the time of Shabbatai Tzvi, the false messiah, it was teeming with supporters of the "savior." The Jews from the surrounding towns called the Rohatyn Jews *Shabse Zwinkes*. During World War I, Rohatyn was taken over by Russian forces and Jews were subjected to rapes, killings, and mass deportations. Later, the town often changed hands.

It was liberated by the Austrian army, taken over by the Poles, Bolsheviks, and Ukrainian army of Petliura, and later regained by the Poles.

We rented a one-bedroom apartment from a Mr. Gutman. It was located in a small alley, not far from the main market square, the *rynek*. The rooms were small but the garden was large. The garden reached a stream. Little did we know then that the location of this house would save our lives.

Before the war, Rohatyn had about 4,000 Jews. During the war, it was flooded with Jewish refugees from western Poland, refugees who had escaped Hitler's clutches. As a result, the Jewish population doubled. The doubling of the population created a shortage of bread, matches, salt and other goods. Every morning I had to get up at 6:00 and get in line to buy half a loaf of bread. The school day began at 8:00, and I was always afraid of being late for school.

The bread shortage was due to the rigid, centralized Russian distribution system. The Soviet bureaucracy used prewar statistics and the swelling of the town's population was not taken into consideration. A town listed as having 8,000 people was entitled to 4,000 pounds or bread daily, even if it actually had 12,000 inhabitants.

Although my mother worried about my father no longer being able to take his annual trips to treat his ulcer and rheumatism, his health had actually *improved* since the business had been nationalized. He had been delivered from worries about the double set of accounts and other daily pressures. As a result, his health blossomed. During all those years in Podhajce, my parents had worked very hard. The store had been open from 6:00 in the morning to 11 o'clock at night, without a lunch break. Despite the new stresses we were under as refugees in Rohatyn, my father miraculously was feeling better. As the Good Book says, in every disaster there is a silver lining.

<u>Martin's Note</u>: *Symon Petliura became the supreme commander of the Ukrainian Army and the president of the Ukrainian People's Republic during Ukraine's short-lived sovereignty in 1918–1921, leading Ukraine's struggle for independence following the fall of the Russian Empire in 1917. Ironically, many Jews supported the founding of the Ukrainian People's Republic, which called for a multinational state in which Jews were to enjoy equal rights.[3] During Petliura's rule of the Ukrainian People's Republic, however, at least 50,000 Jews were killed.[4] Although these are usually described as pogroms, they were attacks on Jews by the Ukrainian national government's army, rival armed groups loyal to the Ukrainian national government and counterrevolutionary Whites who wanted to restore the Romanov dynasty.[5]*

Scapegoating the Jews was used as a "political tool that helped different warring parties to unify their disparate forces and whip up popular support for their cause."[6] Local populations also participated in the violence. Jews usually were attacked because of their alleged Bolshevik or Red Army sympathies but also just for plunder.[7] A scene of peasants searching the bodies of massacred Jews, in the Ukrainian town of Proskuriv,[8] was to play out, again and again, during the Holocaust. In addition to plundering and killing Jews, Cossack soldiers fighting for the Whites gang-raped Jewish women and girls as young as ten with abandon.[9] They weren't the only group to engage in mass rapes. The scale and horrific nature of this multi-year wave of anti-Jewish violence made it comparable to the Khmelnytskyi massacres that began in 1648.[10]

The Petliurist anti-Jewish violence could be shockingly gruesome. In one instance, a Petliurist soldier cut out the eyes and tongues of a Jewish tailor and his two daughters (the oldest of whom was fourteen) before killing the three of them.[11] Indeed, Veidlinger argues that the savage attacks on Jews in the Ukraine during this period "inured the population to barbarism and brutality," thus making the Shoah easier.[12] In 1926, Petliura was assassinated in Paris by Sholom Schwartzbard, a young Jew, who claimed it was in reprisal for the deaths of fifteen family members killed in pogroms in 1919. Schwartzbard was acquitted at trial. (During the trial, Schwartzbard was accused of being an agent of the NKVD.)

CHAPTER 6

The Germans, the Ukrainians, and the Pogrom (Summer 1941)

Life in Galicia had changed under Stalin. The unpleasant reality, the shortages and the terror, were papered over with a flood of words and slogans. Life had become incomprehensible and absurd. Two years of life under the Soviets set the stage for a life full of nightmares. The worst was about to come.

On June 22, 1941, the Germans attacked Russia and one week later, German planes bombed Rohatyn. I was sitting with my mother in the kitchen, when we heard the noise of the approaching aircraft. Soon I heard the piercing noise of falling bombs. *My God*, I thought, *it sounds like its coming straight at us. In a minute, we'll all be dead.* I looked around and saw my mother laying flatly on the floor—she was pale white, all the blood drained from her face. The piercing noise stopped, followed by a big explosion. A minute later, the planes were gone, and an eerie silence prevailed.

Thank God we survived. If you hear the noise, you are still alive, I said to myself, looking around to assess the damage. Through the windows, I saw smoke rising from the direction of the *rynek*, where a building had been hit.

Now the situation was changing very fast, from minute to minute. A few days later, the NKVD started burning documents and killing its political prisoners. The German invasion prompted the NKVD to kill nearly 10,000 imprisoned Polish citizens rather than let them fall into German hands. [*The NKVD also killed Ukrainians it had jailed on suspicion of having informed for Germany.*[1]*—MK*] But even before the NKVD had a chance to finish its work, the German Army entered the town. The resulting Russian retreat resembled the retreat of the Polish Army, albeit on a more massive scale.

When the Germans entered, the Jews accepted this necessary evil with hope. Making a living was everybody's concern. Little did we know what was in store for us.

The German authorities were swiftly established. The Ukrainian population received the Germans like liberators, believing the German propaganda and expecting the creation of an independent Ukraine. Besides promises, however, they got nothing. It looks like the Germans compensated them by permitting them to start a pogrom and beat Jews.

Martin's Note: *In the 21 months before Operation Barbarossa, the German invasion of the Soviet Union, as many as 30,000 Jews had perished because of the Nazis.[2] The invasion of Soviet-occupied territory and the Soviet Union in June 1941 marked an extremely deadly turning point for Jews. After the invasion, a new German policy of systematically destroying all Jewish communities was soon put into place.[3] Einsatzgruppen (mobile killing squads) expanded from "shooting all adult male Jews to 'root and branch' genocide, targeting women, children and entire families."[4] Following the German invasion, German-instigated pogroms took place in virtually every Galician town or village, from the capital Lwów to towns like Tarnopol, Drohobycz, Brzeżany, Sambor, Stryj, Kolomyja, and others, as well as in dozens of villages and hamlets in which the Jewish population was simply wiped away by its peasant neighbors.[5] By August 1, some 24,000 Jews in eastern Galicia had been massacred.[6]*

The violence took place during the last days of June and during July 1941, in waves: simultaneous with or even before the arrival of the German troops.[7] The first wave was during the "prison actions" (after the discovery of prisoners massacred by the NKVD just before the Soviet withdrawal, which was blamed on the Jews, naturally).[8] For example, German soldiers made Jews in the city of Lwów, which then had Poland's third largest Jewish population, carry the decaying bodies of the Soviet-executed prisoners from one place to another and wash and bury the bodies, sometimes using only a toy shovel or their bare hands, while Ukrainian locals cursed their Jewish neighbors and threw stones at them.[9] Sometimes Jews were forced to lick the corpses and were then beaten to death with various instruments.[10]

In late July, during the "Petliura days," the Nazis offered the Ukrainian populace an opportunity to avenge the assassination of the Ukrainian leader by Sholom Schwartzbard. One example: Following the mass murder of Jews in Lwów in early July, local Ukrainians seized thousands of Jewish men and women in late July and killed at least 2,000 more.[11] The acts of violence and murder were associated with the looting of the Jews' property, the burning of synagogues, and widespread sexual assaults on Jewish women.[12] They occurred with or without the presence of the occupying forces. Germans participated only in about half of the incidents.[13] The perpetrators were generally Ukrainians; for the most part, Poles kept away from the pogroms or are mentioned as occasional participants.[14]

Rohatyn survivors Aryeh and Cyla Blech write this about the Ukrainians in their city in 1941:

> The first to demonstrate their animal instincts and anti-Semitic sentiments were the Ukrainians. Their dirty work consisted of denigrating Jews, extorting money, jewels and food from them, and further, beating them, delivering blows without mercy and without any reason other than for sadistic pleasure. When the SS later undertook their anti-Jewish work, they found willing and devoted helpers in the Ukrainians.[15]

In Rohatyn, according to multiple accounts, on or around July 12, 1941, Ukrainians wielding sticks, and perhaps also Germans, grabbed Jews on the street and in their homes, beat them and drove them to a synagogue where they were forced through two rows of Ukrainians, a sort of brutal "receiving line," where the Ukrainians further beat them as they ran through.[16] Then the Ukrainians/Germans there forced the men inside the synagogue and locked them in, with the threat of burning them alive after any money or valuable items like watches were taken from them.[17] Most accounts posit that the community gathered money and other valuables to buy the lives and release of the people inside.

This was no idle threat. Rather, it was part of the Nazi playbook. Just days earlier, in Tarnopol, German and Ukrainian police forced about a hundred Jews in a synagogue and set it on fire.[18] In Przemyślany (Psheh-mish-lah-neh), a town only thirty-four kilometers north of Rohatyn, on July 15, 1941—just two weeks after the Germans invaded the town and around the time of the Rohatyn synagogue pogrom—the Germans, with the active assistance of the local population, burned a synagogue and all of the ritual objects inside it. About ten Jews were thrown into the fire and died in the flames. The fires spread to the Jewish houses nearby, and about forty homes were destroyed.[19] In Białystok, a city in northern Poland, the Germans, around the same time, "set . . . a kind of example" for the local populace to follow by carrying out large-scale killings of Jews themselves.[20] German policemen killed about 300 Jews and then left their bodies lying in the streets. The police then drove several hundred more Jews into a synagogue and set *it afire, shooting those who tried to escape.*[21] *In 1946, the Central Commission for the Investigation of German Crimes in Poland reported that the Germans set "several hundred" synagogues ablaze or forced the Jews to do it themselves and then sometimes fined the Jews for "setting" the fires.*[22]

Similarly, though not involving a synagogue, on July 10, 1941, it appears that eight Gestapo men decided that all the Jews in the German-occupied town of Jedwabne [Yed-VAB-Neh], Poland should be killed.[23] *After a brutal, murderous pogrom, a group of Poles locked 300 Jewish men, women, and children—their neighbors—in a barn in and burned them alive.*[24] *Jedwabne is west of Białystok.*

Just three days earlier, local Poles in the shtetl of Radziłów, who had greeted the incoming German army as liberators from the Soviets, also had forced their Jewish neighbors into a barn and set it on fire, shooting those who managed to get out. According to an eyewitness, it was more difficult to name townspeople who did not plunder their neighbors' houses as the people were being incinerated.[25]

In the summer of 1941, at the same time the Nazi-incited pogroms were taking place in Rohatyn and elsewhere in the Polish Ukraine, they were also taking place in other countries now occupied by the Germans. Lithuanians, Latvians, and Estonians eagerly assisted the Nazis in murdering Jews in their countries.

Germany's so-called Order Police constituted about 500 out of the 3,000 men assigned to the four Einsatzgruppen, which were usually led by Nazi party and SS members of long standing.[26] *The various German police forces were under the control of SS commander Heinrich Himmler, who "hybridized them": Police officers were recruited by the SS, and SS officers were assigned to the police.*[27] *German policemen killed more Jews on the eastern front than did the Einsatzgruppen.*[28] *For example, on April 28, 1942, German policemen killed thirty-two Jews in the ghetto in my maternal grandfather's hometown of Ostrowiec Świętokrzyski (usually simply referred to as Ostrowiec).*[29]

CHAPTER 7

The Judenrat (Jewish Council)

The German units that entered the town behaved well. No anti-Jewish incidents were reported.[1] On the contrary, homesick German soldiers, who could not interact with Poles or Ukrainians because of the language barrier, eagerly socialized with Jews. I remember how my father played chess in the alley with German soldiers, and shared with them his recollections from World War I.

We were more afraid of the Ukrainians than of the Germans. The Ukrainian Militia developed a habit of catching Jews and forcing them to do work. It was work without pay, slave labor. Our lives became difficult and unpredictable. Jews were afraid to walk the streets, and we were glad when the Judenrat, the Jewish Council, was created. The formation of the Jewish Council brought some normality to our lives.

It happened unexpectedly. We heard that a German captain told Shlomo Amarant, the head of the *kehilla*, the Jewish community, to call a meeting of the Jewish leaders, including the Rabbi, the former members of the *kehilla* council, and other notables and have them present at the Old Synagogue in two hours.

Two hours later, the people were assembled and twelve people were selected to serve as the Judenrat, the Jewish Council, which would represent the Jewish Community before the German authorities.[2] (The Nazis decreed that only Jewish men should serve on these councils, and the Rohatyn Judenrat, like virtually every Judenrat, was all male.[3]) The German captain told them to organize a Post Office, *Arbeitsamt* (a labor exchange), Bread Distribution, Jail, Burial Society, and a Jewish [Auxiliary] Police Force. With one stroke, the Germans had created a new Jewish aristocracy, and divided the community into the powerful and the powerless. The Judenrat and the Jewish police were given the power of life and death over the powerless Jewish masses.

Amarant became the chairman of the Judenrat and on his shoulders rested the responsibility of creating and staffing all the necessary agencies and dealing with the flood of German orders. Meir Weisbraun was named the commandant of the Jewish Order Police. His qualifications were his having achieved the rank of sergeant in the Polish Army. He became the most powerful man in the ghetto.

Meir was an unusually handsome man, well built, with a black mustache and wavy black hair. He organized a Jewish police force of fifty people. The policemen looked like a sheriff's posse; they wore badges, hats, and truncheons as a sign of authority. Meir designed for himself an elaborate uniform; with a silver braided hat he looked like the baron from Strauss's operetta. He was a simple character, without too much education, but good-natured. He really wanted to help the Jews and save lives. In the beginning, he wanted to play the role of a redeemer of Israel. Later, he believed that he could save the bulk of the Jewish population by sacrificing to the Germans the old and the crippled.

A flood of German orders started to arrive soon. Jews were not allowed to have radios, telephones, furs or even bicycles. All equipment had to be turned over to the Germans. Violators would be punished by death. Next, an order demanded from the Jewish community a contribution of one million zloty. If the money was not delivered in seven days, 200 hostages would be executed.[4] The next blow to the Jewish community was the verdict that everyone twelve years or older had to wear a white armband with the Star of David. Violators would be punished with death.

The Judenrat soon established an extensive bureaucracy: The labor office assigned people for slave labor. The General Department distributed skimpy bread rations. Most important was the Police Department. Ironically, the Jews welcomed the creation of the Judenrat. Life became more secure, more predictable. Every family had to supply slave labor a few days a week, but it was possible to substitute one member for another. The Jews also got representation in front of the capricious Nazi authorities—or at least we thought so.

Martin's Note: Governor-General Hans Frank ordered the creation of Judenrats in the General Government.[5] In addition to sparing German manpower that would otherwise have been needed to manage the ghettos they established across Poland and elsewhere, the Judenrats also channeled Jewish resentment toward the Jewish administrations and away from the councils' Nazi overlords.[6] There were "continual changes in the personnel of the Jewish Councils.... Council members escaped, took cover, resigned, were arrested, were killed on the spot, or were deported; and others were nominated to take their places."[7]

Regarding the flood of restrictive German orders, the confiscation of radios was intended to prevent Jews from getting independent news from outside the ghetto.[8] The prohibition on bicycles was important because Jews were generally barred from using public transportation. Cars were seized by the Nazis and were replaced in large ghettos like the Warsaw Ghetto with rickshaws.[9]

The Nazis ordered Jews to turn in all clothing with fur—the so-called "fur decrees"—to clothe their troops for the cold Russian winter. Thorne writes that Jews in Sambor and in many towns and villages burned their furs to keep them from being used to help the German war effort.[10] The practice of destroying furs or giving them to Polish acquaintances was dangerous. For example, the yizkor book for Kolymja notes that the Judenrat there knew which Jews possessed furs and "if someone chose not to give up the furs or tried to hide something, he was arrested by the Judenrat and put in the Jewish jail [the jail run by the Judenrat]."[11] The Germans' punishment was even worse. According to Wohl, two Jews in Rohatyn were killed when furs were found in their homes. The Ostrowiec yizkor book (Sefer Ostrovtsah) similarly notes that the SS shot a man for hiding a fur at a Christian friend's house.[12] Thorne writes that this was commonplace.[13] In Podhajce, a woman named Visha Roth was killed when the Pole she hid her fur with turned her in.[14] Close to Podhajce and Rohatyn, in Tarnopol, when the Germans ordered the Jews to surrender all their items of fur clothing at the end of December 1941, the Gestapo took twelve Jews as hostages. After the Judenrat had collected and handed over the furs, the Gestapo conducted a search and discovered fur clothing in the home of the Schwarz family. The Germans killed all five family members.[15] As discussed later, furs were particularly important to the survival of my mother.

CHAPTER 8

First, the Ghetto; Then, Awful News

A few weeks after the pogrom, a new blow fell on the Jewish community: the creation of a ghetto. Shlomo Amarant was told that the Jews would be confined to their own quarter. The boundaries were the river Gnila Lipa, the stream running into the river, and the marketplace. (See arial map.) All Jews living beyond the outlined boundaries had one week to vacate their houses.

People could take their personal belongings and simple, old or unpainted furniture. Everything else had to be left behind. Any Jew caught outside the boundaries of the ghetto would be shot on the spot. After the ghetto was established, only Jews with work permits would be allowed to leave it.

When the news leaked, pandemonium broke loose. Everybody wanted some exemption. Two days later, the first movers appeared on the streets. People carried their belongings on their backs, on pushcarts, and on wheelbarrows. It looked like a modern version of the Exodus from Egypt.[1]

Before people could move, however, the Judenrat had to assign them a place. The ghetto was in the poor section of the town, and the creation of the ghetto created terrible overcrowding. The rule of thumb was that one family was assigned no more than one room.[2] A kitchen was also counted as a room. The scene in the Judenrat was hellish. People were cursing, crying or pleading for more space for their families.

Our family was lucky. Because our apartment was already within the boundaries of the ghetto, we didn't have to move. Nevertheless, we had to share our kitchen with three sisters—three spinsters. The apartment was very small. It contained a small bedroom, painted in an odious green color. The bedroom contained only one bed and a sofa. That was all the furniture that fit. The kitchen had a wood-burning stove, a small window looking into the alley, and a bunkbed installed by our new tenants. It's no wonder that we spent all our free waking hours in the alley.

Despite all the pleading, within one week the ghetto was created. All streets leading out of the ghetto were blocked off and only two exit points remained open. At the crossing points, railroad crossing type ramps were installed. The Jewish police manned them. The Germans cleverly used their victims to enforce Nazi restrictions.

Staying alive in face of the German attempt to starve the Jews to death became the main preoccupation. The ghetto was sealed off tightly and most Jews were left without any means of support. Only a fortunate few, like tailors and shoemakers, could earn a living. The majority, the shopkeepers and the traders, lost everything. People started to sell personal belongings to buy food or fuel. After a few weeks, one could see people walking with swollen legs, the outcome of starvation.

At the beginning, you couldn't buy food even if you had money, but as soon the Germans tightened the noose, the Jews found ways to bypass it. For example, Bloch found some old grindstone and installed a primitive flour mill in his basement. He charged ten percent for using his mills. Now, people that bartered their clothing for wheat could grind the grain into flour. After the creation of the ghetto, all food supplies were cut off. There were many babies in the ghetto for whom fresh milk was essential for survival, and the desperate parents paid any price for a liter of milk.

One day I came back from work outside the ghetto bringing one kilogram of wheat. My mother was elated.

"I'm so happy! Our potatoes are running out. Now we can have a real meal."

She took the wheat and started to grind it in a small manual coffee grinder. Every ten minutes, she ground a small drawerful of rough wheat.

Shmuel, our neighbor, came into our kitchen and seeing my mother working the coffee grinder asked her what she was doing. "What am I grinding?" She answered with a smile. "I'm grinding wheat and making kasha. I'm preparing our supper."

Shmuel then told her about Bloch's underground flour mill, and suggested she try using it to grind the wheat. When I got to Bloch's place, Bloch took out one tenth of the wheat, and guided me to a dimly lit cellar.[3] In the middle of the cellar stood the old grindstone. He explained how the mill was used. "You grab the stick with your right hand and turn the stone. With your left hand you feed in the grain. One more thing, I have a kid standing guard, and watching out for Germans. When you hear a loud whistle, run for cover. Good luck, Shiko."[4]

The work on the grindstone was backbreaking. The mill was comprised of two heavy round stones, the top stone had an opening in the center for feeding the grain, and the bottom stone had a small opening through which the rough flour was discharged. The top stone had an implanted handle for turning the stone. The friction was tremendous; you had to spend almost as much energy operating the grindstone as you could get from the flour.

My mother was a terrific cook, and from this raw wheat she made an excellent meal—kasha. The next day, I discovered that peasant women were selling fresh milk on the street across the ghetto boundary. Although it was dangerous, I started to buy milk. I haggled the price, standing at the border of the ghetto, I later threw the empty container to the seller to be filled up and jumped the stream to pay and retrieve the milk. It was a dangerous transaction, but starvation was worse.

The creation of the Judenrat brought some stability to our lives in the ghetto. The Judenrat supplied all the labor required by the German authorities and walking on the streets became less hazardous. I, myself, worked about five times a week on slave-labor assignments, because I substituted for my mother and my father. [*My dad was only fourteen or fifteen and seriously underweight from deprivation.—MK*] At that time, a great differentiation occurred in the ghetto. People were divided into two groups: the powerful and the powerless. People without connection to the Judenrat were powerless. Our family, being outsiders without connections, belonged to that group. We were giving the worst slave-labor assignments.

In addition, there was a terrible erosion of Jewish values. Brutality came to surface. You saw this with power-drunk, truncheon-swinging Jewish policemen.

For a long time, we had lost contact with our family. After the Germans took over the town, all mail service stopped. Suddenly, we received a letter from my grandfather. B., known in Podhajce as the town's fool, delivered it. He had walked on foot from Podhajce and walked for three full days.

Reading the letter, my mother burst out in tears. The news was horrible. Ukrainians had killed Mom's sister, Ethel. She had lived in a small town called Mikulince.[5] When the Germans entered the town, her husband, Awrumce,[6] had been taken away to dig trenches. My Aunt Ethel went out to look for him and never returned home. Her body was never found.

In the letter, there was a small photo of an old man. "This is your grandfather," said my mother, handing me the photo.

"Grandfather?" I asked in disbelief.

My grandfather had a luxurious white beard and sidelocks. In my eyes, he always looked like the prophet Isaiah. Here was a picture of an old man, without teeth, without the magnificent beard, looking like an old peasant. His eyes were lifeless, sad.

My mother cried, "I never thought to live to see my father without a beard, shaved like a beggar."

Martin's Note: Dawidowicz describes the "nightmare experience" everywhere that Jews were forced into ghettos:

> Endless processions of weary men and women, babies in their arms, children at their sides, with bags, sacks, bedrolls on their backs and around their necks, the miserable remnants of their belonging loaded on carts, wheelbarrows . . . , leftovers of their past life, artifacts of a vanishing civilization, pushing, shoving, screaming, groaning, shuffled into the ghettos.[7]

Timothy Snyder writes that the ghettos represented a separation of Jews from the protection of law: "They had no power to decide where their bodies would be, and no claims to possessions." Beginning in Poland, he says, the Germans established ghettos in every country where they sought to destroy the state.[8] The Nazis regarded their ghettos as temporary concentration camps.[9]

Starving the Jews in the ghettos was official Nazi policy. Speaking of the Jews' food rations being reduced to half of those of the Poles, Governor General Frank said that "it must be done in cold blood and without pity; the fact that in this way we condemn 1,200,000 Jews to death by hunger is only of indirect importance. If the Jews should not starve I sincerely hope that it will inspire further anti-Jewish regulations."[10] The "terrible erosion of Jewish values" from starvation my father references wasn't limited to acts of the Jewish police. Sometimes, even parents and their children fought over tiny scraps of food.[11]

Regarding the end of the chapter, to my astonishment, Horowitz writes in the Mikulince yizkor book of the murder of "Mrs. Milch of Podhitze," who almost certainly was my father's Aunt Ethel:

> *The town was full of German military. Soldiers came to Jewish homes and took what they could, particularly food stuffs. A town council was elected, headed by the Ukrainian Fedewich. The Ukrainians considered themselves the rulers and did whatever they wanted. They harassed the Jews, beat them, looted their property, insulted them, and cut off their beards and side curls. One day, the Ukrainians arrested a few Jews in the orchard alongside the brewery. They ordered the Jews to dig a grave for a horse. The bloodthirsty Ukrainians then buried the Jews in the same pit and threw the horses on top of them. Among those killed were Fruma Hochberg, Mark Fidler, and Mrs. Milch of Podhitze.*

German "refinements of cruelty were reserved especially for pious Jews and rabbis, whose traditional Jewish garb . . . and whose beard and sidelocks identified them as quintessentially Jewish. . . . Germans seized bearded Jews and beat them. A more sophisticated entertainment involved plucking beards, hair by hair or in clumps."[12] In the Chełm yizkor book, Lazar Kahan writes: "When the Germans released the rabbi [of Chełm] after the shameful torturing they caught Jews with beards, they cut and tore out beards and even set fire to the beards of several Jews. Then they dragged Jews with burning beards to the fence and poured water on them without end. . . . The Jews were drenched and, as it was cold, they . . . became sick. . . ."[13] In Radom, my mother's hometown, the Nazis burned the beards mostly just on one side of men's faces and then made them pose in grotesque positions.[14] Dawidowicz also mentions beards being set on fire and Germans hacking beards off with bayonets.[15]

CHAPTER 9

The Labor Camp: Skipping Out on Skalat

I was standing in the alley when Dudzic W., a Jewish policeman, appeared. He handed me a slip of paper from the Judenrat. I was directed to report the next day to the Judenrat and bring along a week's supply of food. The policeman handed me the form and disappeared before I could read it. It turned out that the Judenrat was ordered by the Germans to supply 120 Jews for the work camp in Skalat, and I had been selected to be one of them.

The question arose: what do I do now? My family decided that I should run away and hide outside the ghetto until the transport left. My father, being a pessimist, insisted that I leave immediately. He said, "I don't trust the Germans and I don't trust the Judenrat. You better run immediately. They might come at night to catch you."[1]

Without thinking too much, I grabbed a piece of bread and jumped the border stream. After leaving the ghetto, I instinctively walked toward the outskirts of the town, hoping to find shelter there. I was a stranger in the town. I didn't know too many people, so I decided to hide in the fields. It was before harvest time, and the cornfields and the wheat fields were high. I walked briskly, passing the village and turned into the fields. I found a field of rye and settled down for the night. I took off my jacket, made myself comfortable and went to sleep.

It was dark when I awoke before sunrise. I was cold and trembling convulsively. My clothes were damp from the dew. I looked up and saw the sky with all its shining stars. *What do I do now?* I looked around and, in the distance, I saw the outline of the village. A few scattered, whitewashed peasant huts. Maybe I could steal into a barn or bury myself in a haystack? I liked the idea. I saw myself lying in a fresh-smelling haystack, gazing at the stars.

I got up and slowly approached the village. As I came closer, I saw an open barn. It looked abandoned— a perfect place to hide. Walking briskly, I warmed up a little and my strength came back. I walked faster. I'd almost reached the entrance to the barn when a dog attacked me, barking viciously. Instinctively, I stepped back. The dog jumped on me, barking, but he immediately fell back. He was attached to a long restraining leash. Now, all the village dogs joined in on the barking. I saw a light flicker on and a peasant appeared in the doorway. I swiftly turned back and ran to my original hiding place. The haystack was beyond my reach.

The rising sun dissipated the morning fog, bringing some relief to my misery. Now, I felt pangs of hunger. The bread was gone. *What do I eat now?* I looked around and saw the stalks of wheat. I tried them. The grain was not ripe but soft and green. Slowly, I separated a kernel and chewed it. It wasn't bad. It took me a long time to satisfy my hunger. A few gulps of water from the stream satisfied my thirst. *Tonight, I will return to the ghetto, so let me enjoy the warmth of the sun, and being close to nature*, I thought.

At midnight, I got up to return to the ghetto. *The transport must be gone by now*, I reassured myself. Without any further adventures, I retraced my escape path, jumped the stream, approached the house, and knocked on the window. In a minute, my father came out from the house.

"Shiko, for Heaven's sake what are you doing here? They are looking for you! Go back! It will take a few days to assemble the transport. You'd better run."

"A few days? How will I manage? How will I know when the danger is over?" I asked.

"When the danger is over, I'll leave a lit candle in our window. This will be the signal Now, wait. I'll bring you some food." My father went inside the house and a moment later I heard loud voices. I recognized the voices of Jewish policemen. I couldn't wait for the food. I ran quickly and returned to my hiding place.

I stayed in the fields a whole a week. It was hell. The cold of the nights, the dampness of the morning dew, the unbelievable heat of the day. It was hell, but I learned how to cope. I slept during the day and foraged at night like animal. At night, I kept moving to keep warm. After a week, I returned to the ghetto, dirty, unshaven, and shivering, but happy that I had avoided the German camp. I was happy to return to the ghetto, to the dangerous place that gave me a feeling of "security."

The Labor Camp: Skipping Out on Skalat | 77

Martin's Note: My dad and his family had reason to fear that he would never be heard from again if sent to a labor camp. Hillel Zeidman, a survivor of the Skalat Ghetto, writes in "The End of Skalat," in the Skalat yizkor book that people in the Skalat work camp endured "crushing labor" and that, on June 20, 1943, a majority of the camp's surviving inmates were exterminated.[2] Podhajce survivor Shlomo Teicher paints a nightmarish picture of the Borki Wielki work camp, where 4,000 Jews died over the camp's eighteen-month existence. He writes of SS and Jewish policemen beating inmates to unconsciousness (with the SS sometimes going further and killing them), of sick people being executed, and of the Germans shooting every tenth prisoner in reprisal for an escaped inmate.[3]

Writing about the Janowska [Janover] labor camp in Lwów, Thorne says: "All those transported here had a death sentence pronounced on them. Without their awareness of it, they were already in the grave."[4] Thorne also writes:

> "At times, Jewish 'foremen' from the ranks were called on to help hold down the victims, and if they—in their distaste at the job— did not grip prisoners as prescribed, they too were beaten. And once or twice a week, to intimidate the prisoners and keep them in a constant state of fear, they randomly pulled an inmate from the ranks and shot him on the spot.[5]

There are different views as to the Nazis' objectives here. In September 1941, Einsatzgruppe chief Otto Rasch suggested that Jews be worked to death as a more "practical" alternative to mass shootings.[6] The German Crimes in Poland, Vol. I states that, "[T]he aim of labour camp policy was not so much to squeeze the last ounce of work out of the Jews as to kill them by overwork and physical torture."[7] Christopher Browning, however, argues that statements such as this one are an oversimplification and that there was a tension between Hitler's and Himmler's ideological desire to exterminate all Jews and Germany's need for slave labor connected with its war effort.[8] Mary Fulbrook, a British professor of German history, falls more in the "extermination through work" camp (no pun intended). She notes that the SS hired out slave labor to German industry and asserts that the employers "needed only to have a guaranteed supply of cheap labor, not necessarily retaining the same individuals over time."[9]

In researching this book, I learned, to my surprise, that one of the most popular tourist attractions in Poland, the Wieliczka (pronounced Vyeh-Leech-ka) salt mine outside of Krakow, was once a Nazi labor camp.[10] *In fact, it was a sub-camp of Płaszów, made famous by* Schindler's List. *I have toured Wieliczka twice, in two different decades (2005 and 2018). In neither tour was Wieliczka's connection to the Shoah mentioned.*

CHAPTER 10

The First Action (March 1942)

The Action in the Ghetto of Rohatyn, March 1942

By Alexander Kimel

Do I want to remember?
The peaceful ghetto, before the raid:
Children shaking like leaves in the wind.
Mothers searching for a piece of bread.
Shadows, on swollen legs, moving with fear.
No, I don't want to remember, but how can I forget?

Do I want to remember, the creation of hell?
The shouts of the Raiders, enjoying the hunt.
Cries of the wounded, begging for life.
Faces of mothers carved with pain.
Hiding children, dripping with fear.
No, I don't want to remember, but how can I forget?

Do I want to remember, my fearful return?
Families vanished in the midst of the day.
The mass grave steaming with vapor of blood.
Mothers searching for children in vain.
The pain of the ghetto cuts like a knife.
No, I don't want to remember, but how can I forget?

Do I want to remember the wailing of the night?
The doors kicked ajar, ripped feathers floating in the air.

The night scented with snow-melting blood.
While the compassionate moon is showing the way.
For the faceless shadows, searching for kin.
No, I don't want to remember, but I cannot forget.

Do I want to remember this world upside down?
Where the departed are blessed with an instant death.
While the living condemned to a short wretched life,
And a long tortuous journey into unnamed place,
Converting Living Souls, into ashes and gas.
No, I Have to Remember and Never Let *You* Forget.

* * *

Martin's Note: *At the Wannsee Conference of January 20, 1942, the Nazis decided on their "Final Solution" of the "Jewish problem"—the extermination of all 11 million Jews living in Europe, including the United Kingdom and neutral countries.[1] The Einsatzgruppen received clear orders from the chief planners to make Europe* Judenrein *and they took their jobs seriously.[2] This would now play out in ghettos across Eastern Europe.*

I will never forget the Nazi "action"[3]—the killings that took place on March 20,1942 in Rohatyn. The German raiders surrounded the ghetto and brutally murdered 3,400 Jews.

In March 1942, I was part of a group of Jews that was led to a bleak, desolate place outside the town, a large plateau, with sparse grass and dwarf bushes. At the site, a tall German with a red, square face told us we were going to dig underground storage facilities.

We were given tools and soon the area looked like a gigantic construction site. People were diligently digging, breaking up the excavated boulders and carting away dirt. I was given a big hammer and worked at breaking up big boulders before they were carted away on wheelbarrows.

After a backbreaking day, I returned home and my father told me: "Shiko, I arranged a job for you with the German Army. You are going to work as a carpenter."

The next day, early in the morning, I left for my new job. I was anxious and worried. *How will I manage? What do carpenters really do?* I wondered. It was dark outside, and lights shone through the small windows. The

The First Action (March 1942) | 81

dilapidated streets were covered with a blanket of white snow. The ghetto looked quiet and peaceful.

At the job, I was assigned to help a German soldier named Hans, who heartily laughed at my clumsy handling of the saw. "To make a straight cut, you have to pull the saw gently. Don't jerk it. Don't use force," Hans admonished me.

We were building a fuel depot for the Wehrmacht. I was so involved in my work that I didn't pay attention to the intermittent shooting that erupted at midday. At lunchtime, I sat at the roadside with Willie Bloch, the other Jewish carpenter. A passing Ukrainian peasant warned us, "They are killing the Jews in town. Why aren't you boys hiding?"

"Killing Jews? What are you talking about?" I didn't believe him.

"Look there. See for yourself," he said.

I turned around. In the distance, I saw heavy German trucks disgorging people, who were then driven uphill on foot. I heard the shooting intermittently, but I didn't believe that killings were taking place. I didn't know what to do, but before I could decide, Willie took off and ran in the direction of the railroad station, and I followed him.

We found shelter in a storage room filled with cement. We sat in the far corner, hiding under a mound of cement. The shooting grew louder and louder. Soon it turned into a continuous barrage. I leaned against Willie and felt his heart beating wildly. We sat there for a very long time which seemed like an eternity. At five o'clock, the shooting stopped. Covered with cement dust, we crawled out from our hiding place and, oblivious to our appearance, walked back to the ghetto.

I walked in a daze. Despite the shooting, the possibility that people had actually been killed somehow didn't occur to me. I expected to find everybody alive and everything in order. I blocked out the unpleasant reality from my awareness. On the way home, I saw a horse-drawn wagon loaded with stained clothing. The wagon driver, whip in hand, walked alongside the wagon.

"Where are they taking this soiled clothing?" I asked the Jews who were walking behind the wagon.

"Come give us a hand. We are taking the corpses to the mass grave for burial," came the answer.

What he said must not have fully registered with me. *For burial? What are they talking about? Nobody buries stained clothing,* I thought. As I looked closer, I was shocked. These were not bloodstained clothing but corpses— real, human corpses.

I didn't want to go but I couldn't refuse. I started to walk behind the loaded wagon. Squeaking and shuddering, the wagon turned from the main road onto a hilly dirt road. I recognized the place. This was the road I had been on two days ago when I went to build the underground storage facilities. The cart, overloaded with corpses, swayed. The horses slowed.

"Let's push," yelled the driver. I went closer, grabbed the wooden railing of the wagon, and to my horror, I recognized the face of one of the corpses. It was Arnold, a classmate of mine. *Oh my God! This is Arnoldek! I just kidded him yesterday.* I felt a tremor passing through my body. Arnoldek was a heavy-set, good-natured boy. At school he had sat next to me, on the same bench. He loved candy and his rustling of crushed candy wrappers used to drive me crazy. Now he was dead. I couldn't believe it. Arnoldek's head stuck out from the spikes of the side ladder. I gently pushed it back. I was astonished at my own calmness. No feelings, just emptiness. Limitless emptiness.

When we arrived at the open pit, the place I was digging just two days ago, the scene was ghastly; the tremendous pit was filled with bodies, floating in a sea of blood; some people were still alive, moaning and moving. Some people begged for help. The Germans were gone, but the pit was guarded by Ukrainian militia, and they wouldn't let us help the wounded. We were told to dump the bodies into the pit, and later we had to collect the bodies of victims who had been shot while trying to escape.

Moshe the Shoemaker called out for people to recite the Mourner's Kaddish. We lined up in front of the pit and began the ancient prayer. It was a Kaddish said for the actual dead, for the "dead" who were still alive—and for ourselves because we expected to be shot after finishing our job. During the recitation, I felt a wave of resentment. The words of the prayer burned holes in my heart: "And the name of the Lord be sanctified and extolled." For me, praising God at that place and time was a blasphemy. It was a mockery. I couldn't continue.

After the Kaddish, the group slowly started moving towards the ghetto. We moved in deep silence. I felt an empty stupor. As I approached the boundaries of the ghetto, my heart pounded. I jumped the border stream and ran toward the house. I was looking for my parents. The kitchen was empty. On the kitchen table I found a pot with peeled potatoes soaking in water. The potatoes were covered with black spots. Seeing this, I almost fainted. My mother would never leave potatoes covered with water because they spoil. I was certain that my poor mother was dead.

I ran out of the house and saw my mother standing in the alley. "Mom!" I yelled. "You're alive!" I embraced my parents and burst out crying. "Where did you hide?" I didn't see my sister. "Where's Luba?"

My mother started to sob. "Oh, my darling daughter must be dead! I won't survive this!" We tried to calm her down, to no avail. Her loud cries brought the neighbors into the alley.

Avraham, our neighbor from across the street, came out with an ashen face. He had aged ten years in one day. "I came home and all my family, my wife and three children are gone. I will never see them again," he said. He quietly started to cry.

For the first time in my life, I saw a grown man weep uncontrollably. I knew one of his daughters well. Esterka was a petite, charming girl with red hair and a freckled face. She was always neatly dressed in a black school uniform with an immaculate white collar. She was my age.

Esterka had two main concerns in life: her freckles and her grades. She considered the freckles big blemishes and spent all her lunch money on exotic creams. In school, she had difficulties with algebra and used to ask me for help. Esterka was now gone. Freckles and algebra would no longer trouble her.

I felt embarrassed. I didn't know what to do or what to say. Silently, I left the crying man and went in search of my sister. At the Judenrat, everything was in disarray. Nobody could help me. I decided to return home. When I returned, my mother was standing in the alley, embracing my sister. Seeing this, a wave of euphoria swept over me. I was excited. *We made it! We are all alive!* I said to myself. I was joyful, but then I was ashamed. I was ashamed to be so happy at this terrible time.

This feeling of shame has stayed with me throughout my adult life. Only in the later years did I fully realize the precariousness and limitations of human existence. Today you are here, tomorrow you are gone. A man can't control his feelings, and, in time of danger, he rarely can control his deeds. Man is from dust and to dust he returns. I became more understanding of myself and more forgiving of others.

I also often think of my friend Willie Bloch, with whom I survived that dreadful day. Willie was a fighter. In December of 1942, Willie escaped from a cattle car transporting Jews. He survived the ghetto, as well as the cold and hunger of the forest. But in 1945, Willie Bloch died in the Battle for Berlin.

I couldn't say Kaddish then. But for Willie, Arnoldek, Esterka, and countless other victims, I do say Kaddish now.

The Aftermath

There was a painful aftermath to the action. The agony of the ghetto was unbearable. Every family was affected: mothers lost their children, children remained without parents. Our family was lucky. We all survived. My parents had hidden in a dilapidated shed.

People were suffering and sharing the pain by telling their stories—how they survived, how their loved ones had perished. [*People had been pulled from their apartments, with (according to one account) Germans and Ukrainians shooting the elderly, the sick, children, and pregnant women on the spot.[4] A few people successfully fled the ghetto but most did not. Armed men stood at all the exit points and hundreds attempting to escape were shot.[5] The rounded-up victims had been assembled in the town square and forced to stand motionless in the freezing cold for a long time and then lie face down on the ground, after which they were loaded onto freight trucks and driven to the mass graves. There, virtually all were machine-gunned to death. (The Blechs write that it was immediately known that the Gestapo had come that day with "a special battalion assigned specifically to the destruction of the Jews," referring to the* Einsatzgruppen.)[6] *This is generally referred to by scholars as the "Holocaust by Bullets," and more Jews died this way than were killed at Auschwitz. Some people who had been lined up to be shot in front of the mass grave were wounded but not killed by the bullets. Some of them fell into the grave and somehow managed to climb out later, though dead bodies had been lying on top of them. Some of them made it back to the ghetto and lived. Some didn't. Sterzer says an eighteen-year-old refugee from Germany made it back to the ghetto, but the Nazis learned of this and demanded that the Judenrat give her up. She was then killed.[7] There were also some less gruesome stories of survival.—MK*] My sister's friend, Salek Stein, explained that he survived because he was a member of the Italian Fascist party. He had gotten a membership card while studying in Italy before the war because it had entitled him to certain discounts. (It was impossible for Jews to study medicine at university in Poland then.) Caught by a German, he showed him the Fascist card and talked the German into letting him go.

After the March action, our lives in the ghetto changed. We were preoccupied with staying alive. Gone was the communal spirit. The most striking change was the acceptance of violence and the development of indifference towards others.

Big changes also took place in our alley. Gone was Hecht's mother. The Lustigs also lost their mother. Gutman lost both his parents. Soon afterwards, the Germans ordered the shrinking of the ghetto boundaries and in addition brought into the ghetto new victims, Jews from outlying towns: Bursztyn [pronounced "Burr-Shtin"],[8] Bukaczowce, and Bolshovce.

The alley had to adjust to the new conditions. Gutman moved in with the Lustigs, vacating the kitchen for a new family. Hecht got two new tenants, Brandeis and Naftali. At the creation of the ghetto, one family per room or kitchen was the rule of the thumb. Now the rules had changed. Each room had to accommodate the maximum number of people.

Strangers were living together in the same room. All intimacy, personal space and dignity were gone. The overcrowding, coupled with shortages of food and firewood caused many outbursts and fights. Luckily, our bedroom and the shared kitchen were so small that no additional tenants were added.

CHAPTER 11

Building a Bunker, Breaking the Ice (Literally), and My Burning Shame

Having murdered half the population, the Nazis ordered the shrinking of the ghetto. Again, I witnessed the familiar moving scenes. Fortunately, our house was located within the borders of the shrunken ghetto.

One day I was standing in the alley when a young man appeared in the Hechts' house with a small piece of paper in his hand. He said he had been sent by the Judenrat to live with us.

Shmuel Hecht took the paper, verified the signature, sighed deeply, and said: "There must be a mistake. There is no room here. We have a small room, but it's taken. Mr. Brandeis lives there. It is unsuited for two strangers."

Ania, the wife of Shmuel Hecht, came into the kitchen carrying a pot with washed, unpeeled potatoes. Peeling potatoes was considered a sin in the ghetto because it was a waste of edible skin. She looked intrigued with the appearance of the young stranger when came into the room. His name was Naftali Rosen.[1] He was from Bursztyn, which the Nazis had declared *Judenrein*, forcing him to move to Rohatyn. He told us that both of his parents had been shot and killed in Bursztyn.

Shmuel was concerned about crowding. He turned to Naftali and said, "The Judenrat made a mistake; the room is too small for two people. You wait here. I'm going to argue with the quartermaster." An hour later he came back and announced that no mistake had been made.

I liked this Naftali. He was a dynamic, well-read man with an excellent knowledge of Jewish history and philosophy. He had been thrown out of the yeshiva after the discovery that he read Spinoza. He was diligent in dealing with the Germans. He often volunteered to shine their shoes and, doing an excellent job, frequently was rewarded with bread or cigarettes. "I don't care what I have to do, but I am not going to die from hunger," he used to say.

After a while Naftali started to smuggle food into the ghetto. Only people working outside the ghetto could leave its walls. Naftali would dress into two suits, exchange one suit for bread and smuggle the food into the ghetto. It was a dangerous but rewarding game.

Naftali dreamed of joining the partisans to fight the Germans. But he was poor and, to support himself, he joined the ranks of "slaves for hire." The Germans imposed a compulsory labor regime; every day the Judenrat had to furnish 300–400 people for slave labor. We were used for all kind of menial jobs such as cleaning the sewers, firing the boilers, cleaning the houses of the "master race," etc. The Judenrat distributed the work on a rotating basis. The work was unpaid, but sometimes the decent Germans gave the slaves some bread—from the nasty "masters" the Jews received only kicks or beatings. The wealthy Jews hired the poor ones to work in their place. It was beneficial for both sides: the poor could support themselves, and the rich avoided dangerous or unpleasant assignments.

After the action of March 20, people in the ghetto were concerned with safety. Hunger was not the biggest enemy. We realized that the Germans couldn't starve us to death easily, but they could kill us with bullets. Building hideouts, or bunkers, as we called them, became a main preoccupation. When people met, they greeted each other with, "How's your bunker?" or "Do you have a bunker?" One day, Shmuel Hecht asked Naftali for advice on where to build a hideaway. "We have to protect ourselves—another action is a possibility," he said. Naftali and I walked around the house to look for a solution.

The next day, Shmuel assembled all the heads of the families and presented our ideas. The house was built on an old cellar. The entrance door to the cellar was located in the backyard.

"If we block up the door and fill in the steps leading down to the door, the cellar will be completely camouflaged. The entrance to the bunker will be through a new trap door located under the wooden cabinet," suggested Naftali.

"How will we enter the bunker?" my father asked.

"The trap door will be located under the wooden cabinet. First, you open the cabinet, then raise the hinged bottom, and pull open the trap door. The last man in closes the bottom and lowers the trap door into place."

"That isn't a good idea. The neighbors will see immediately that the door is missing. It's too dangerous," Gutman objected. Our neighbor, Lustig, whose wife had perished in the action, seconded him. "Yes," he said. "It's not a good idea. The Germans usually search the inside of buildings. The chances of detection are much higher if the entrance is from the interior. We should build a bunker in the backyard with the entrance from the shed."

"In the winter, footprints in the snow will alert the murderers," Shmuel objected.[2]

"The entrance to the bunker can't be inside the house. In case of an action, we might find the door locked and that'll be the end of us."

"So where do you suggest we build the bunker?" Naftali asked, annoyed.

"I think that we should dig a tunnel in the garden, with the entrance from the storage shed," came the response. At the back of the garden, there was a solid-brick shed, used for storing garden tools. The shed was far from the house, and we worried that our footprints would be visible in the winter or during a rainy day. Our objections were overruled, though, and the bunker's construction began.

All the work was done at night. The men did the digging while the women stood watch. The big problem was the disposal of the dug-up dirt. It had to be spread evenly in the garden and covered with dried up grass and weeds. Due to lack of space, only five to six people could work at the same time.

We sank a big three-foot diameter hole in the floor of the shed and from there we excavated the tunnel under the surface of the garden. The work proceeded at a feverish pace.

One night, it was my turn to work as a digger. I was working in the pit, filling the pails with heavy brown clay, when suddenly there was a knock on the door. Chana Lustig, the girl who was standing guard, stuck her head through the door, whispering, "Stop digging! The police are here!"

Before I could get out from the tunnel, the door opened and a man with a bright flashlight entered the shed and directed the light beam straight into my eyes. The light blinded me and I couldn't see who it was. Thoughts started to race through my head: *Oh my God. This is the end. It was a mistake to dig here. We are too much in the open. Everybody sees us digging.*

"What are you doing here? Stop this nonsense immediately. Otherwise, the Germans will be here."

I recognized the voice. It was Meir Weisbraun, the commandant of the Jewish police. It turned out that our Polish neighbor, B., had observed our nighttime activities, and he had alerted Meir.

The project had to be abandoned immediately and we returned to the original concept. During the dark night, we scooped up all the dirt dug out during the construction of the abandoned bunker and filled in the stairs leading to the cellar. Then we cut a two-foot-by-two-foot opening in the floor and constructed a wooden box filled with dirt, and masked with wood flooring. Above the trap door, we installed a long old cabinet filled with rugs and dirty linen. The bottom of the cabinet was provided with hinges and could be raised to provide access to the trap box. The bunker itself was equipped with benches, a barrel of water and a sanitation pail.

We also cut an opening through the metal door and installed a small vent pipe, masked with a pile of leaves. The leaves soon decomposed and smelled like manure, providing additional protection.

Now, my work with the Wehrmacht had come to an end. The front line was pushed out a thousand miles, and the fuel depot was relocated to Vinnytsia, about 160 miles southwest of Kyiv, and I returned to the slave-labor assignments and to the harsh, unrewarding work. One day, I was sent to work in the county office building.

In the county office building, I reported to the janitor, Maxim, as ordered, and I came down to his office in the cellar. It was a warm, cozy place. My first job was to stoke with coal the oven of the central heating system. It was not a difficult job and even pleasant work. The red glowing coal engulfed me with warmth that had been so much missing in my life. But soon Maxim gave me a new assignment.

"Take this stoker iron and clear the sidewalk of ice and snow," ordered Maxim.

The stoker iron was a very heavy rod weighing about forty pounds. It was about six feet long, finished with a square head, used for breaking up the burning clumps of coal. It was inappropriate for breaking up ice on a sidewalk. At that time, I was fifteen years old, a growing, undernourished youngster, and I didn't have the energy needed for this inefficient job. A small axe would have been a perfect tool. I returned to the "office," and asked Maxim if I could have a small axe. He told me to work as I had been told. "*Schnell*," he added. "Fast." It was one of the only words in German he knew. Frustrated, I returned to my job.

My Burning Shame

One of my most painful memories from the Holocaust is the moment I refused to share my bread with a hungry man. To escape the slave-labor assignments, I got a job on the railroads. I cleared weeds from the tracks, checked the rails, and replenished washed-out gravel. It was hard, physical work. The pay wasn't much and, in addition, we had to kick back a quarter of it to the Polish supervisor who hired us.

After a few months, this work came to an end, and I was transferred to work in a stone quarry that produced gravel for the railroads. It was even more difficult work. I had to get up at 5 o'clock in the morning, walk to the railroad station, and take an hour's ride to the quarry. I spent a whole day crushing stone boulders with a twenty-pound hammer. The work was exhausting and, worst of all, I was burning lots of precious, irreplaceable calories. As a result, I was always ready to eat and devoured any piece of food I could get my hands on.

One day, during the lunch break, a neighbor of a mine, an older man who had lost his family in the March action, approached me and asked me to share my bread. The whole morning, I had been looking forward to lunch. I wanted to eat and feel the delicious soft chewed pulp of bread. Now, I could not, physically or emotionally, part with the food, and I refused. I refused, and the image of the old man walking away from me like a beaten dog stayed with me all my life. I was ashamed of my refusal then, and I am ashamed of my actions now.

CHAPTER 12

The Yom Kippur Action (September 1942)

Several months after the March action, life in the ghetto had returned to "normal." People were preoccupied with the fight for survival. As the Talmud says: "Danger to life overcomes everything else." On the streets of the ghetto, you saw people poorly dressed, with the look of hunger etched in their faces. People moved slowly, thinking, dreaming, about food. The smallest edible piece of garbage was consumed with delightful abandon. [*In May 1942, "[h]unger was rampant and a typhus epidemic broke out. Day to day, ten to fifteen Jews died of hunger and sickness."*[1]—*MK*]

One day, my father asked me if I would go to Yom Kippur religious service to be held at the home of our neighbors, the Orensteins.[2] For me, it was hard to pray. Looking at all this destruction, how could I? At that time, I didn't realize yet that God doesn't need the admiration and prayers from the mortals. It is the mortals who need God, to bring sense to their lives and give it some structure.

When we entered the next morning [*September 21, 1942—MK*], we found the "synagogue" full of anxious, scared people. For most of them, it would turn out to be their last Yom Kippur. An elderly Jew, dressed in a white robe resembling a shroud, conducted the services. His emaciated, drawn-out face was covered by the prayer shawl; his two burning eyes and had an eerie, unearthly look. The congregation tearfully responded to the ancient prayers.

Reb Nachum started reciting the prayer where one asks God to be written into the of Book of Life. On the Day of Atonement, God decides who will live and who will die, who will die from hunger and who will perish by violence. At the part of "*Me l'chaim, v'me lamavet*"—who will live and who will die—the congregation responded with loud cries and weeping.

We were midway through the services when there was a knock at the window. "The killers are here! Run for your life! Run for your life!" Pandemonium broke out. Screaming, weeping people went running to the bunkers. Our house was close to the Orensteins', and we reached our bunker in time, before the Germans appeared. The last to check in was Shmuel Hecht. He closed the hatch door and camouflaged the entrance. Someone thanked God we were all in. Despite the seriousness of the situation, I felt a wave of resentment. Why are we thanking God? A Jew gets sick, we thank God, a Jew recovers, we thank God. And now, the Jews are killed like flies, we also thank God. We have no self-esteem. This is the reason that we let ourselves be brutalized.

We sat in complete darkness, in silence. I was sitting on a wooden bench between my parents. Despite my religious rebellion, I did fast that Yom Kippur and I felt the pangs of hunger. I concentrated on this feeling of hunger; it gave me relief from the gripping anxiety.

Soon, we heard heavy German boots kicking the furniture, stomping on the floor in search of the bunker. At one point the German was above me. I heard the floor squeaking when he walked. *Why are all the people breathing so loudly? God help us! God save us, at least this time,* I prayed silently. The old cellar was built solidly, the floor squeaked but protected us. The Germans did not find us.

The Yom Kippur action lasted two days. Normally, an action lasted only one day. It turned out that the Jews had perfected so much their hiding methods that it was impossible for the Germans to fill the waiting train, so they extended the action for another day.[3] The bunker was equipped with a metal pail used for sanitation, but we didn't have any food or water.

The next day, I grew restless. I changed seats with my mother, who was now clutching my father tightly. I was afraid for her. She had a heart problem and every time she got scared, she shook like a leaf. I had not eaten for two days. I decided to leave the bunker to explore the situation and maybe find some food. Chaja [pronounced "HIGH-ya"], Hecht's sister, joined me. We slowly opened the hatch and, like pilots, climbed out of our cockpit.

I approached the window. The deserted streets were drenched with warm sunlight. Nature was cooperating with the murderers, making their job easy and pleasant. Looking through the window I saw two Germans approaching. I wasn't sure if they saw me. A few seconds later there was loud knocking on the entrance door and loud German voices yelling their blood chilling: "*Juden raus! Juden raus!*" (Jews Out! Jews Out!)

The Yom Kippur Action (September 1942) 95

I ran to the bunker entrance and opened the hatch door and turned to Chaja: "They saw us. Jump quickly! Jump!"

Chaja turned around and I saw her pupils enlarged by fear. After a moment of hesitation, Chaja jumped. I heard a loud thump, when she hit the floor. I was getting ready to jump when I heard the German approaching and yelling, "*Juden raus! Juden raus!*"

I froze for a split second. In times of danger, you think with lightning speed. *If I jump now, I will endanger the lives of twenty people down below,* I thought. I caught a glimpse of my father standing below the trap door. He wanted to catch me. There wasn't enough time. I closed the trap door and swiftly masked the entrance.

In a daze, I walked out of the room. I faced two raiders. Fortunately, they were alone, not accompanied by local people. An idea hit me, and I decided to try a trick. I turned to the Germans and told them in deliberately broken German, "No Jews. All Jews kaput here. I found them. Me Ukrainian helping Germans find Jews. Let's go!"

I looked at the two Germans, the raiders. One was a young boy and the other overweight man hardly fitting into his tight uniform. *So this is what Angels of Death look like?* I thought. In my imagination, Angels of Death were always skinny.

Despite my dangerous situation, I felt my fear leave me. Down in the bunker, I was buried; here, I could run. When we left the Hechts' house, it was a bright, sunny day. In the distance, I saw a column of Jews led by two armed Germans. It looked so peaceful, like people on an outing. No cries, no pleas. Even the children behaved like zombies.

I was afraid that I would be recognized by people in the column and incriminated. I had to get rid of the Germans. We were passing in front of the Melcer house. I turned to the Germans and told them in Ukrainian that I was going to look for the Jews and motioned them to wait for me. I darted through the house and left by the rear door. In the next house I ran into a tool shed, covered myself with old rugs and hid there.

After dusk, when the shooting had stopped, I slowly moved out from this pile of rubbish, and crawled to the ventilation pipe from the bunker. There I whispered, "Mom, it's me, I'm alive. I'm alive." Through the ventilation pipe I heard my mother crying.

After the reunion, we emerged from the bunker to assess the damage. It was extensive. About 1200 Jews had been driven to the railroad station, loaded onto cattle cars and shipped out.

Where? We didn't have the slightest idea.

96 | The Pessimist's Son

Martin's Note: _They were transported to the Bełżec death camp. Aryeh and Cyla Blech, write: "Around forty Jews were able to jump from the wagons, and those that returned to Rohatyn told how, even before the train . . . arrived at Bełżec, many died of suffocation, a few lost their minds and others lost their lives jumping from the moving train."_[4]

As described by Snyder, Bełżec was a "death factory," where nearly all Jews were killed upon arrival.[5] It, Treblinka, and Sobibór were established as part of Operation Reinhard, the plan to murder every Jew in Poland and all those the Germans could transport there.[6] Bełżec had a 99.99 percent mortality rate—much worse than even that of Auschwitz-Birkenau. Based on the account of Rudolf Reder, one of only two or three persons who survived Bełżec and the only one who lived long enough to testify about it, Fulbrook paints this horrific scene:

> Reder "always saw a spark of hope light up" in the eyes of those about to be murdered [because they had been falsely told they would bathe first and then be sent to work]. But it was not long before they discovered what truly lay in store, as "the little ones were wrenched from their mothers, the old and sick were tossed onto stretchers, men and small girls were prodded with rifle butts further and further along the path . . . straight to the gas chambers." Women and girls had their heads shaved, while many people were already corralled in the gas chambers, where some had to wait in the dark for a full two hours before all the chambers were filled. Suddenly the women would realize what was going on, and "without any transition from hope to total despair— laments and shrieks erupted." Around twelve SS men "used truncheons and sharp bayonets to drive people into the gas chambers: around 750 were crammed into each of the six chambers, which were so tightly packed . . . that it was difficult to close the doors, at which point the engine was finally switched on. Reder recalled: "I heard the desperate cries, in Polish, in Yiddish, the blood-chilling laments of children and women, and then one communal terrifying cry which lasted fifteen minutes. The machine ran for twenty minutes, and after twenty minutes all was silent." [Reder and others dragged the corpses] "using leather straps, to the huge mass graves prepared in advance, and the orchestra was accompanying us. It played from morning till evening."[7]

About 435,000–500,000 Polish Jews were murdered in Bełżec.[8] *Snyder writes that the death factory there was created by the Germans so they could kill Jews "west of the Molotov-Ribbentrop line, where the Germans lacked the personnel for mass shooting campaigns and where they were unwilling to arm Poles as auxiliaries." Bełżec was guarded and operated chiefly with non-Germans chosen from the SS training camp at Trawniki, in the Lublin district of the General Government. The first Trawniki men were captured Red Army soldiers, largely Soviet Ukrainians.*[9]

Rachel and Moshe NasHofer write that the Yom Kippur action in Rohatyn was carried out by "Gestapo murderers from Tarnopol . . . with the help of the Jewish police."[10] *As a general matter, many of the Jewish police throughout Poland were hated by their fellow Jews as Nazi collaborators.*[11] *In one case, longtime Jewish inmates in Auschwitz-Birkenau asked newcomers in July 1944 from the Starachowice labor camp complex whether there were any Jewish policemen among their transport who had behaved badly and then badly beat one who was so identified.*[12]

CHAPTER 13

Caught Again: The December Action (1942)

Did the ghetto receive warnings about the impending doom? Not directly. There were plenty of signs and hints, but they were difficult to accept.

A few months later, there was another action, in which I was caught again. On a December morning before dawn, I was standing guard together with Chana. I heard the distant rumbling of trucks followed by a suspicious noise coming from the border of the ghetto. I decided to check it out. I told Chana to sound the alarm if I wasn't back soon.

Slowly, I proceeded to the border. It was still very dark. My heart was pounding wildly. *Don't play the role of a hero. Just proceed with your task. It's nothing.* I tried to calm myself down when, just 100 feet from me, I saw troops getting out of military trucks. Before I could turn around, a German command stopped me cold in my tracks.

"*Halt, Jude! Halt!*" When I turned around, I saw a German directing his gun towards me. I approached him slowly.

What do I do now? I asked myself. Somehow, I had this notion I would survive.

I turned to the German and engaged him in a conversation. At that time, I spoke fluent German. When I heard the noise of war planes flying overhead, I asked him: "What plane is this? Is this a Messerschmitt or a Stuka?"

"It's a Messerschmidt," replied the German.

"Which one do you prefer, the Messerschmidt or the Stuka? Which plane is better?" I asked again.

For about five minutes, we discussed the merits of each plane. Those five minutes lasted an eternity. Then, I turned around and said, "I have to go. Goodbye."

I walked slowly, feeling tension in my back. *How would it feel to be shot? Would it be painful?* Those were the thoughts that raced through my head.

Breathing heavily, I walked slowly toward the corner of the street. When I reached the corner, I ran home as fast as I could. I never stopped to look back. The German did not shoot. To this day, I don't know if this was due to my socializing or that the Germans were not allowed to start shooting until they had completely surrounded the ghetto.

When I arrived home, the alley was dark and empty. It looked like Chana had sounded the alarm and that everybody was in the bunker. I quietly opened the door to the Hechts' house and almost tripped in the darkness. When I reached the bunker door, the masking door was closed. I tried to nudge it, without success.

What do I do now? Where should I hide? I was distressed. Then I remembered the ventilation pipe. It ran outside the house. Through the ventilation duct, I established contact with our bunker and after a few minutes I "relaxed" in the dark, damp bunker. When I reached the bunker, my mother was crying. She had been worried about me and our cousins, Elke and Libby.

Elke and Libby had lived in the nearby town of Bursztyn. It was the town my father came from. After the March action, in which the Germans and their accomplices murdered about seventy percent of the ghetto's Jews, the Germans replenished the pool of the victims by resettling the Jews from all surrounding towns, like Bursztyn, Bukaczowce, and Bolshowce, to Rohatyn.[1] Our cousins lived on the next block. As a matter of fact, Mechel, Libby's husband, was a member of the Judenrat in charge of the burial society.[2] He smuggled food into the ghetto in reusable caskets. The Germans, afraid of typhus, never opened the caskets. The food may have been contaminated by the typhus victims—but nobody in the ghetto cared.

It was pitch-black in the bunker. The air in the bunker was damp and humid. I felt a body tripping over my feet and a loud thump followed. It was Lustig trying to get in the dark to our sanitation pail to relieve himself.

I don't remember how many hours we sat in the bunker. It felt like forever. Shots and cries penetrated our hiding place and, with each one, we felt closer to death.

After a long, long day, the cries stopped and we slowly emerged from the bunker to assess the damage. It was winter, and the ground was covered with red and white snow. Deep tracks in the snow indicated the marching columns. Here the victims were led the marketplace and later to the railroad station.

I ran toward the house where my cousins lived. I knocked at the windows. No answer. *They must still be in the bunker,* I thought. But I didn't know where their bunker was. People kept their bunker entrances secret. In the ghetto asking such questions about people's bunkers was considered to be in very bad taste.

Religion in the Ghetto

In the ghetto, despite the hunger, killings, persecution, and humiliations, the observance of the Jewish religion was stronger than ever. This was a sign of both the amazing strength and weaknesses of the Jewish people.

All Torah scrolls were distributed to private homes. Rooms used for sleeping were converted to prayer halls during the daytime. There, people congregated to say Kaddish, and to pray. In the ghetto, everybody was reciting the Mourner's Kaddish. It was the glue that kept generations together. The Jewish families were tightly knit. There was no sacrifice the Jewish parents wouldn't make for their offspring, and in return the children kept the memory of them alive by saying Kaddish.

Later, after the death of my mother, the only suit that I owned was torn during the *kriah*, the symbolic tearing of clothing as a symbol of mourning. I was expected by the community to say the Mourner's Kaddish daily, but its words burned holes in my heart: "And the name of the Lord be sanctified and extolled." For me, praising God when there were so many innocent victims was sacrilegious. It was a mockery! Why had God abandoned us? The people from the alley prayed in the Hechts' house. Each morning, the sleeping room was cleaned, the table served as the pulpit and for reading the Torah, and all men, dressed in prayer shawls with phylacteries, prayed with devotion.

Looking at those people rhythmically swaying and reciting the thousand-year-old prayers, even when they faced death, made me frustrated—frustrated with their submission, and frustrated with their inaction. I had never smoked, but I started to smoke cigarettes—on Saturdays only. It was my form of rebellion.

Martin's Note: Rohatyn survivor Abraham Sterzer says that on December 8, 1942, the Gestapo from Tarnopol "together with the gendarmerie" surrounded the ghetto and searched for Jews with the help of the Jewish police. Many sick people didn't succeed in hiding, he writes, and they were immediately shot or taken to the ghetto square. By five in the evening, the Germans had succeeded in gathering more than 2,000 Jews who were led by armed escort to the railway station and from there crammed into freight cars to Bełżec for extermination.[3]

Regarding my father's religious rebellion, observant Jews are not permitted to smoke on Saturday (Shabbat). My father's immediate family was not especially observant, but he grew up in an Orthodox community in Podhajce. My father asked, "Why had God abandoned us?" Did God even exist? The Holocaust shook the faith of many, including my dad.

Another perennial, but less theological, question is whether Jews resisted as much as they could. My dad's frustration in this regard was shared by many. Rabbi Thorne discusses the anger of a Jew at his people for allowing themselves to be slaughtered without attempting resistance. "What will the world think of us, dying like sheep? . . . Jewish history is full of heroes who fought back!" the man yelled. He planned to use a pistol he had and three bullets, intending two for Germans and then one for himself. He was, however, killed before he could shoot the gun.[4] *In his next chapter, "Why There was No Resistance," Thorne offers some explanations, one of which is: "Could we hope to hold back the evil that the nations of Europe could not—we, the ghetto Jews, who had been reared not to live by the sword but by the spirit, according to the Lord's word?"*[5] *He, however, wrote this while still in hiding and before the Warsaw Ghetto Uprising (spring 1943), the Białystok Ghetto Uprising (September 1943), the revolts in Sobibór (1943), Treblinka (1943), and Auschwitz (1944), and many heroic acts by Jewish partisans and so on.*[6]

CHAPTER 14

The Baby and the Bunker

"Ania is pregnant! Ania is pregnant!" [Ania is pronounced "Anya."] The startling news about Shmuel Hecht's wife hit the alley like a bomb. Pregnancy in the ghetto was like the kiss of death, for all of us. The news of the pregnancy created an upheaval and havoc in the small community that shared the bunker. "Ania's folly is endangering the lives of all of us," lamented my father.

Lustig, our neighbor, agreed. He noted that we had built the bunker together and that we all shared the night watches. Because we shared the bunker, the eight families living in the two adjacent houses were dependent on each other for the safety of their lives. The bunker was not a defensive fortress at all. It was a small old cellar, where the entrance door was bricked up and ventilation was provided by a pipe hidden behind the shrubbery. Inside the bunker, all the barrels containing pickles and sauerkraut had been removed and long wooden benches installed. A small trap door, located under an old piece of furniture, provide a camouflaged entry to the bunker.

The initial consensus was that Ania must have an abortion, but Ania stubbornly refused. In addition, having an abortion was not so simple in the ghetto. All the doctors had been killed. Shmuel Hecht had been told by a midwife that she could do the abortion but that it was very risky, especially in light of poor sanitary conditions and no medicine.[1]

For years, Ania couldn't conceive, and now nature was playing a dirty joke on her. Her husband, Shmuel, was a tall, gentle man, liked by everybody. After his father died of cancer, he took over the grocery store, and having a good rapport with people, he improved the business. He had run the store [*before the ghetto had been established—MK*], but it was his mother who had made the decisions. Shmuel was a decent person and a good son. When his mother arranged the match, he obediently married sweet Ania, with whom he fell in love.

The marriage was a good one; they cared for each other, and his mother did not interfere in his marriage, except *noodging* him about a grandson.

"When will I have a grandson? What are you waiting for? I'm getting old," she used to say.

But Ania was infertile. She had been told by a doctor that her chances of conceiving were very slim.

After a few years, his mother started to push Shmuel to divorce Ania, which he could do under Jewish law. Shmuel refused, telling his mother that he preferred Ania without children than another wife with children. It was the first time that Shmuel had disobeyed his mother. His wife was very grateful to her husband for his love.

Ania was a plump, pleasant woman, with blue eyes and blond hair. She spoke in a low-keyed voice, rarely argued, and yet always managed to have her way. After the death of Shmuel's mother, she became the source of strength to Shmuel. He sought her opinion on matters large and small, and dutifully accepted her decisions.

Now, they argued vehemently. Ania desperately wanted a baby and she believed in fate, or *beshert*, as Jews call it. She believed that Providence was actively directing the lives of individuals, and that humans had to accept this divine intervention.

Ania's decision split the small community into two camps: one camp, mostly men, wanted Ania to have an abortion, while the other, mostly women, said it should be her choice.

My father, Leon, said it was a crime to bring a child into this world, that a baby had no chances of survival and that its birth would endanger the lives of all of us. He admonished people to remember the Blochs' tragedy. At the last action, the hapless mother had unintentionally smothered her own baby. The other camp was headed by Chaja, Shmuel's sister, who said that an abortion by the midwife willing to do it would be a death sentence for Ania.

Meantime, the situation in the ghetto grew ominous. News of killing in the surrounding towns was pouring in: Brzeżany, Tarnopol, Buczacz, and so forth. Killings, killings everywhere. The only good news came from the Russian front. The Battle of Stalingrad was in full swing. The German loss there lifted up the spirits of the ghetto.[2] Maybe the war will come to an early end and we will survive, people thought.

The resurgence of hope made the question of a safe bunker more pressing. My mother, Pesia, came up with a good idea that averted open warfare between the two camps. She argued that we needed a more modern bunker, a piggyback, double bunker—like one of our neighbors had built recently. My mother also said that it was *beshert* that we have a new bunker.

Once *beshert* was invoked, the arguments were settled. An honest Jew would never dare to challenge his destiny. The new-bunker idea was accepted, a community crisis was averted, and Ania remained pregnant.

Our small community hired Shmulek Barron, an excellent bunker builder, to manage our new bunker's construction. Shmulek surveyed our houses and proposed two alternative plans.

"You can extend the existing bunker and build a piggyback bunker. It will be far from the entrance, and nobody will hear the baby crying. By using the existing cellar, the excavation will be easier and there will be less dirt to dispose of."

"Yes," interjected my father. "But we will have to cart all the dirt through the small opening. It will be a tough job."

The other alternative was to excavate the floor of the existing shed and built a false floor. It was an easier job, but it would require heavy wood beams and other shoring materials.

Everybody liked the second alternative, provided we could find the needed lumber. The floor of the shed was excavated to a depth of about seven feet, and from there a six-feet wide bunker, was dug under the house. The excavated earth was spread evenly in the garden. All the work was done at night; each pail with the earth had to pass through a human chain, before being deposited. Supreme precautions had to be maintained—the work had to hidden from the Germans and from neighbors.

The soil under the house was heavy clay, easy to excavate, and didn't require shoring up. Long benches, sculpted in clay, were created on each side. After the second bunker was finished, a false floor was built in the shed. The entrance to the bunker was constructed from the cellar, under the house. The cellar had an outside door entrance, easily accessible to all alley dwellers.

The new bunker complex was well masked. The masking door was located under an old commode. Upon opening the trap door, one entered a short tunnel leading toward the first bunker, which was used for hiding clothing, supplies and valuables. Under a pile of dirty clothing, there was another masking door leading toward the new main bunker.

Before the bunker was finished, however, the problem of ventilation arose. 'We need fresh air or we'll suffocate here. It will become a grave, not a bunker," complained my father.

"I thought about that. Don't worry. We will drill a hole close to the wall and install a ventilation shaft alongside the wall masked as a storm leader," Shmulek the Builder answered.

To say "don't worry" to my father was a signal that something was wrong and that he should start worrying. He strongly believed in Murphy's law—and worry he did.

Shmulek fashioned a special drilling tool from a hoe. The hoe was bent into the shape of a propeller. At the end of the pole, he attached a long handle.

When we started to drill the ventilation shaft, the drilling went smoothly for some time, but then we hit stones. The flimsy tool started to churn, and then broke. A small hole remained, but my father found it inadequate.

"We will suffocate here. It will be painful way to go," my father said. "It is better to be shot than to suffocate. We need better ventilation."

"Don't worry," said Shmulek again. "I think we hit the foundation wall. We have to drill at a larger angle. We are going to make sufficient provisions for ventilation."

We started to drill again, and this time the full length of the pole disappeared without penetrating the surface. "What happened now?" worried my father.

"Leon, don't break my neck. I'm ready to quit. Don't worry. I will find a solution," Shmulek pleaded.

He extended the drilling pole by attaching a second pole, and the drilling started again. After days of drilling, we reached the surface. It turned out that the ventilation opening was about five feet from the wall.

"We won't be able to mask the ventilation pipe," my father complained.

"Don't worry," came Shmulek's standard answer. "We'll mask it with a bush."

"We have to make another attempt and drill through the foundation wall," Father suggested.

"We don't have the tool to drill through the stones. Either we stay with a smaller hole or with the larger hole five feet away from the wall."

My father insisted that another attempt be made, but the majority overruled him. My father was known in the ghetto as the *Schwarzeher*—the Pessimist—and people avoided him because of it. He used to say to the Jewish policemen, pointing to their police hat, "Throw away that funny hat and find a place to hide. This *shako* won't save you."[3]

Unfortunately, nobody listened to my father's advice. Nobody wanted to see the danger of a faulty ventilation system. We would pay the price later.

The Baby and the Bunker | 107

We were all involved in the construction of the new bunker and forgot about Ania and her pregnancy. One day, Shmuel came to talk to us.

"Ania is getting heavy, and she can't pass through the trap door to the bunker," he said. "If there's an action, we'll all be lost."

It was Lustig who came up with an ingenious solution. He said that Ania should remain underground until she gave birth in a month. The idea was accepted, and soon an underground maternity ward was created. The wooden benches were removed and replaced with a small bed. Lowering Ania into the bunker became a complicated operation. Ania was already too big to pass through the masking door. We had to remove a piece of furniture to enlarge the hole. After Ania passed through, the hole was filled to the original size. Ania didn't like being alone underground, and Shmuel was very upset.

The next day, my mother lowered herself into the bunker and paid a visit to Ania. Now, *she* came back very upset.

"We can't leave her there alone," my mother declared. "She is going to die. It's a damp place, the bedding is wet. The kerosene lamp smells but doesn't give any light." Later in the day, she told Shmuel that she would keep Ania company at night and sleep in the bunker:

Shmuel was overjoyed that Ania would have some company and thanked my mother profusely. Now, like a bird guarding the nest and feeding the chicks, Shmuel was constantly on the run: he cooked, washed, and endangered his life exchanging clothing or bedding for bread. As a result, Ania got the required nutrition so the child would be healthy. Ania was nearing the end of the pregnancy; she was due any moment. The baby was kicking, she was anxious. "Who will deliver the baby in a bunker? Can the midwife be trusted?" she asked her sister-in-law Chaja. There was no doctor in the ghetto.

Shmuel wanted a doctor. One night, my father came home with good news. He said Shmuel was lucky because a Dr. Hudish from Kolomyja had jumped from a death train and was now in the ghetto.[4] Father had spoken with him and he was willing to attend Ania's delivery.

The next day, Dr. Hudish was lowered into the bunker. He examined Ania and prepared her for the delivery. "The patient is fine. She is due in about a week, but the conditions of the bunker are appalling," said Dr. Hudish, coming out from the bunker. After ordering additional bed sheets and a better kerosene lamp, Dr. Hudish asked for some specialized delivery tools. An unusual, urgent request for the equipment went out in the ghetto.

A few days passed but the instruments could not be found. A week later, despite the lack of the instruments, Dr. Hudish delivered the baby. In the midst of death, a new life started. The miracle of procreation had taken place in the most unusual circumstances.

It was a girl. The baby was born in a caul, a very good omen. The mother felt fine and soon she was able to rest in a new bed. The baby named, Aviva, meaning spring in Hebrew, gained weight in the next two weeks. The new bunker was finished by now, and the pressure was off the Hechts. The neighbors now were engaged in their own struggles to stay alive. But then Chaja, Shmuel's sister, got sick. She was running a high fever and couldn't swallow food.

Dr. Hudish said it was typhus and that they should keep her away from the baby. That was easier said than done when an entire family occupied one room.

It seems that Chaja caught typhus when sleeping in the damp, dirty cellar. Constant worry about Ania and lack of proper nourishment had lowered her resistance. In the ghetto, typhus was a deadly sickness; only a small percentage in the ghetto survived the disease. After a short illness, Chaja passed away. There is an old Jewish saying that "Every baby brings its own luck." So far, Aviva had not brought any luck to her family.

The funeral preparations were brief. The *Chevra Kedisha*—the Burial Society—was notified. Chaja's ration coupons were turned in to the Judenrat, and a simple reusable wooden casket was rented. The most difficult thing was to obtain permission from the German authorities to let the funeral procession leave the ghetto. The old Jewish cemetery was far away from the boundaries of the ghetto.

On a clear, windy day, the short funeral procession with the earthly remains of Chaja Hecht proceeded slowly through the abandoned muddy streets of the ghetto. Only four casket bearers and the closest family members were allowed. The funeral passed almost unnoticed. I was one of the pallbearers.

The arrival at the old cemetery was a painful experience for me. The age-old part of the cemetery was destroyed; the stones with ancient Hebrew inscription had been uprooted and used as building material. An enterprising farmer had started to work the grounds, preparing it for seeding. Even the dead were persecuted. This was total annihilation. Jewish flesh was to be used as fertilizer.

The new section contained rows upon rows of graves with simple stakes with wooden markings. No stones were allowed. It looked like Chaja found only a temporary resting place—soon the peasants would pull out the stakes and work the fields. From dust ye come, and to dust ye return.

The burial ceremony was short. Shmuel recited the mourner's Kaddish. The body wrapped in a shroud, was taken out of the reusable casket and placed in the grave. A standard makeshift sign was placed, declaring that this was the resting place of Chaja Hecht. The funeral participants dispersed quickly, each trying to scrounge around and maybe buy some bread or potatoes.

But mysterious are the ways of *beshert*. Little did Shmuel know that Chaja's sacrifice hadn't been in vain. On the way from the cemetery, Shmuel decided to step in and see Xenia, who lived in a nearby house, to maybe get some bread for Ania and the baby. Xenia was a part-time madam, and a retired prostitute. "She's a nice woman, and she owes us some favors," Shmuel told me. "Come with me. Maybe we'll get something to eat."

Xenia was a heavy-set Ukrainian woman in the fifties. Her face showed traces of a worn-out beauty that was covered with layers of powder and rouge. She was an intelligent woman. Without much of an education, she had risen through the ranks of the common prostitutes to become a madam.

Xenia's neighbors were afraid of her big mouth. She could easily puncture people's illusions and reputations. "Your lame husband is no good. I can tell you a thing or two," she used to scream in a full voice. It also was rumored that Xenia had German protectors. Her abundant supplies of chocolate and cigarettes seemed good proof of those contacts. Now, Xenia received Shmuel warmly. "How is your mother?" she asked.

"She's dead," answered Shmuel.

"I am so sorry to hear it." She also had known Chaja Hecht and was sorry to learn the circumstances of Chaja's death. She prepared a package for Shmuel: cheese, butter, bread. Shmuel hesitantly told her about the baby and his predicament.

"I'll take the baby. No problem," declared Xenia after a minute of silence. Shmuel stood speechless, thunderstruck, then he slowly dropped to his knees, grabbed Xenia's hand, and started to kiss it.

"Thank you! Thank you!" he cried, tears streaming down his face.

After a few minutes, he regained his composure. The good news slowly sank into his consciousness. He took the packages and swiftly ran out to share the good news with Ania. In the ghetto, the running, smiling Shmuel created a sensation. Who in the ghetto had ever seen a smiling, joyous man returning from a funeral?

At home, Ania understood fully the good news Shmuel brought, but she was not happy. She didn't want to give up her baby. She also wasn't excited about the prospect of having her baby raised by an old prostitute.

Shmuel argued that Xenia was offering life to their baby, and that she was a loving person. Anything is better than death, he told Ania.

And so, preparations were made to transfer the baby. On an agreed-upon day or, rather, night, Shmuel took Aviva tucked in multiple layers of clothing and wrapped in a blanket, waded the shallow river, and handed over the baby to the waiting Xenia.

Xenia told the neighbor she was closest to that one of her "daughters," as she referred to the women working for her, had gotten pregnant, and that the father of the child wouldn't let the mother have an abortion. Xenia implied that the father was a powerful German officer. The next day, the whole neighborhood was criticizing Xenia behind her back for harboring a German bastard. On Sunday, the baby was christened and given the lovely name of Luba.[5]

Xenia settled down to a new life, with her new baby. Some neighbors suspected the baby was Jewish, but, aware of Xenia's big mouth and knowing of her German connections, they kept those doubts to themselves. Luba was growing up peacefully, surrounded by all the love given her by her new mother, Xenia.

CHAPTER 15

My Mother Dies

Chaja was not the final victim of "bunker typhus." However, Ania, amazingly, did not catch the disease. Instead, my mother was the next victim. One day she came down with fever and developed all the typical symptoms. We immediately called the doctor. My poor mother had a heart condition. Before the war, she had gone to Vienna and been diagnosed with a heart murmur. Now she started to lose strength quickly. We desperately tried to get medicine, without success.

One day my father came home very disturbed. The Germans had ordered the Judenrat to create a makeshift hospital and gather all the typhus victims. Any person with typhus found at home would be shot on the spot, declared Hermann, the Gestapo man in charge of the ghetto. The Judenrat evacuated a large building, and the Jewish police were gathering the sick and placing them in the makeshift hospital.

My father was very uneasy and worried. "The hospital will be overcrowded. There are no doctors, no nurses, and no medication," he said. This will be a morgue, not a hospital."

"What are our options? Can we keep her here?" my sister asked.

"Maybe we should put her in the bunker? There she'll be safe." replied Father.

"There's no ventilation, no light there. Mother will die there. And besides, we have to get Hecht's permission. The bunker is in his house. Will he agree?" Luba asked. The matter wasn't settled, and Mother remained at home.

A few days later, my mother passed away. Believe it or not, I was happy that she died unconscious, that she died in her bed, surrounded by loved ones. I was happy that she had been spared a torturous journey. Even today, I can't believe how strange happiness in the ghetto was.

Martin's Note: My father didn't provide a date or even an approximate date for his mother's death, so the precise timing is unclear. But according to one account, the typhus epidemic reached its climax in the winter of 1942–1943, and the Judenrat was ordered to open the hospital. The Yad Vashem Encyclopedia of Ghettos says that the Nazis killed all the patients in April 1943, and a page of testimony my father provided to Yad Vashem says his mother died in 1943. So my paternal grandmother presumably died sometime from January 1943 to April 1943. She was forty-three or forty-four.

CHAPTER 16

Luba Goes to Podhajce

When it dawned on us that Hitler was going to kill all the Jews, we desperately tried to save ourselves by any available means. One day we received a letter from Lwów, from my father's cousin. Her husband, David Treiber, had left for Cuba before the war, and she, being considered a Cuban citizen, was interned in Lwów in a luxurious camp for foreign citizens. "There is a possibility for Luba," she wrote, "to marry in name only a foreign citizen and thus be saved."

My father loved the idea. There was only one difficult condition—a huge fee. It turned out that we had the money, but it had been left in Podhajce. At the beginning of the war [*before the Soviets began nationalizing businesses and properties—MK*], my father sold all the goods from the store. Each month, he traveled to Lwów, to buy dollars, the hard currency.

When we left for Rohatyn, we left the money with our friends in Podhajce, the Goralniks. Now, it was decided that Luba would bring the money back. But it was more easily said than done. Traveling was forbidden for Jews. A Jew caught outside of the ghetto would be shot on sight. Nevertheless, Luba decided to take the chance, and my father immediately started to worry.

"How is she going to get to the railroad station? Getting tickets is dangerous. We have to find some solution," he worried.

Father worried until he found a solution. Meir the *Balagule* suggested that his friend Danilo, another coachman, would take Luba to the next railroad station. "There she can board the train, disguised as a Ukrainian girl, and nobody will pay attention to her," he assured my father.

Luba was courageous. Disregarding the dangers of the journey, she went to Podhajce, where she stayed with our grandfather. There, she got the box with valuables from the Goralniks.[1] They were very honest people, good friends, and they didn't want any rewards for their troubles. As a precautionary measure, Luba divided the money into two parts. One part she took with her and the other part she buried in the same metal box in our grandfather's shed. G., a cousin, helped her bury the treasure.[2]

When she came back, the negotiations for the *pro forma* wedding continued, but the problem arose about the validity of the wedding. Would the Germans recognize a Jewish religious wedding? Are there any legitimate Jewish civil authorities that they would recognize? Probably not. It was a gamble. In the meantime, another possibility opened up for us. Father heard that there was a smuggling ring that took Jews to Hungary. The price was very high, though.[3]

"We need the rest of the money," declared Father. "Luba will have to go again."

And so, Luba made the perilous journey a second time. Unfortunately, however, this time she came back empty-handed. The buried money was gone. The only person who could have taken the money was G., but he vehemently denied taking it. Our grandfather, greatly upset, had turned to G. and said, "G., as God is my witness, I'm ready to swear on the Torah that you took the money." But it was to no avail. G. was unmoved and there was no recourse available to us.

The money was gone and, with it, so were Luba's wedding plans. But as Reb Nachum used to say, "mysterious are the ways of the Creator." Maybe that saved my sister. Toward the end of the war, the Germans liquidated the foreign camp and killed all the people.

In the ghetto, I saw so much suffering and I realized that human endurance and human cruelty are both limitless. One day, I came home from work and found a young boy, about ten years old, lying on a bundle of straw in the alley. The boy was sick. His face was red. He was trembling from fever, breathing hard, and continuously moaning.

"Who is the boy?" I ask my sister, who was feeding him some soup.

Luba said he was the son of Mechele the *Stolar*.[4] His father and his family were taken away and now this poor orphan was homeless.

"How can we help him?" I asked.

"He's sick with typhus and everybody is scared to touch him," she replied.

I remembered the story of Mechele the *Stolar*. He was a hero. During the last action, the Germans discovered a bunker and, being afraid to go in, they threatened to firebomb it unless the Jews came out. Mechele the *Stolar* volunteered to give himself up. He said goodbye to his son and left. He sacrificed his life, saving about fifteen people. And now his son lay motionless, sick with typhus, on some straw in the alley.

The boy survived without medication on the meager food spared by women of the alley.[5] He survived and had almost recovered when the Jewish police took him to the hospital supposedly set up for typhus victims. He was shot when the Germans liquidated the hospital. Human endurance is limitless, but so is human cruelty.

Martin's Note: At one time, when the hospital was full, Hermann, a Viennese Gestapo officer, "entered the hospital, assembled the doctors, other workers and the nurses, shot the patients in their beds and then the personnel. Then he ordered the Judenrat to clear away the dead bodies" and re-open the hospital. Sylvia Lederman similarly writes that "[w]hen the Germans did away with all the sick people in the hospital, their vacant places were immediately filled with new victims and the process began all over again."[6]

This murder of the ill was not confined to the Rohatyn Ghetto; indeed, it was a universal Nazi practice. On September 1, 1942, the Gestapo and SS removed more than 2,000 patients from a hospital in Łódź, including eighty pregnant women, and sent them to Chełmno, where they were gassed to death. Those who tried to flee were shot.[7] In October 1941, the Germans set fire to the Kovno Ghetto's hospital in Lithuania while patients, doctors and nurses were inside.[8] In the Drohobycz Ghetto, during a November 1942 action, the Gestapo "marched through the wards [of a Jewish hospital] and shot everybody in their beds."[9] This kind of conduct is also recounted in the Kolomyja yizkor book. In addition, in my mother's hometown of Radom, on the orders of the SS, the Jewish police took fifty-nine sick people out of the hospital, only in their underwear. They were put in a semicircle in a garden and shot.[10] A Jewish policeman accompanied Nazis to such a hospital "cleansing" in Buczacz.[11] On August 26, 1942, doctors and nurses who protested the Nazis' murder of patients in the Jewish hospital in Wieliczka were themselves shot.[12] In addition, when the Germans entered Lwów, "they immediately murdered all the mentally ill in the hospital."[13] In ghetto actions, Germans frequently shot on the spot small children, pregnant women and the handicapped or elderly who had been rounded up, because the Nazis regarded them as "useless eaters." Those not shot on the spot were typically transported to death camps.[14] Indeed, Snyder writes that the term "useless eaters" was used for all Jews "[w]hen food rather than labor was the primary anxiety" of the Germans.[15]

And of course, in Nazi labor camps, the Germans frequently murdered sick people whom they deemed unable to work enough, though sometimes they allowed ill inmates to recover so they could resume their forced labor. Browning writes about prisoners in the typhus isolation word in the Strzelnica work camp in the Radom district:

> *The block was quickly overflowing, so [Commandant] Althoff arrived in the night and killed every patient but one [a sixteen-year-old boy who managed to escape.] As those patients who could rise from their bunks staggered toward the doorway [as they had been ordered to do], Althoff opened fire on them with his submachine gun.... Following the massacre ..., Althoff and two Ukrainian guards fetched some more typhus suspects and lined them up front-to-back to see how many could be killed with the fewest bullets.[16]*

In the spring of 1943, conditions at the Strzelnica work camps improved somewhat because the German factory managers were "facing a self-induced labor shortage in their own camps caused by the profligate killing of sick Jews, at a time when the replacement of Jewish workers was becoming increasingly difficult" as the result of the Nazis liquidating ghettos.[17]

With respect to the camp for foreigners in Lwów, it seems my father is referring to part of the Janowska camp. In the winter of 1941, it held Jewish citizens of the United States, Belgium, France, England, Holland, Hungary, and Yugoslavia, who had ended up on the territory of occupied Poland and were living in Lwów at the time.[18] While my grandfather may have been desperately grasping at straws for any possible way to keep his children alive, the idea that foreign citizenship might protect a Polish Jew wasn't far-fetched. Indeed, in the Bochnia Ghetto, Jews with foreign passports or visas were required by the Germans to register with the Judenrat, and a forged visa from Palestine enabled Schonker and his immediate family to escape the ghetto before it was liquidated.[19] A major theme in Snyder's Black Earth *is that Jews with citizenship in countries where the state still existed (such as France) fared much better than stateless ones.[20]*

CHAPTER 17

An Unpleasant Surprise

"Wake up, Shiko! Get up! Something strange is happening. I don't know what is."

I jumped out of bed, dressed quickly, and, in a minute, I was ready to run. In the ghetto, constant danger made us very alert.

"Listen to this noise, son. What is it?" my father asked.

I heard a rambling, muffled noise. Its source was difficult to determine. I also felt a light tremor, like a small earthquake. My sister woke up. Father was the first to figure out the source of the rambling noise.

"Oh God!" he yelled. "It's the bunker! The noise is coming from the bunker. We have our money buried there. Run!" He ran out of the house and I followed him. The gray sky that hung over the ghetto opened and poured heavy torrential rains over the hapless dwellers. Water, water was everywhere. Although we were drenched, we felt secure. The Germans never conducted an action in bad weather. Why should they get wet? They figured the Jews would wait.

Luckily, the heavy cellar doors leading to the trap door were not locked. Forgetting all the necessary precautions, we opened the trap door and got into the first bunker. I had a flashlight on me and in the light of the flashlight my father pushed away the pile of dirty, soiled linens, which smelled of rot, and opened the trap door.

We entered the main bunker and we were met with a rain of clay. Pellets of wet clay were coming down like rain. I raised my head and saw a small stream of water coming down through the base of the ventilation opening.

I directed the beam of the flashlight up to the ventilation shaft, trying to figure out how to stop the water.

"Let's get the money. Stop fooling around. Help me dig," commanded my father. One big piece hit my head and splashed all over my face. We worked feverishly, pushing for fifteen minutes and got the metal box out.

My father tucked it under his arm and ran out from the bunker. I closed all the doors and quickly followed him.

When I came back to our room, my father was working on his next problem. "Where do we hide the money? It's all that's left." He was worried.

"Let's put it in the straw mattress," Luba suggested.

"No. Everybody hides money in a mattress. This is the worst place to hide it." Father pushed away one bed and tried to pry open a floor plank. Suddenly, there was a big rumbling underground, the floor shook violently, and, seconds later, the outside wall collapsed. It just slid down like a house of cards. Our room was completely exposed to the outside. We had just experienced a small, very small, earthquake.

Father stood with the metal box in his hands, looking in amazement through the gaping hole created by the collapsed wall.

A minute later, my father came to his senses. With a swift motion, he pulled out the bed cover, hung it over the enormous hole, and hid the box under the straw mattress. Now, he straightened himself up and started to worry: "We have no bunker to hide in, no place to sleep and all the money is exposed."

In the morning, the rain stopped, and the sun came out. Lots of curious people came to survey the strange occurrence. The gawkers, standing three feet from my bed, looked straight into our room. The collapsed wall created a sensation in the ghetto. Droves of onlookers were passing by, and everybody had some question to ask or comment to make. At midday the crowds of onlookers disappeared. A minute later I got really scared.

Somebody forcefully pulled the blanket covering the wall opening, and, by the irregular outline of the open wall, a German appeared. It was like a picture frame. The German, dressed in a green uniform, looked at us through the middle of the hole. Alongside him stood a Jewish policeman. "What happened here?" the German asked.

"It looks like the flimsy foundation was undermined by the heavy rains. This happened already in some other place." explained the Jewish policeman, who was trying to help us. After observing the open bedroom, the German left.

"Shiko, come with me to the Judenrat, and Luba will stay here, on guard. We have to get a place to live," my father said.

In the Judenrat, the clerk, Izio, was very understanding. "Most I can give you is a corner of Leah's house. We're overcrowded, unless you can wait for the next action," he tried to joke.

"What a joke. I'm laughing to death, Izio," Father said.

Izio's face became serious. "It's a big room and will hold a few more people. That's all that I can think of."

"What do you think, Shiko? You know the place. Your friend Willie used to live there."

I called my father aside and told him: "Don't take it. It's a dangerous house—directly on the border and without a bunker. I'm not ready to commit suicide. Are you?"

We returned empty-handed. At the alley, the gawkers were gone and our neighbors were already discussing building a new bunker with Shmulek, the bunker builder. "The only solution is to use the first chamber and build another bunker next to the outside wall of the shed. Both chambers will be connected with a masked tunnel."

My father was fuming: "Shmulek, I told you that the vent line was no good. It was the water penetrating through this line that caused the collapse. The outlet was too far from the wall, where all the rainwater was collected."

"Leon," replied Shmulek. "You insisted on a large vent line. The small vent line was good and more secure. It's your fault. Don't blame me!"

Again, Father lost the argument when the majority opted to accept Shmulek's plan. The work was about to start when Lustig asked:

"How long will it take to build the bunker?"

"About three months. We have to dig an underground structure, move a lot of earth. It takes time."

"Three months? The Germans won't wait three months," Lustig said, worriedly. "How long will it take if we use an open-excavation method?"

"About a week, with the proper manpower"

Shmuel Hecht suggested that we build the bunker next to the collapsed wall. "We will use open excavation under a pretext that we are shoring up the damaged foundations."

Everybody agreed, and in daylight open construction of a bunker started. It was a historic first in the annals of bunker building. The rubble from the collapsed wall was arranged to provide a type of retaining wall. The dug-out dirt was placed behind the wall. The excavations proceeded around the clock.

To get some semblance of privacy, we redecorated our apartment. We nailed two brown woolen blankets to the wall and covered up the hole. We now lived in a tent-type dwelling.

Now our situation became worse. We lived with an open wall close to a dangerous "illegal" construction site. Luckily, after three days of intensive work the excavation was completed, and it was time to cover up the bunker. Shmuel Hecht was charged with providing the heavy planks needed to support the new ceiling. The hole was about twelve feet by ten feet. Soon, Shmuel came back empty handed. Ten-foot planks were not available in the ghetto, at any price. In the rush of the emergency digging, nobody had done all the necessary planning. Bitter recrimination started again. My father, of course, blamed Shmulek.

Luckily for him and for us, Shmulek found a solution: "We'll divide the bunker into two chambers by using old armoires, filled with dirt and stones, as support columns. This will shorten the span to about five feet."

"Yes," interjected Father. "We'll build two separate, oversized graves. It's too small for fifteen people."

The hole was enlarged to twelve feet by twelve feet, and furniture was used as support columns. The bunker was ready to be covered when the next emergency developed. The first bunker, the entrance bunker, which was situated under the floor of the shed, had to be connected with a tunnel passing under the weakened foundations. This tunnel had to be properly reinforced to prevent a new collapse. The problem was how to reinforce the tunnel. A steel plate was needed. But where could you get a steel plate in the ghetto?

The ingenuity of people in danger is difficult to imagine. An amazing solution was found. Lustig rolled the "solution" up to the bunker. It was a heavy oak wood barrel used for collecting rainwater. "You cut an opening through the bottom of the barrel and you have an ages-old tested tunnel."

Within one week from the start of the construction, the bunker was completed. Now, the retaining wall was removed and the rubble and bricks were scattered over the surface, to provide additional masking.

Now, we had to solve our next problem. We needed a place to sleep. How do you squeeze a family of three into an anthill?

The house of Gutman consisted of two one-bedroom apartments, four rooms in total. About five families lived in those four rooms. Now we had five families living in three rooms. My father found a solution, using the only power of persuasion available to him—money. In the kitchen of the next apartment lived Elke, a widow with two children. They all were living hand to mouth and needed money. My father offered them a substantial sum, and Gutman moved into a closet in Hecht's apartment, while Elke and her kids moved in with the Lustigs. Our family moved into a small kitchen with the added luxury of a separate entrance. The emergency was over. We could relax and wait, in luxury, for the next action.

CHAPTER 18

The Resistance Group/ "The Hope"

The youth in the ghetto dreamed about resistance. We dreamed about fighting the Germans. I remember, one night holding watch, when we heard the rumbling of planes flying overhead. Looking upward, I said to Chana, "It's a pity that the Allies don't send commandos with weapons. If we were given leadership and weapons, we would fight the Germans like lions." Unfortunately, nobody was interested in our fate, and we were not needed.

In April 1943, the ghetto was cheered up by the tremendous news of the Warsaw Ghetto Uprising. The fact that the Jews could mount armed resistance against the Germans was met with huge jubilation. This good news exploded like a volcano, spewing joy.[1] At the same time, however, ominous news was making the rounds about killings and liquidations of ghettos in surrounding towns.[2]

Naftali wanted to be part of the resistance. He said that, if we could get some weapons, we could organize a group of young people ourselves to fight the Germans. I thought for a moment and suggested seeing Meir the *Balagule* because he might help us find guns. We located him in one of the makeshift synagogues.

The "Generals"

Before the war, Meir the *Balagule* owned a horse and wagon. On the side, Meir traded horses, mostly rundown ones. He knew many peasants and horse traders, who even then were his loyal friends.

We went to the synagogue and found Meir. In the ghetto, the few surviving elders, people over sixty years old, congregated daily in the synagogue, discussing the conduct of war and politics. We called them "the generals."

When we entered, there was a heated discussion. Regarding the fall of Stalingrad: "The English should attack Romania. Why go to Africa? Romania is the weak link of the Nazis."

"You'll hit them there and the Nazis lose all the oil—without oil they are kaput," argued one of the generals.

"They should bomb all the German power stations. Without the power stations, without electricity, the Germans will give up," replied another general.

Meir, who saw us entering the synagogue, interrupted the heated discussion. "What can I do for you boys? You didn't come to pray. It is business on your mind, isn't it?"

We took him aside and told him: "'Reb Meir, we need to buy weapons—revolvers, carbines, ammunition. We know that you have connections. Can you help us?"

Meir looked at us intensively, studied our faces for a few seconds, and said:

"Listen, boys, you're barking up the wrong tree. You have no chance."

"I guess we'll have to look elsewhere."

The ghetto was continuously flooded with rumors—good, life-sustaining rumors. Rumors that nourished the soul and lifted the spirits. For example: Roosevelt announced that each peasant who saved Jews will be given five acres of land. The German army rebelled against the insane killings. In Przemyśl, the German army stopped a train on the way to the concentration camp. Stalin had ordered the Russian partisans to accept Jews.

Another favorite topic in the ghetto discussions was punishments for Hitler, to be meted out after the war. Somehow, in the ghetto, there never was any doubt that the Germans were going to lose the war and that Hitler would be severely punished. What where the punishments discussed? Hitler should be cut in two and each piece buried separately. The most popular punishment was that Hitler be put in a cage, driven from town to town, so that each Jew could spit in his face. Another punishment discussed was the Hitler should be buried up to his neck and stay buried until he died.[3]

Later, Naftali and I joined a small group of Jews who wanted to build bunkers in nearby forests and buy rifles. We went with our group about twelve miles outside the ghetto and met up with a farmer named Anton whom someone knew. The leader of our group, a man named Mr. Fink, who used to be my physical education teacher in Rohatyn before the ghetto was established, negotiated hard and paid Anton 200 dollars for an Italian rifle with fifty cartridges.[4] Anton promised us to procure more weapons at a lower price. We then went to the forest. We tried to build a bunker there and dug furiously, but we hit sandy soil, which ended that attempt. Before heading back to the ghetto, we tried to load our new rifle.

Click. Click. Zap.

The cartridge jammed the rifle mechanism. The cartridge did not fit the rifle. Upon close examination, it turned out that Anton had sold us an Italian rifle but with Russian cartridges. It was a fiasco. We returned home without the money, without a usable weapon, and with fifty useless Russian cartridges. What a failure.

The Concert

After I returned from the "Forest Expedition," I was depressed. My life was nearing an end, without hope for survival. In addition, all hope for resistance or fighting back was gone. To add salt to the wounds, it was a beautiful spring. Nature, awoken from its long winter slumber, was blooming and blossoming with vitality. Even the few grass blades of grass that survived the harsh winter, multiplied into expanding green patches. Springtime, the time for love and procreation of life, was for us a time to prepare for death.

The concert was an event that I will never forget. In a small dark room, about fifteen teenagers gathered to listen to a violin recital by one of our friends. I looked at those emaciated faces, creased with pain, the downcast eyes reflecting the distress of their souls. They were like withering branches cut from healthy trees. The violinist played cheerful Russian folk songs like *Katyusha* and *Kapitan*, and suddenly he switched the tune and the well-known melody of *Hatikva* ("The hope," in Hebrew), which would become the national anthem of Israel, filled the room. "*Od lo avda tikvateynu*—Our hopes are still alive."

The tune and the words brought me to tears. I stood up saluting and, through my tears, I looked at the once-beautiful youth condemned to death and asked myself: *Why? Why is this happening to us?* A scene from the Bible appeared before my eyes: The blinded Samson bringing down the Philistine Temple. At that moment, I wouldn't have minded being blinded myself if only I could bring down the cruel world I was existing in.

Martin's Note: Soviet partisan units were made up mostly of Red Army soldiers whose units were destroyed in the early stages of Operation Barbarossa, paramilitary groups under the control of the NKVD and local Communist party activists. Soviet partisan groups were often reluctant to accept Jews into their ranks. Many Soviet partisan commanders held negative stereotypes that Jews were cowards who couldn't be trained to become fighters. In addition, many Soviet partisan groups required their members to supply their own guns, which Jews rarely could do. There also were rumors that Jews seeking to join partisan groups were secret German spies.[5] Polish partisan groups also discriminated against Jews.[6] Sometimes Jews got around this by posing as Gentiles.[7] For example, Shmuel Gutman recounts how he passed as a Pole in a Polish partisan group that blew up a set of train tracks.[8] However, there were some instances in which Jews worked openly with non-Jewish partisans. One moving story involved the town of Skalat, where my father was to have worked in the Nazi labor camp. (See Chapter 9.) In June 1943, Gen. Sydir Kovpak, a Soviet partisan leader, led his brigade to attack the Germans occupying Skalat. They freed 300 half-starved Jews in the labor camp, many of the younger of whom joined the Kovpak forces.[9] One Skalat survivor-turned-Kovpak Partisan spoke of the great pride he took in being part of a Jewish squad in the resistance.[10]

At a secret meeting on May 15, 1943, the Rohatyn Judenrat and Jewish police realized that armed struggle was the only way out of their situation, and they decided to buy arms and make it possible for certain armed groups to go out to the forest.[11]

CHAPTER 19

Escape and Liquidation (May–June 1943)

The situation in the ghetto grew ominous. News of killings arrived daily: Brzeżany, Kolomyja, Przemyślany, killings everywhere. My father was as determined as ever to find a peasant who would hide us. Father was a congenital pessimist, and events up to then had proven him right. He was very persistent and finally found a possible way out. Reb Meir with his connections gave him the lead.

"I know a Polish gentleman, a real gentleman. Get in touch with him. I would trust him with my life and the life of my family. Unfortunately, I don't have the means," said Reb Meir.

Those words were music to my father's ears. He was ready. "How do I get in touch with him?"

"You have to go to see him. He lives about twenty kilometers [twelve miles] from here. Łopuszna is the name of the village. It is a small village. Danilo the coachman will take you there."

My father liked Meir and trusted him. A few days later he went to see Koenigsberg [the name of the gentleman] and struck a deal. He came home very excited.

"I found a place! I found a peasant who'll hide us. Koenigsberg gave us a Polish peasant—his name is Matusiak and he's going to take us in. We'll pay him twenty gold dollars a month. In a week we're leaving the ghetto! With God's help, we will survive!" My father smiled. I had never seen him so excited and happy.

My sister and I were less excited. "Matusiak can take the money and kill us. What protection do we have?" we asked.

"I met the man and I trust him. Secondly, as soon as we arrive in the village, we'll hide the money. We'll bury it. He'll never know where it is."

Luba was not convinced. The truth is that she had a boyfriend and didn't want to leave him. I decided to join my father.[1]

After two days of preparations, we were ready to leave the ghetto. I packed my backpack, in a military fashion, with a rolled-up blanket on top of it. Then, I checked once more the backpack and discovered that my sister had put my *tefillin* (phylacteries) inside.[2] Without saying a word, I took them out and, not wanting to let fall into German hands and be defiled, I burned them. I burned my bridges behind me. I was ready to go.

After two weeks of staying with Matusiak on the *khutor* (a hamlet), we settled into a routine. It was a beautiful summer with warm and dry days. Warming in the sun, listening to birds singing, and not being afraid. This was paradise. During the days, we stayed in the forest and at night we slept high on the mountain of straw in the barn. The food was abundant, although simple. Potatoes with sour cream filled my stomach, although I did not lose my psychological hunger.

One day I heard the rattling noise of the peasant wagon. We immediately backed off the dirt road. A wagon in this part of the country, in the middle of the day spelled trouble. Hidden in the forest underbrush we observed the road. "If the Germans are coming, we have to crawl away and hide in the forest," warned my father.

I looked closer and I recognized Danilo, the peasant who had brought us here. "I am afraid that he is bringing bad news," my father said.

"Father, please don't exaggerate. Be a little optimistic," I suggested.

"Optimistic? How can a Jew get good news these days? When he dies and loses his fear."

Father was right. Danilo was bringing us bad news. It was a letter from Luba. It was short and to the point:

> My Dearest,
> The situation in the ghetto worsens from minute to minute. I feel like "The last days of Pompeii." I'm running scared. Please came back to get me.
> Love, Luba.
> P.S. I hope you come in time.

Without hesitation, my father took his walking cane, put on an old vagabond coat brought by Danilo, and left on the dangerous journey back to the ghetto. I remained alone.

The next day, Matusiak brought me the shattering news that the liquidation of the ghetto had begun. I never expected to see my family again. I remained alone in this cruel world.

The whole day I spent lying on the forest floor, reminiscing about the past, and trying not to think about the future. I couldn't even touch my food. Even my chronic hunger was gone.

When my father arrived in the ghetto, he found the mood drastically changed. Gone were the jubilation and excitement caused by the Warsaw Ghetto Uprising. It was a foreboding mood; people expected to be killed in a few days and were paralyzed by fear and helplessness. Rumors flew endlessly. The ghettos in surrounding towns were being liquidated and mass hysteria spread, as the community waited for death.

The resistance group finally decided to leave the ghetto for the forest, but they couldn't do it without causing a panic. If the resistance group left, the panic would be unbearable. Meir Weisbraun, the chief of the Jewish police and leader of the group, faced a dilemma: The group had weapons and could survive in the forest, but he couldn't abandon a sinking ship.[3] Fearing that people might leave the ghetto and take the weapons with him, he ordered the concentration of the weapons at one central point.

My father had never believed in resistance. "Russia, America, and England can't do it, so what are our chances?" he would say. "Luba, pack your stuff and let's leave the ghetto immediately," he said to her upon his arrival.[4]

"Father, the Gestapo liaison from Tarnopol telegraphed to say that the *rochim*—the murderers—will stay home this weekend. Please, let us stay one night at least," she begged him.

"I left Shiko in the forest," my father answered. "He's all alone."

"One night won't make a difference. I want to enjoy the comfort of my own bed, for one more night. *Please.*"

The idea of sleeping in a bed, after all those nights in the barn, appealed to my father and he agreed. "One night and no more. Tomorrow morning, we're leaving for the forest."

The telegram turned out to be one of the psychological-warfare hoaxes perpetrated by the Gestapo. Ten hours later, the ghetto was surrounded, and its liquidation began. Instead of sleeping in their own bed, my father and my sister were sitting in the bunker waiting to be killed.

Luckily, they had been alerted in time and everybody had reached the bunker safely. Before they settled down, the drama of the liquidation unfolded: muffled screams, shots, the familiar shouts of *"Juden raus!"* interspersed with the powerful explosions of bombs.

The *Judenrein* action—the liquidation action—differed from previous actions. Now, the Germans didn't send the Jewish police to bring out the victims; instead, they firebombed the bunkers. The Germans never entered a bunker themselves. They were afraid. After two hours of vigil, Shmuel Hecht who was sitting near the trap door, motioned for silence. "I hear German voices above. They found us. Please keep quiet!"

"Oh my God!" cried my sister, who felt guilty for bringing our father back.

"Quiet!" hissed Shmuel, "I recognize the voice of our neighbor, V.[5] The son-of-a-bitch is giving us up."

They sat in silence and in total darkness, listening to the muffled voices from above. "Nobody is here," V. was reporting to the Germans. "This bunker is used only for storing clothing and valuables."

Afterwards was a complete silence, interrupted by close shot. "This jerk brought the Germans to the bunker," hissed another neighbor.

"We don't know—maybe the Germans forced him to enter the bunker, but he saved us," someone said. The question of whether V. saved their lives or brought the Germans to the bunker was left to history to decide. The immediate problem facing the occupants was what to do? The action started at five o'clock in the morning, it had already lasted a full day. It was midnight. Staying put in the bunker could only prolong the agony for another day. There was no hope.

There were about fifteen people in the bunker. Fifteen scared and resigned people, hoping and praying for an easy death. They wanted to get it over with.

After a while my father got up. "I'm going to have a look. I'm not ready to die. Not yet."

"Let's wait a little," begged Luba.

"No, time is not on our side. Waiting is suicidal. The Germans are tired by now from all this shooting."

"You are right, Leon. It's time to go." Shmuel Hecht grabbed his wife's hand and pulled her. "Ania, let's go." In a few minutes, they had climbed through the door.

Now, Luba was persuaded to leave. When they emerged from the bunker, a wave of hot air hit them. The Hechts' house was on fire. Red flames illuminated the area. A real inferno. The Germans and Ukrainians patrolled the area, shooting at anything that moved.[6]

Escape and Liquidation (May–June 1943) | 129

"Bend down and crawl slowly behind me," ordered Father.

Behind the house there was a big garden, with planted potatoes. At this time, the potato plants were blooming, and some reached a height of two feet. Father pulled out a few potato plants and camouflaged himself.

"Luba, do the same and follow me."

The house was located near the border stream. Illuminated by the hellish red light, two potato plants were slowly crawling toward the stream.

After crossing the stream, they turned around and huddled under a bush for a short conference. "I'll go first and you follow me, at least a hundred yards behind; if I run into trouble, you run."

"Where are we going?"

"To Danilo. He lives on the outskirts of the town. Follow me."

After crossing the town, without turning to look at the burning ghetto, they safely arrived at Danilo's house. Danilo lived in a whitewashed hut with two small windows and a thatched straw roof. Behind the house, there was a big stable. In the front yard, a vicious dog was running on a long leash.

When Father and Luba approached the house, the dog started to bark viciously, jumping in their direction. The barking drew a savage response from all the neighboring dogs. My father and sister had to withdraw and hide in the fields.

"I have to get to Danilo before daylight. We can't stay here. What are we going to do?" My father was at his wit's end. "To escape the ghetto to be caught by Ukrainians."

They again approached Danilo's house. The loud barking started again, but this time they were lucky. The small window opened, and Danilo stuck out his head.

"Danilo! Danilo!" hissed Father. "Please let us in."

Danilo recognized him. A minute later they were resting in the safety of the stable.

The next day, at sunset, they left for the forest. Danilo drove the wagon, on the front seat beside him sat Luba, and Father sat in the rear, his feet dangling through the ladder-type railing. He was dressed in an old Russian military coat, and a pointed cavalry hat called a *budionovka*. With his unshaven and lined face, he looked like an old vagabond beggar. My sister was dressed in a colorful skirt and a white embroidered blouse. She looked like a young Ukrainian girl going to visit her beau in the next village.

The Pessimist's Son

After driving in complete silence for about half an hour, they encountered another wagon driven by an old peasant: "The Germans set up a roadblock, two miles from here. They're looking for Jews," he said.

Danilo proceeded for a while without saying a word. My father started to worry. "He is delivering us to the Germans," he said to Luba. Suddenly, Danilo jerked the reins of the horses and turned around. They were now going back, in the direction of the ghetto.

"Where's he going? I'm afraid to ask," my father said. Luba kept silent.

After proceeding for about half a mile, Danilo made a sharp right turn into a very narrow road that separated two properties. It was a private road. As they went, they passed peasants working in the fields. At each encounter, Danilo greeted the peasants with a customary: "Bless the Lord, Jesus Christ."

The sun rose. It was a bright, warm summer day. The singing birds proceeded with their courtship, women in white kerchiefs diligently raked and cleaned the potato fields. Nature and people were at peace with themselves, and only a few miles away an enormous tragedy was taking place.

After a half an hour ride Danilo turned into a dirt road that led them to the main road, bypassing the roadblock. Now, Danilo turned his toward Father, asking quietly: "Don't you trust me, Leon?"

In a few hours, they safely arrived at the *khutor*.

<u>Martin's Note</u>: *This is an excerpt from the description of the liquidation of the ghetto on the Rohatyn Jewish Heritage website (citations omitted):*

> **1943 Jun 6~8**—*Liquidation of the Rohatyn Ghetto, and an attempt to kill all remaining Jews there. Gestapo and Ukrainians surround the ghetto, set houses on fire, and throw grenades. Much of the ghetto is leveled by fire, leaving only the Judenrat building and a few other Jewish buildings standing. The few thousand Jews who survive the initial round-up are marched in a column on the road north out of the Rohatyn city center, weeping, some carrying small children. From the side of the road, a Ukrainian schoolchild sees her Jewish girlfriend in the column, and they yell out to each other, "Farewell!" Many armed men manage the column, which stretches so long that bystanders can barely see the end of it. Throughout that day and for the next two, armed guards encircle the Jews, force them to undress, then shoot them over a large mass grave north of the town center, near the new Jewish cemetery and*

a monastery. Over the next days, the corpses in the pit are covered with lime and then with earth, but the stench from rotting flesh persists, unbearable to passers-by. [Days later,] there are corpses everywhere. The Jewish survivors are grief-stricken; some attempt suicide.[7] *[In my father's video testimony, he says that very few people in the ghetto killed themselves. Sterzer says the same thing.*[8] *My father doesn't specifically say anything about survivors of the liquidation attempting suicide.—MK]*

From Pinkas Hakehillot Polin:

The Germans and the Ukrainians put the ghetto houses on fire and threw grenades inside. Those who were caught were brought to pits which were made a day before near the new cemetery on the way to Parnuvke, next to the monastery, where the slaughter went on for three days until June 9 1943. Some of the victims, especially the children, were not shot, they were buried alive.[9]

In the next few weeks, the hunt for hiding Jews continued, during which bunkers were found. Three of these bunkers were known by their builders as "Stalingrad", "Sevastopol" and "Leningrad" as symbols to the strongholds against the German army in the Soviet front. These bunkers were equipped with food supplies for a long period of time, and around 60 people were found in one of them. But these hideouts were exposed because of informers, and German sources reported of armed resistance in one of them.[10]

* * *

The Germans may have gone back to shooting Jews in front of mass graves instead of sending them to death factories like Bełżec, as they had done in the second action, because that they had closed Bełżec (the closest death camp to Rohatyn) by June 6, 1943.[11] *At Bełżec, the Germans secretly exhumed all the mass graves and cremated the bodies to hide their crimes.*[12] *The Nazis also took other steps to hide evidence of their genocidal work.*[13] *After its closure, the site was "looted by local people looking for valuables—gold teeth, money—that the Nazis might have missed."*[14]

CHAPTER 20

In Hiding

We were sitting at dinner one day, when the dogs started to bark loudly. Somebody was trying to get into the house. Matusiak got up and motioned us to hide. "Please go to the barn. A stranger is coming." Without thinking much, we ran out through the back door.

We heard a raised voice. Matusiak was yelling: "It's not true! You're crazy, with those stories! How can you do this to me? You're my neighbor."

Fifteen minutes later Matusiak came to the barn. He was shaken. "I think you have to leave. The neighbors suspect that I'm harboring Jews."

"Mr. Matusiak, I am sure that nobody saw us here. We are very careful. Let us stay." Father pleaded.

"It's dangerous for you and me. A neighbor of mine came to warn me. Other neighbors saw the new dress and new clothing for the children my wife bought and this made them suspicious: 'You're throwing money around. You must be hiding Jews.'" Matusiak was a poor farmer, and my father paid him fifty gold dollars monthly, an astronomical sum of money. He had spent part of the money, and that was enough to arouse suspicion. Our vacation was over. Inside a minute, our whole world had collapsed.

"Let's join the Jewish group in the forest," I suggested.

"No," my father answered. "Sooner or later the Germans will pick them up. They have no chance to survive undetected in the forest. In the winter, each footstep will be imprinted in the snow. Either the Germans or the Ukrainians will kill them. We have to find another peasant to hide us."

The next day, Matusiak came to see us. "You can stay a few days more, but stay inside. Don't run around in the forest. Tomorrow, I'm going to see Koenigsberg. He knows lots of people and he might be able to help you."

This lifted our spirits. Koenigsberg had been our liaison with Matusiak. Despite his German name, Koenigsberg was a Polish patriot, and a real gentleman. He was the richest man in his village, Łopuszna. Koenigsberg owned twenty-five acres of fertile land, horses, and cows, but his main wealth and income was derived from an oil press. He owned a press where linseed was pressed into precious oil.

A week later, arrangements were made for our transfer to the Koenigsbergs. They lived in a large house situated at the main road in the center of the village. The farm sloped downward, toward the river. On the right-hand side were stables for the cows and horses. On the left, there was a little shack with the oil press and beneath it the big barn, packed with straw to the rafters.

This barn became our hiding place. Our "dwelling" was a hole about six feet by eight feet. We were surrounded by straw, breathed air filled with straw, and ate food mixed with straw. Straw was everywhere. The only connections with the outside world were the slots in the old, dried-up gray wooden planks. Through those slots the sun shone in the morning, lifting our spirits. Sometimes it rained, and I could catch some of the raindrops and feel the wetness on my skin. It made me feel alive, not like a corpse buried in a straw catacomb.

Luba stayed in the main house. She helped out Mrs. Koenigsberg with her chores and taught their three daughters: Janina, Ursula, and Cesia.

The ability of humans to adapt to any conditions is amazing. Soon, we settled into a routine. In the morning, we washed with a washcloth made damp from a bottle of water and then took turns in the morning walking in our "straw palace." Only one person could walk at a time. Later, after one of the Koenigsberg daughters delivered our meal, we played chess.

Food delivery was a complicated operation. Usually, Cesia took a metal pail filled with chicken feed and started to call the chickens: *Tu! Tu! Tu!* [that is, "Here! Here! Here!"]. The chickens followed her when she threw the grain to them while walking toward the masked pass-through hole. Making sure that nobody saw her, she tapped on the door and passed us a pot of soup. Whenever I heard the *Tu! Tu! Tu!* call, my mouth watered.

Cesia was the youngest daughter and after a while I fell in love with her and her *Tu! Tu! Tu!* I never thought that you could fall in love in a straw-filled cubbyhole.

Once a week, Koenigsberg briefed us on what was going on in the world, brought us some newspapers to read, and lifted our spirits. According to him, it was only a matter of months before the war would end. I don't know if he himself believed those stories, but he was a gentleman.

We scrutinized every word of the newspapers, which were published by the Germans for the local population. The Polish was atrocious, but the propaganda amazing. Goebbels had a way of interpreting each defeat as a victory. The Germans were never defeated; rather, they always retreated to better positions, inflicting heavy casualties on the enemy, advancing to the rear. We were delighted to see that the "better positions" were closer and closer to us. We became masters of reading between the lines. The places of German victories became engraved in our minds: Tobruk, El Alammein, Orel, Vitebsk, Kursk. We lived by those names, dreaming that one day we would be able to see all those places.

Soon, we developed an additional competitive game—de-lousing. Despite our efforts to keep clean, lice started to plague us. So every morning after washing, we killed the parasites. We developed a competitive game: who could kill the most parasites in the allotted time.

We also played chess, endlessly fighting over each move. "You can't make this move with the tower. I am at the end of the game. I'm able to check you. It's unfair." Sometimes Father got excited and screamed loudly. I usually gave in. I didn't want to lose my life because of a chess game.

All this time, Luba was living as domestic help or as a governess-tutor in the main house. I think that Mrs. Koenigsberg was a sickly woman who needed help. Luba was staying all the time in the house in order not to arouse suspicion. During the whole time we were there, we never saw her.

The Koenigsberg place was always full of people, wagons, and horses. I think that the oil press saved our lives. Nobody would suspect that Jews could be hiding in place as busy as Forty-Second Street in New York.

As the summer passed, the days were getting shorter. We made ourselves a straw curtain to mask the openings in the barn's planks, and we started to use an archaic lamp. It was a small bottle filled with oil with a wick immersed in it. The main problem was safety. A small move and the whole barn could be set on fire. I always had to hold the lamp in my hand, until our host gave us an old metal pail with holes punched in the side—a homemade lantern. We lived in our cubbyhole, detached from the world.

We also discovered a fascinating new pastime—story-telling. My father started to tell me stories from his life. They fascinated me and I listened rapturously to them as they were told and retold, almost memorizing them. They evoked in me a feeling of peacefulness. It was a vision of a remote world where life was secure and slow-moving. I especially liked the stories from World War I.

My father was drafted into the Austrian Army and served as an artillery observer on the front in Italy, on the River Isonzo. It was a stationary war, fought for years in the mountains of Tyrol, where the Austrians tried to push the Italian army. My father took part in the Twelfth Isonzo Offensive.[1]

Twelve offensives on one spot. It sounded idyllic—human madness at a slow-moving pace. My father, serving as an artillery scout, directed artillery fire.

"I used to jump out of the trenches with my binoculars and the hand-cranked telephone, pulling the telephone wires with me. Then, I crawled to the end of the ridge, hid under a tree or under a bush and observed the movement behind the enemy lines. One day I spotted a caravan of mules, negotiating a winding mountain path. The mules were loaded with wooden cases of artillery shells. I thought, 'The mules are carrying shells for the Italians to use against us,' I picked up the telephone set and, cranking the handle, called in the firing coordinates."

"After a few shots, I was able to zero in on the caravan. The animals were hit and started to fall off the cliff. The next day, the Italians zeroed in on our battery and opened fire with a barrage. I was out at my post at the ridge. When I crawled back, I found half of my comrades dead. I found my best friend Simeon Sharp badly wounded and bleeding. He died in my arms.

"I was in a shock. I looked at myself. My tunic was all stained with the blood of my friend. I suddenly realized that this was a war. It wasn't only the mules that fell off cliffs. I decided to quit."

"How can you quit a war? Did you desert the army?" I asked.

"No, I quit legally," Father said. "I applied for a furlough. Our battery was put out of operation, and we were withdrawn from the front line to a small Hungarian town near Lake Balaton. I went to the rabbi and he directed me to a Jewish girl that was taking care of soldiers. She gave me a small bottle of acid. I think it was sulfuric acid. Smear it on your leg for a few days and you'll develop the symptoms of a wound."

"Our battery was reorganized, we received new horses and additional soldiers. *Kannonenfutter*—cannon fodder, as the Germans called it. We returned to another position on the Isonzo. I waited for an opportunity. When our position was slightly hit, I smeared my leg with the acid and screamed in pain. The acid was burning a real hole in my body. I screamed with pain until a Red Cross orderly put me on a wagon and took me to the field hospital.

"In the hospital, before I was examined by a doctor, I smeared my wound with a few drops of acid. I stayed in the hospital for months and the wound would not heal. Until my doctor became suspicious and figured me for a faker. He put my leg in a cast. 'I assure you, Kimel,' he said. 'Your leg will heal in one week. I'll take care of you.' And, really, my leg started to heal.

"I was ready to give up. The cast was tight and I couldn't reach my wound with the 'magic bottle.' One night, I had a dream. I saw my friend Sharp dressed in a *talit* [*a prayer shawl—MK*]. He said, 'Leon, I am praying for you. Don't give up. Find a way.' I woke up and in my confusion jumped out of bed. The jerking of my encased leg sent a wave of pain through my body, and my cast slipped a little bit. That was all that I needed. My friend saved my life.

"I took the magic bottle and went to the toilet there. In the middle of the night, I worked feverishly to reach the wound. I dipped a piece of toilet paper in the fluid . . . and I was happy when I felt the burning, piercing pain. I was back in business. Three months later, I was discharged from the hospital and declared an invalid, not fit to serve in Austrian Imperial Army. That's how I left the war theater."

Soon, autumn arrived. The autumn of 1943 was unusually cold. Frost covered the crops. One night, I woke up shivering. I tried to dig into the straw, but it didn't help much. I had to get up and start moving around to warm up. My father also woke up and immediately started to worry. "We can't stay here—we'll freeze to death. I think Koenigsberg is trying to get rid of us. What does he need this aggravation for?"

The next day, we spoke with Koenigsberg. "Mr. Kimel, I'm aware of the problem. We have to build an underground bunker, but I don't know where to dispose of the excavated dirt. With people waiting for the press milling around, digging is dangerous, and we need to find someone to do the digging. But don't worry, Mr. Kimel, we will find a solution."

When my father heard the "don't worry," he immediately prepared a long list of things that might go wrong, and started to worry, one item at a time. Koenigsberg soon came to inform us that he had started the digging. He found a nice Ukrainian man, Stephan, who would do the digging at night. My father immediately revised his "Worry List," introducing new items: First, the Ukrainian might denounce us to the Germans and get a reward. Second, his wife might blab the secret out. Third, the Ukrainian partisans might try to get our money. Fourth, Stephan might kill us himself.

After two weeks of intense anxiety, we were transferred to the new underground bunker. The bunker in many ways resembled the old bunker "at home." An area of about twelve by ten feet was excavated to a depth of about seven feet, and a false ceiling was built. Inside, our main furniture was a homemade platform bed filled with straw and covered with a blanket. The new place was warm, but we lost the wooden slots connecting us with the outside world and letting sunshine through. We had to use the oil lamp for illumination and the only connection with the outside world were the two vent lines.

In the autumn of 1943, the German Army was retreating on all fronts. Even the newspapers became more open and required less and less reading between the lines. Goebbels changed the propaganda line. After discovery of the Soviet Union's Katyn Massacre, Germany became the defender of culture against the onslaught of Stalin's Asiatic hordes.[2] Reading the newspapers became a feast. New names were engraved into our consciousness. The Russians started the summer offensive. New Russian names we learned were Zhukov, Rokossovksy, Konev.[3] We started to believe that we would survive. In the winter of 1943, Russian forces entered the old Polish territories, and the front line drew closer. The roar of German tanks and planes became constant. We learned to distinguish the noise of Panzer tanks from Tiger tanks. Most of all, we learned how to determine the directions in which the tanks were moving. When they were retreating, we celebrated; when going eastward, we wished them an easy death.

Soon the front drew nearer and nearer. In March of 1944, the Russian forces liberated Tarnopol. We started to count the hours until our liberation. When my father abandoned his chronic pessimism, I became suspicious. There is a Ukrainian proverb "*Ne kaze hop . . . ,*"—meaning "Don't count your chickens. . . ."

One night, we were awakened by a noise above our trap door. What is it? Were we liberated? Soon, the door opened and Luba appeared. "What happened? Are the Germans gone? Where are the Russians?" My father and I asked her.

"They are almost here. The Russian patrols were spotted about ten miles from here, but the Germans brought in reinforcements. They are combing the forest now and killing any surviving Jews," Luba shared the news with us.

"Worst of all, Koenigsberg is afraid of the Russians and decided to retreat with the Germans," she said.

"Oh my God, we'll be left alone!"

"No. Stephan is going to take care of the farm: the cows, the horses—and us. Koenigsberg is going to leave us food and water for two weeks. The Russians should be here any moment."

We had mixed feelings. We were sad to see Koenigsberg go. He had been our patron saint. But we were excited about our upcoming liberation.

Soon, Koenigsberg brought us dried bread and two containers of water. "I have to go. I'm afraid that the Russians will send me to Siberia. They called me a *kulak* before. I'll settle down in western Poland. Stephan is going to take care of you." We thank him for saving our lives and kissed him goodbye. Father also gave him some extra money. Little did we know that our ordeal was just starting.

<u>Martin's Note</u>: *My father regarded Matusiak as being primarily motivated by profit, but he believed that Koenigsberg acted out of humanitarian motives.*

Many Jews hidden by peasants were found out because the peasants' neighbors grew suspicious about the surprising newfound wealth of the hiders (here, the Matusiaks). Snyder refers to the hiders as rescuers and argues that such rescuers risked their lives and those of their families and that they did not do so for profit. In his view, the economically rational act when approached by a Jew would have been to take their money and then turn them in.[4] In fact, something like that happened frequently. In many instances, "rescuers" sheltered Jews until the Jews' money ran out and then murdered them.[5] Indeed, this almost happened to a cousin of my mother.[6] Gross takes a different view from Snyder, noting that sheltering Jews during the occupation could be "very lucrative." He argues that Polish shelterers were taking a calculated risk and that the "likelihood of being killed in such circumstances were rather low" as German police rarely found hiding Jews and Polish police usually would pillage the shelterers' house as punishment and kill the discovered Jews but take no further action against the shelterers.[7] The greater fear, according to Gross, was that a peasant's neighbors would rob or steal from him or her if they suspected he or she was harboring Jews.

Grabowski agrees with Snyder that harboring Jews was very dangerous. He finds that Poles aiding Jews faced possible fines or prison time prior to the summer of 1942, when the pace of ghetto liquidations increased, and that they thereafter faced a real risk of the death penalty.[8] In his study of rural Dąbrowa Tarnowska County, however, Grabowski agrees with Gross that assisting Jewish refugees was, in his words, a "very profitable profession," and Grabowski finds that far more

Jews were hidden by Poles motivated by money than by altruism.[9] Like Gross, Grabowski argues that "it was not the Germans but next-door neighbors who inspired the greatest fear both in those who rescued, and those who were being rescued." He continues:

> Many [village neighbors] considered Jewish life worthless and felt little hesitation to share their insights and suspicions with the police. . . . Simple envy often played a large part, too. According to many, those sheltering Jews were making a fortune in the process. Such "unjustified" enrichment bothered neighbors and friends, who considered themselves unfairly excluded from the redistribution of wealth that was happening around them. Jewish wealth thus was regarded as common property, and individual attempts at hiding Jews were considered egoistic assaults against the community. Since everyone could suffer because of possible German reprisals, there was no reason why only the chosen few should gain.[10]

Regarding Koenigsberg and his decision to flee before the return of the Red Army, kulak was a Russian term for a prosperous peasant in Russia or the Soviet Ukraine, a sort of oxymoron, and the term also could include wealthy farmers.[11] In and around 1930, 300,000 Ukrainians were among 1.7 million kulaks deported, often to Siberia, as part of Stalin's forced collectivization plans. In 1937 and 1938, the NKVD murdered over 378,000 people labeled as kulaks, whom Stalin deemed enemies of the state and counter-revolutionaries, and sent about an equal number to the labor camps. Soviet Ukraine was a major center of the killing, and the NKVD shot nearly 78,000 people to death in the Soviet Ukraine as part of its kulak operation.[12] Koenigsberg (who was a Pole, not a Ukrainan) must have been called a kulak when the Soviet Union occupied eastern Poland before the Soviets were forced out by the Wehrmacht. A disproportionate number of people killed through Stalin's kulak program were ethnic Poles, and the NKVD had a saying, "Once a Pole, always a kulak."[13] It is no wonder that Koenigsberg fled when he heard the Red Army was returning.

In connection with Koenigsberg's village, Jack Glotzer writes about hiding in the woods of Łopuszna. This includes being pursued and shot at by Germans and Ukrainians, and a massacre by the Ukrainian group known as Banderovtsy (Banderites), named after Stepan Bandera, the Ukrainian nationalist.[14] Bandera's organization, the Organization of Ukrainian Nationalists (the OUN), equated

Jews with Communists and accused Jews of cooperation with the Bolshevik regime and of crimes against the Ukrainian nation.[15] *The day after the invasion of the Soviet Union, the political director of Bandera's faction of the OUN had written to Hitler, expressing hope that Operation Barbarossa would "destroy the corrupting Jewish-Bolshevik influence in Europe and finally break Russian imperialism..." and bring about the "restoration of an independent national Ukraine."*[16] *It declared an independent Ukrainian state allied with Germany with a closing note: "Glory to the heroic German army and its Führer, Adolf Hitler." Bandera's men led OUN auxiliary units that marched into eastern Galicia in June 1941 with the Wehrmacht.*[17] *On July 5, 1941, however, the Nazis arrested Bandera because it suspected him of planning a revolt against Germany. With its hopes for Nazi support for Ukrainian independence dashed, the OUN soon was proclaiming it was fighting both German and Soviet imperialism.*[18] *(Other Ukrainians, however, collaborated with the Nazis in the hope they would gain favor with the Nazis and change their minds.*[19]*) The Banderites attacked Jews, Poles and pro-Soviet Ukrainians. According to Bauer, they were more numerous and powerful than the Soviet partisan groups or the Polish units of the Armia Krajowa.*[20]

CHAPTER 21

The Final Ordeal, Then . . . Liberation!

———————

"Those are Germans. We're surrounded." My father was crouching at the ventilation pipe, listening to outside voices. I saw cold drops of sweat on his forehead. "The German Military Police took over the farm, and we're buried under the lion's den. We're lost! Buried alive and finished!" said my father quietly.

My father was a pessimist, always expecting doom, but now we really were in an especially dangerous situation. During the months of the German occupation, we had been hiding in a bunker on a small farm, waiting for liberation as though we were waiting for the coming of the Messiah. The Russians were about twenty miles away, and we maintained an around-the-clock vigil. Waiting.

The farm had been taken over by the German Military Police, and we had become their uninvited (and unknown) guests. Luba had now joined us in the bunker. With only a three-week supply of bread and water and the place swarming with Germans, we faced a slow, torturous death. Death by starvation.

Through the ventilation pipe, our only link with the outside, we listened to the dramas unfolding on the outside. One day, I heard a familiar voice, pleading with the Germans. "I am a Jew. Please give me a bowl of soup and a shower and kill me later." I recognized the voice. I knew the man. It was L., the son of a neighbor.

I knew him quite well. At the beginning of the German occupation, we had worked together on many slave-labor assignments. He had been a nice fellow, until he joined the Jewish police and became one of the movers and shakers of the ghetto, became corrupted with power. He was the best example of how power corrupts and makes monsters out of ordinary people.

He survived the liquidation of the ghetto and had been hiding in the forest, but he couldn't take the daily misery, cold and hunger and surrendered. I never found out if the Germans wasted a bowl of soup on a Jew who would soon be dead. With bullets, they were generous. Listening to his voice, I was sad and scared. *What's going to happen to us? Are we going to break down and surrender?* I wondered. Soon our situation worsened. We had to cut our rations to half a glass of water and slice of bread per day. Yet, despite the strict rationing, we were down to a loaf of bread and half a gallon of water. I started to save some water. Every day, I put a few drops of water into a bottle, for a rainy day.

For a rainy day? I couldn't understand why people look for shelter when it rains. How I would have loved to stay in the rain, open my mouth and let the delicious raindrops wet my parched lips! *It would be delightful*, I thought. I started to long for the simple pleasures of life. I dreamed that I was basking in the warm sunshine and felt the gentle pressure of the blowing wind. Was I ever going to see sunlight again?

I had lost a lot of weight. The skin on my cheekbones became taut and thin, and I had trouble sleeping. Worst of all was the thirst, the ever-nagging thirst. My hunger subsided, but I felt a constant draining of my strength. I often would doze off, losing my sense of time and space. One time, I woke up and looked around. I saw my father and sister crouching restlessly on a bundle of straw. In the flickering light of the oil lamp, the underground bunker looked like an Egyptian tomb. My poor father had aged. My sister had developed protruding cheekbones; the shine of her black hair had disappeared. Her beauty was gone. It occurred to me that we might die here.

Oh God! I thought. *What's going to happen to us? Let me die first.*

One time, I saw my father resting motionlessly on the bundle of straw. It seemed to me that he had stopped breathing. "My God," I cried in desperation. "What are we going to do? We can't bury him. The only metal objects that we have are flimsy spoons. What are we going to do? We can't stay with a dead body." I realized that we would have to surrender. With some luck, I might get a bowl of soup. The possibility of getting a bowl of soup cheered me up. And Father was still alive.

I became very lethargic. I lost the will to live and started to hallucinate. Once, I dreamed that I was liberated, and spent my time going from well to well, drinking cool, delicious water. Then, the pain from my swollen lips woke me up. Luckily, the Germans started to retreat. The front lines grew

The Final Ordeal, Then . . . Liberation! | 145

nearer to our hiding place. We often heard the distant thunder of the artillery. One time, I don't know if it was day or night, I was awakened by a loud, persistent noise like a lawn mower. Soon I heard explosions, shots, and excited yelling of the Germans. We faced a new danger: the Russian *kukuruznik*, the "corn thresher."

The *kukuruznik* was a light, primitive biplane made of an aluminum frame covered with canvas. The low-flying plane was invulnerable to German flak fire. Machine gun bullets only made holes in the canvas. The plane would keep flying, attacking the Germans with incendiary hand grenades. When the German police post became the target of the attacks, we were in danger. Our bunker was located under a barn, filled with straw, about 100 feet from the building housing the Germans. Listening to the explosions, I experienced mixed feelings: I wanted the Germans to be hit, but I was also afraid that a small mishap would occur and that we would roast to death.

The next night, thunderous explosions awakened me. The whole bunker was shaking. The Germans placed pieces of field artillery adjacent to our bunker. We were in mortal danger. *The Russian Katyusha rockets will surely hit us*, I thought. Life was so unpredictable. After all the struggles for survival, to die from a Russian Katyusha would be ironically tragic.

But we were lucky. After a few hours the shooting subsided, and in the strange silence we heard a Russian song. "*Na pozitsiiu devushka. . . .*" Slowly, I crawled to the vent pipe, and I could not believe my ears. I heard Russian voices. We were liberated. I felt a wave of excitement. I jumped up yelling "Father, Luba, we made it! We're liberated!" I was amazed at my strength.

My father and my sister jumped out. We embraced and kissed each other, and swiftly emerged from the bunker into the bright, blinding sunshine. I walked as if in a daze. When I opened my eyes, I marveled at the miracle of creation. The big oak tree I saw was green, a dark vivid green. The flock of white geese with their orange beaks looked so peaceful, so alive. Even the gray sparrows chirping on the thatched roofs looked like wonders of nature.

Suddenly, I saw Stephan, the field hand, carrying a pail of water. I ran toward him, pushed my head into the pail and drank the water nonstop.

When I got up, I saw my sister talking with a Russian soldier. It looked like a dream. A Russian soldier. What a sight! I swiftly ran toward the road and seeing a Russian riding on a horse, I yelled to him: "I am a Jew. I survived! Thanks for the liberation!"

"Poshiol, prokliatyi narod! (Go away, you cursed people!)" the soldier yelled back.[1]

I felt sick to my stomach. Running toward the house, I realized that I had diarrhea. Nevertheless, the first month of our liberation was the most exciting time of my life. I met many other survivors and immediately felt a strong bond and kinship. It was such a wonderful feeling to experience closeness and trust after all those harsh years. Stories of miraculous survivals were engraved in my memory.

CHAPTER 22

Our Return to Civilization

The first days after liberation were bitterly euphoric. I was euphoric because I was no longer a hunted animal—a hunted animal afraid to show his face in the daylight, afraid to walk at night, waiting to be shot. Now I could walk free of fear. I could read a newspaper, look at a blue sky, take in the sun, wet my lips in the rain. I was not afraid to lose my most precious possession—my life.

It was also a bitter feeling. Remembering those who perished, especially my mother. I was also sick with diarrhea. After years of starvation, I couldn't eat. I was still losing weight. In addition, we had to face the problems of daily living in a war-ravaged country. Without resources, without education, a profession, without a place to live, we were facing a doubtful future. The euphoria balloon had been punctured.[1]

After a few days, we returned to my hometown, and there I faced the first crisis.

Being liberated was so much different than I'd expected. As a survivor, I expected some preferential treatment. All endangered species get *some* protection. Here's the protection I got: Two weeks after the liberation, I was summoned to the Mayor's Office, where the mayor told me I was being sent to work in the coal mines of Donbas.

"I'm a ghetto survivor, seventeen years old, undernourished, sick with diarrhea, and weighing exactly 36 kilograms. How can I work in coal mines?" I protested.

"Never mind, you'll manage. We Russians don't differentiate between Ukrainians, Poles, or Jews. Everybody has equal rights and obligations," answered the mayor.

At that moment, I realized that my struggle for survival wasn't over. It had just entered a new, subtler phase. The next day, I enrolled in high school, claiming that I was only fifteen years old. I simply deducted my years in hiding.

The Pessimist's Son

After we returned to my hometown, I found it a desolate place—the town destroyed, nearly all my family and friends gone.

We settled down in an empty office building that soon afterwards was taken over by Judge Boris for his makeshift courthouse. In this improvised courthouse, Judge Boris dispensed justice Soviet style: The goddess of justice, although blindfolded, easily recognized which offenders had bribed the judge.

We lived above the courthouse and living there had its drawbacks. We faced a constant stream of peasants ringing the doorbell and bringing gifts to the Judge: chickens, eggs, and butter. All those gifts were required to grease the wheels of the justice system. Most of the time, I was able to straighten out the callers, but from time to time we were left with a basket deposited before our door. Judge Boris was keenly aware of our interference with the justice system and tried get us out from the courthouse to another apartment, but none were available.

One day, answering the doorbell, I found myself facing two uniformed NKVD officers. "You are invited to visit our office," said one of the officers. And in Soviet Russia, nobody could refuse such a polite invitation.

I was a little scared. *Judge Boris is losing his patience. I wonder what the charge will be?*, I said to myself.

The NKVD headquarters were located in the old courthouse. On arrival, I was led to a dimly lit room, and interrogation started. State your name, age, place of birth, occupation, and so forth. Then suddenly the officer raised his voice and said: "You are accused of being a nasty collaborator, a member of the Jewish police."

"Me, a Jewish policeman? You must be kidding. I was thirteen years old at that time, and therefore too young to be a policeman. You can check with the school principal."

The NKVD man picked up the phone, called the principal of the school, spoke with him for some time and left the room for a few minutes to confer with his boss. When he came back, he said:

"You can go now. It was a mistake."

When I reached the door, he stopped me with the question. "Do you know G.?" *G.? G.? Who could it be?* I wondered. *It must be a trick pulled by Judge Boris.*

"No. I don't have the slightest idea who that is." I told the NKVD man.

Upon leaving the courthouse, I ran home to reassure my father that I was ok. Suddenly, it came to me: "G." was the mispronounced name of G.,

Our Return to Civilization | 149

the same cousin who had helped Luba bury the money and stolen it. He had been a policeman. Now it was time to pay him back.

I turned back to return to the courthouse, but on my way, I had second thoughts. I recalled a quotation from the Bible about Noah, stating that in his generation Noah was a righteous man. I also recalled the commentary stating that, if Noah had lived in another generation, he wouldn't be righteous. Can one apply normal ethical standards to people living in extremely abnormal conditions? Shall I be the judge? No. I turned back and went home. Soon, I ran into G.

"The NKVD is after you. They took me by mistake. You better hide," I advised him.

And hide he did. I wouldn't see him again for decades.

As Reb Meir used to say, "Mysterious are the ways of our Lord." Indeed, things that happened were impossible to predict.

In Łopuszna, the place where we survived, out of the 350 Jews who hid in the forest, sixteen survived.[2] The others succumbed to hunger or disease or were killed outright by the Germans or by Ukrainian partisans.

Unexpectedly, Ania, Shmuel, and their baby, our neighbors from the ghetto also survived. They were helped by Xenia. The reunion of the baby with her birth parents was very dramatic. The baby (then a toddler) called Xenia "Mom," and didn't want to go with her parents. They lived together for months until the girl, then eighteen months old, got used to her biological parents.[3] Dr. Hudish, who had delivered Aviva, also survived, as did his wife. I met up with them, years later, in Israel.

Another surprise: Maxim, the janitor of the German County Office who was so nasty towards me, saved the lives of about ten Jews, hiding them in the attic of the County Seat. Willie Bloch, the perennial survivor who had jumped from a cattle car, also survived—only to be drafted into the Russian army and killed one day before the end of the war and the attacks on Berlin.[4]

In Podhajce, we got the dreadful news that Chaim Lehrer, my dear grandfather, whose eyes had looked so lifeless in that last photo of him we saw, took his own life after Roncia, his beloved, music-loving wife and my adored grandmother, was killed. That was a very painful double blow.[5]

Martin's Note: According to information my dad provided to Yad Vashem, Chana Lustig, the girl with whom he stood guard in the Rohatyn Ghetto, was murdered in the liquidation at the age of about thirteen. My dad's first cousins, Elke Rubler and Libby Rubler Jupiter, also were murdered, as was Libby's husband, Mottel/Mechel.

With respect to Donbas, Ludwipol survivor Yehuda Raber writes that name Donbas was notorious because of the harsh conditions there, and that it was where the Soviets sent all who had acted against the Soviet regime.[6] (My father, however, doesn't appear to have been assigned there as any sort of punishment.)

My dad doesn't provide a lot of information (which would have been second hand) about what happened in Podhajce after his family left in 1939. Based primarily on various accounts in Sefer Podhajce, here is some of what befell the Jews of Podhajce under German occupation, some of which is similar to what transpired in Rohatyn:

In June 1941, the Germans entered Podhajce. As elsewhere, the Ukrainians were quick to act violently against Jews. In Podhajce, they "set up local S.S. units, and with the protection of the Germans, they began their systematic murder of the Jewish population."[7] The Nazis established a Judenrat, whose members were appointed at the recommendation of the mayor. They collected punitive fines— money, furniture, and bedding—from the Jewish population.[8] The Judenrat then had to supply labor for the Germans. Based on the respective yizkor books (which is not a scientific sampling), the Judenrat of Podhajce seemed more despised than that of Rohatyn.[9]

Shoshana Haber describes the creation of the ghetto in Podhajce in 1942:

> Everyone, including the elderly, women and children, took all kinds of belongings in their hands, on their back and on their heads. The Germans and their Ukrainian assistants stood at the side and laughed. A number of those being transferred received death blows because they lagged behind in the transfer of their property. . . . The worst part was at the end of the transfer, at nightfall, when the Germans realized that there were too many Jews, and the place was not large enough for them on the two streets that were designated for the ghetto. . . . Then they began to shoot at anyone they wanted to as they were entering the ghetto. Several hundred Jews were murdered that day.[10]

The first Nazi action in Podhajce took place on Yom Kippur 1942 (September 21, as one that was taking place in Rohatyn at the same time). According to Nachum Pushteig, approximately a thousand Jews were gathered and sent to the Bełżec death camp.[11] Anyone who resisted was shot on the spot.[12] According to another survivor, "[t]he slaughter was perpetrated by the Germans along with their Ukrainian assistants."[13] In addition to the Ukrainians, ethnic Germans, the

Volksdeutsche, *also helped the Nazis carry out their bloody work.*[14] *Many Jews survived by hiding in bunkers they had built.*

The Germans carried out a second action on October 13. The Nazis brutally murdered some Jews on the spot and sent the rest of those they found to transports to Bełżec. As with the Jews in Rohatyn, some survived by leaping through small windows in the cattle cars.[15] *One account of the second action, however, says that 2,000 Jews were shot in a pit behind the city.*[16]

In the third and final liquidation action, Pushteig writes, Jews were forced to strip and walk onto planks over a pit and the Germans then machine-gunned them.[17] *In the final liquidation action to make Podhajce* Judenrein, *in 1943, several hundred people were murdered. According to a memorial erected on the mass grave in the nearby village of Zahajce, 800 people were shot to death by the Nazis on June 7, 1943.*[18] *(At exactly the same time, the Nazis were liquidating the Rohatyn Ghetto.) Haber describes the gruesome scene this way:*

> As the large graves were being covered, the earth raised itself again and again. An outstretched limb would be raised, a clod of earth was exposed with a stream of blood that began to seethe literally like boiling water—for most of the victims were naked, men, women and children together, and many of them had barely been shot. At times, a stream of blood began to flow from the pit. Surrounding the place of murder were torn money bills that had been ripped to pieces at the last minute so that they would not fall into the hands of the murderers.[19]

Unlike in Rohatyn, the idea of suicide began to spread in Podhjace when rumors of the impending liquidation came. (Some Jews also managed to escape to the woods.) According to Henia Shourz:

> Apparently, 40 people purchased poison, and when the Gestapo guards came to take them from their homes, they poisoned themselves. These people lost their will to live and to struggle against the bitter and terrible fates, so they ended their lives. There was another group of people who were sick of fighting the angel of death every day, and they decided to end their lives. They gathered glowing coals and put them in the furnace. The smoke went up from there and they were asphyxiated. Approximately 20 people died this "easy" death and everyone was jealous of these people.[20]

152 | The Pessimist's Son

Nusia Horowitz made the reverse migration of my father's Aunt Ethel. Horowitz fled with her family from Mikulince after it was made Judenrein, to Podhajce, where her family had friends. She makes a similar point to Shourz's, writing about Podhajce in Sefer Mikulince:

> *Typhus and dysentery took their toll of the [Podhajce] ghetto residents. Sources of food dried up. Jews who sold food were killed and farmers no longer came to the ghetto walls to sell their produce. Hunger took its toll and the noose tightened around our necks. People became apathetic. They became jealous of those that had already died, who no longer had to live this nightmare.[21]*

After the liquidation of the ghetto, the hunt continued after those hiding in the forest. The local Ukrainian population took part in searching for Jews and handing them over to the Germans or killing them on their own. In this way many bunkers were discovered and many dozens of Jews were murdered. During the last month of 1943, a Podhajce self-defense group led by an Israel Zilber (or Silber) helped the Jews hiding in the forest and did its best to supply them with food.[22] At the end of 1943 and the beginning of 1944, the Banderites were active in the forests around Podhajce and murdered many Jews.[23]

In Chapter 1, my father wrote about the over-educated Orenstein children. Tragically, it seems likely the Orenstein children never got a chance to try to put their education to good use. It appears that the Orenstein family's lives were cut short by the Germans.[24] It is difficult to match up some names because of the widespread use of nicknames in Podhajce and my father's sometimes identifying people by only one name, but many Tunises are listed in Sefer Podhajce's *list of martyrs so it is likely the town's matchmaker and family perished as well. It also lists Leibel Weiss and his wife, so it looks like "Leibele Trask (Smack)" and his wife did not make it either. Based on the statistics, one would expect that only about two percent of those who had remained in Podhajce would have survived. My father was one of "only a few isolated" Jewish survivors to remain in Poland after the war.[25]*

After subtracting two years from his age to avoid getting sent to the mines of Donbas in the eastern Ukraine, my father enrolled in school under his new age, continuing a Podhajce tradition. "Everything was beautiful at this time," my father said. "You're alive. You're not in danger." He said that there was an immediate closeness with other survivors. His family stayed in Podhajce for about half a year, and then they went to Tarnopol. My father and family probably moved to Tarnopol because it was a major city in the region. My Aunt Luba's new husband, Oscar Trief, also came from there.

Our Return to Civilization | 153

From Tarnopol, my grandfather, father, aunt and her husband moved to Wrocław (formerly, Breslau, Germany), about fifty miles from Legnica.[26] My grandfather had brothers in the United States, but it was hard to get a visa to America, so he got a phony visa to Cuba and, with that visa, they obtained a transit visa to Sweden. They left Poland and moved there in September 1946. My father worked in a Swedish factory for about six months but returned to Poland by himself to get an education. His father emigrated to the United States, while Luba and her husband (whom my family called "Sunio") stayed in Sweden until 1952. At that point, they had two children, my cousins Harold (born in Wrocław) and Paula (born in Stockholm, Sweden).

Back in Poland by himself, my father didn't "advertise" that he was Jewish, but he didn't hide it either. The people he went to school with or worked with knew he was Jewish. My father applied for an exit permit in 1948, but the "iron curtain" had already fallen and he didn't get one until 1956. My father said that the 1946 pogrom in Kielce (which I discuss later) put the Communist government on notice that it was dangerous for Jews to remain in Poland. As a result, the government allowed Jews to leave the country until Poland closed its borders in 1947. Once the borders were closed, as a Polish citizen during this period of Stalinist Communist rule, my father was not allowed to leave the country, even for a visit.

In Wrocław, my dad had $300 he had earned while working in Sweden. Later, he also got a job in Poland, and his father helped him out with some care packages. In Wrocław, he finished his high school education and then was admitted to the polytechnic institute (university) to study engineering. Documents he saved indicate he received a scholarship from the university. He chose to become an engineer because he knew he wanted to leave Poland and it was a profession he could practice in any country. My dad hid the fact that he had a father in the United States because, he said, the Communist authorities would have expelled him from the university had they known this.

Holocaust survivors received no special treatment or recognition. There wasn't even a term for "Holocaust survivor" in Poland. "You were a Polish citizen, and you had all the rights and privileges of a Polish citizen," my dad said. Given Stalin's stranglehold on Poland, this was consistent with the fact that the number of Jews killed by the Germans in the Soviet Union was a state secret, and that "the Holocaust could never become part of the Soviet history of the war."[27] In this connection, Snyder's analysis is worth quoting at some length:

> [The] high figures of murdered Jews also raised the troubling question of just how the Germans had managed to kill so many civilians in such a short time in the occupied Soviet Union. They had

> *help from Soviet citizens. . . . The shootings east of the Molotov-Ribbentrop line had implicated in one way or another, hundreds of thousands of Soviet citizens. (For that matter, much of the crucial work at the death facilities west of the Molotov-Ribbentrop line had been performed by Soviet citizens. It was unmentionable that Soviet citizens had staffed Treblinka, Sobibór,[28] and Bełżec.) [C]ollaboration undermined the myth of a united Soviet population defending the honor of the fatherland by resisting the hated fascist invader. Its prevalence was one more reason that the mass murder of the Jews had to be forgotten.[29]*

Poland had similar reasons not to dwell on the genocide that had taken place on its soil that had killed three million of its Jewish citizens:

> *Innumerable Poles became beneficiaries of the murder of Jews, the spoilation of their property, and the destruction of their communities. Some had not only condoned deportations and killings; they had been active participants and accomplices. It became almost impossible subsequently for Poles to face up to this. Moreover, the official communist versions of history, emphasizing a combination of heroism and martyrdom, at times almost brushed Jews out of Polish history entirely.[30]*

Jan Gross points to an additional reason the Communist party in Poland, specifically, had for not recognizing what had happened to the country's Jews:

> *Far from championing Jewish "interests" of any kind, the Communist authorities ignored the suffering of Poland's Jewish citizens at the hands of their neighbors both during and after the war. The Communist Party aimed to distance and insulate itself from the "Jewish question" in order to gain a modicum of legitimacy in the eyes of the Polish population, and adopted what at best can be described as an attitude of benign neglect in matters Jewish.[31]*

While studying electrical engineering in Wrocław (where my father earned a Master's degree and was studying for a PhD), he met my mother.

Photographs

1. Pesia and Leon Kimel.

2. Kimel home, Podhajce.

3. Exterior of the remains of Podhajce's Great Synagogue.

4. Ethel (b. Lehrer) Milch, Abraham Milch and Probably Pesia (b. Lehrer) Kimel. (Courtesy of Yad Vashem Photo Archive, Jerusalem. 2983_1.)

5. Eva as little girl between Fala and Natan.

6. The Rohatyn Judenrat. (Courtesy of Prof. Adi Schnytzer.)

7. Luba (b. Kimel) Trief and Oscar Trief.

8. Eva in scout uniform, 1947.

9. Tola and Henri Goldstein on their engagement day, Rouen, France, 1949.

Photographs | 159

10. Alex on bike in Poland.

11. Regina at 14. Legnica, Poland, 1951.

12. Alex at electrical equipment, probably in Poland.

13. Alex's exit visa from Poland to Israel, 1956.

14. Eva and Alex's wedding photo, Legnica, Poland, 1956.

15. Alex and Eva in Israel.

16. Martin's one-year birthday in Legnica, Poland with Eva, Fala, Mieczysław, and Regina, 1961.

17. Fala and Eva.

18. Barry Milch, Martin, Leon Milch, and Leon's Son, Steven, Sydney, Australia, 1989.

19. Alex and Eva skiing.

20. Portrait of Alex and Eva.

21. Gosia Czupak, Pamela (Kimel) Epstein, Alex, Martin, Iwona Pacułt and Eva in Legnica, Poland, 1993.

22. Yechiel "Chilek" Goldstein.

23. From back: Henri-Pierre Sebbon, Martin, Eva, Philip Goldstein, Helene (b. Goldstein) Sebbon, Marc Goldstein, and Alex.

Photographs | 165

24. Eva with David and Sarah.

25. Alex and Eva cutting cake at their 50th wedding anniversary party, 2006.

26. From rear: Harold Trief, Neal, Jonathan, Matthew, David, Miriam, Martin. Front: Pam, Alex, and Sarah.

27. Martin, David, Sarah, and Miriam Kimel before Sarah's Bat Mitzvah.

28. Sarah's Bat Mitzvah with the Himmelsbachs and Epsteins.

29. The Kimels and the Epsteins (and Boomer).

PART 2

Eva's Story of Life, Death, and Survival

By Martin Kimel

My mother, Eva Kimel, was born on June 19, 1931, in Radom, Poland, a city about sixty miles south of Warsaw (population: 85,000–100,000)[1] to Franciszka (Fala) Najnudel (née Goldstein) and Natan Najnudel.[2] My mother had a very happy childhood before the war, with many uncles, aunts, and cousins in Radom. They were considered upper middle class. Her father owned a sawmill in the village of Zawada in eastern Poland near Zamość, close to the Russian border, about eight hours away from Radom. As a result, my grandfather spent long periods away from Radom, working in Zawada. My mother and her family spent summers there. She used to have a lot of fun there building treehouses with the children of my grandfather's partners. But in the summer of 1938, in Zawada, my mother started hearing about goings on in Germany and Hitler declaring war on Czechoslovakia.

My mother's family lived in a pleasant two-bedroom apartment in a three-story building in Radom.[3] My Mom attended a private Jewish school. Each Friday, she attended a Shabbat dinner with her grandparents, and an aunt or uncle came to get her if her parents didn't go. Her mother and maternal grandparents kept kosher homes. (Her paternal grandfather, Lazer Najnudel, lived in Ostrowiec and was ultra-Orthodox.) She didn't remember playing with non-Jewish children before the war. Most holidays were celebrated at her grandparents' house. Her parents spoke to her in Polish and her school instruction was in Polish. But her parents spoke Yiddish at home with each other, and that is how my mother learned Yiddish. My mother said that my grandmother had a good life before the war. For example, my grandmother didn't leave Radom much, but she would travel to Warsaw to have shoes made "to her specifications." When I was growing up, my Babcia would come from Poland for long visits and we always complimented her as *elegancka* (pronounced "eleganska"), which she loved, so I can very much picture this.

CHAPTER 23

Fleeing Radom (September 1939)

When the German army invaded Poland, my mom was eight and her sister, Regina, was only two. After the September 1, 1939 invasion, her father came home one day and said, "Let's go. We're going to Zawada." My mother's extended family owned a fur store, and my mother's grandparents gave my grandmother a trunk filled with furs, which they packed onto a truck with their personal belongings. Then, during the first week of September, my Mom, her parents, Regina, and Lutka Steinman (later, Lutka Grynberg), a first cousin (the daughter of Natan's sister, Sabina), fled Radom, shortly before the Germans began bombing the city.[1] Lutka's sister-in-law wrote that Natan was "resourceful and took care of the whole family's needs."[2] It is good they left ahead of the Germans, who sadistically began beating and terrorizing Jews as soon as they arrived in Radom. As a general matter, the Nazis had a particular fascination with excrement, repeatedly using it to humiliate their victims.[3] They also enjoyed forcing one Jew to beat one another bloody. Many people fled the city and went east,[4] like my mother.

Five (eventually six) Einsatzgruppen, special mobile killing task forces of around 3,000 Security Police (including SS), entered Poland in September 1939. While meant to eliminate the educated class and upper levels of Poland and Polish society, enabling Germany to push Poland into slavery, they killed about 50,000 Polish civilians more indiscriminately.[5] One *Einsatzgruppe* was tasked with terrorizing Jews so they would flee east from the German occupation zone to the Soviet zone.[6] In addition to burning Jews alive in a synagogue in Będzin, *Einsatzkommandos* (smaller detachments) shot at least 500 Jews in Przemyśl and they strip-searched Jewish-looking women in the city of Chełm, breaking fingers to get at wedding rings.[7] As a result, an estimated 300,000 to 350,000 Jews fled to the Soviet occupation zone.[8]

It took my mother's family at least several days to reach Zawada. The trip was made longer because of military checkpoints and roads where civilian cars couldn't enter. The Soviet military was already in Zawada when they arrived, so it must have been September 17 or later. My grandfather went to the train station and spoke with some Russians there. He returned and told my grandmother that the Russians said they could travel by rail to Russia. But my grandmother didn't want to leave her parents and siblings in Poland and refused to leave the country, so they didn't flee to the Soviet Union proper.

They stayed in Zawada only one to two weeks. My grandparents heard that the Germans were still moving east and thought that their family would be safer moving further east, ahead of the Germans. From Zawada they went to the town of Łuck (pronounced "Wootsk," now Luts′k, Ukraine, often spelled "Lutsk" in English). A city on the Styr River, Łuck (the Polish spelling) is a city with a long history. Mentioned in the Ruthenian Chronicles of 1085, from 1320 it belonged to the Grand Duchy of Lithuania; from 1569 to 1795, it was a district center of the Polish-Lithuanian Commonwealth; and from 1796 part of the Russian Empire. Between 1921 and 1939, it was the provincial center of Volhynia in independent Poland.[9] In the 1920s and 1930s, all the large Jewish political parties were active in the city. Jews participated in municipal and regional government institutions. A Jewish public figure in Łuck was even elected to the Polish Sejm (Parliament). In addition to having Jewish religious schools under the aegis of different organizations, the city hosted about fifty synagogues and prayer houses belonging to various religious and professional groups. In 1937, there were 15,879 Jews in Łuck (about forty percent of the population).[10]

My mother's family lived there for a year or so, and my mother attended Russian-language school there. With a lack of kosher food, her family had to eat whatever was available. Her mother gagged when she ate pork for the first time in her life. One of her uncles from Radom had caught up with them and lived with them. In 1940, the Russians had control of Łuck, and word had it they were sending Jews they found there to Siberia. In one incident, they found my mother and Regina as they were trying to hide, and they wanted to deport the girls to Siberia. But local Ukrainians stood up for them, which my mother called "quite brave," and the Russians left them alone. In retrospect, my mother noted, it might have turned out better for her family to have been deported to Siberia, but, as she put it, "who knows?" (Unknown to my mother, her cousin Yechiel Goldstein, Philip Goldstein's brother, was deported in 1940 to a Soviet labor camp in the Arctic Circle. It turned out that the survival rate was much greater for those Jews in the Soviet camps. Roughly fifteen percent of the Polish Jews deported by the NKVD in 1940 died in transit or in the camps; at the end of the war, the remaining deportees were the largest surviving group of Polish Jews.[11]) My mother recalled that her cousin Lutka went her own way, though she didn't remember any details.[12] My mother also recalled thinking that, if she survived, she would one day write a book about her experiences.

Łuck proved anything but lucky for Jews who remained there, and it probably was fortunate that my mother and her family quit that city in 1940. The Germans established a regional center of operations there.[13] In July 1941, the Germans killed 2,000 Jews and called it revenge for wrongs supposedly done to Ukrainians by Jewish Communists.[14] And, of course, the Germans later established a ghetto in Łuck, which they subsequently liquidated. In August 1942, the Germans "ate and drank and laughed" as they forced women to recite, "Because I am a Jew, I have no right to live," before making them kneel naked over pits and shooting them dead.[15]

CHAPTER 24

Ludwipol (Summer 1941)

Continuing eastward from Łuck, my mother and her family eventually settled in the town of Ludwipol (pronounced "Lud-VEE-pol"; now, Sosnove, Ukraine), about 280 km northeast of Lwów (now, Lviv). The Jews had a nickname for it, "Greater Selisht" (*Selisht Gadol*). There were several stories as to how the town was named. One was that a nobleman had lived in a palace on the top of a hill. His name was Ludwik, and his wife's, Pola. The shtetl was one of the smallest Jewish communities in Volhynia, which is generally northeast of Galicia. Ludwipol survivor Asher Gurfinkel describes the shtetl:

> So small was the town, that people would say that when a carriage or wagon entered it, the head of the horse would be at one end of the town and the back wheel at the other end. . . .
> The town had no great beauty and no luxury, and its houses suited its size—they were not large and not tall.[1]

In many ways, prewar Ludwipol was similar to my father's prewar Podhajce—except it was even much smaller and more homogeneous. In 1939, there were about 2,000 Jews living in Ludwipol, out of a total population of only 2,150. In 1941, 2,100 Jews lived there.[2] For my mother, who would decades later tease my father that he was from provincial Podhajce whereas she was from the big city of Radom, it must have been quite an adjustment, and I don't know how it is that Natan and Babcia came to live there. Ludwipol had a bustling marketplace, but the shtetl lacked electricity and running water. Pious Jews studied Talmud and frequented the many synagogues. As in both Radom and Podhajce, Zionism was important. Zionist youth groups proliferated in Ludwipol, and young people studied Hebrew, dreaming of making *aliyah* (that is, emigrating to Israel). Ludwipol's Jews coexisted, sometimes uneasily, with the town's gentiles and peasants in nearby villages. As in Podhajce, weddings (which Roncia loved for their music) were communal affairs:

> Sometimes, usually on a Tuesday, the entire town woke up from its calmness—and from children in their cribs to old people, the entire town accompanies a bride and groom to their wedding canopy. All, invited or not, close family or far relatives, joyfully following the Klezmer, especially the violin singing in the moonlight with a sound filled with Jewish sadness and joy at the same time.[3]

Geographically, Ludwipol had two important features: It bordered a river (the Słucz or Sluch River), beyond which lay dense forests. In the words of one former resident:

> Like a string of precious pearls, pleasant childhood memories of summer days are resting along the small river, as we bathed and swam without the permission of our father. . . . This was the way we lived, we and our father and our fathers' fathers, generation upon generation, closely connected to the landscape of the wide fields and the thick green woods that stretched far beyond the horizon.[4]

Before the war, the various Zionist youth groups would meet and spend time in the forests, which were fewer than two miles from town.[5] Like Ludwipol's Jewish residents, but on the other side of the river, officers from the Polish army barracks and their wives strolled and relaxed outdoors on warm, sunny days.[6]

In Ludwipol, another brother of my grandmother (who was the oldest child of eight) caught up with my mother's family. He had been in the fur business with my great-grandfather, and he traveled to surrounding towns to sell some of the furs in the trunk to raise money for the family. My mother's father got a job in Ludwipol, and my mother attended Russian school there for about two years. She had a big birthday party on the 19th of June—her tenth—with Polish and Ukrainian friends (something that wouldn't have happened in prewar Radom), but three days later war broke out. The German army invaded eastern Poland (which had been annexed by the Soviet Union) on June 22, 1941, forcing the Red Army to retreat.

In August 1941, the German army entered Ludwipol as conquerors.[7] A delegation of Jews was sent out to greet the Germans, hoping to pacify them, but the Germans began to beat them, and the Jews fled. This developed into a pogrom. Ukrainian peasants broke into Jewish houses, severely beating Jews and plundering everything they found. Baruch Gutman, a survivor from that town, writes that, during the pogrom, his brother slipped out of their house, went to the stable, and brought their dog into the house. He then ordered the dog to attack the raiding Ukrainians, driving them out. The Ukrainians complained to the Germans outside, but the Germans didn't understand them.[8]

In the fall, the Germans created a Jewish ghetto in Ludwipol, where my mother and her family lived for about a year. About 1500 Jews lived in the ghetto, though members of the Judenrat and their families along with a small group of skilled workers were allowed to live outside the ghetto.[9] According to one survivor, the Judenrat's members "acted at the risk of their lives to save what could be saved." More than once, the Germans beat the members of the Judenrat.[10] My mother's uncle the furrier got a job working for the Germans in a factory making coats for them—it was slave labor, though it may have been better than other work like repairing a bridge, in which the overseers beat their Jewish slave laborers.[11] But maybe not: The head of the German gendarmerie killed one tailor because he wasn't pleased with a pair of pants.[12] I don't know what work my grandfather did. He may have worked in the local lumber mill, given his sawmill experience from Zawada.

There was no school for the ghetto's children. There was mandatory unpaid work, though. My mother had to pick up cigarette butts and the small children had to pull out grass that was growing between stones. She went to a German kitchen to peel potatoes (apparently sent by the Judenrat for that job). Regina at the time was four-and-a-half. My mother played at times with other children. She recalled playing with a boy one Saturday who was wearing a new suit because it was Shabbat. The boy tore his suit on a fence and became distraught because there was no way to replace his suit in the ghetto.

Living conditions were extremely difficult in the ghetto. It was terribly overcrowded because all the Jews were forced into a small area—a universal fact in the Nazi-established Jewish ghettos. Ludwipol lacked electricity and indoor plumbing outside of the ghetto too, but this was exacerbated inside the ghetto because of the overcrowding. The cold at night was intense and Jews weren't allowed to keep firewood. Nor were they permitted food beyond the starvation rations.[13] Each person received just 100 grams of bread

(3.5 ounces) twice a week.[14] People fought, and sometimes stole food from other Jews because everyone was terribly hungry.

The ghetto had a barbed wire fence around it. It was guarded by merciless Ukrainian police: one woman returning home was found at a routine checkpoint to have seven potatoes she had been given by a villager—she was taken to a police station and killed.[15] There were sirens at night and Germans yelling "*Juden raus!*" Although my mother, as child, may not have known about it, in the winter of 1941 Heinz Lohnert, the Nazi commissar, ordered all the Jews to turn over all silver and other valuables or he would have every Jew killed.[16] Furs, sweaters, woolen socks, and boots similarly had to be turned over also for the German army at the front.[17] It is unclear whether my grandmother or her brother still had any furs with them or what they did with them if they had any. Furs had become worth more than gold, diamonds or dollars.[18] At that point, it is possible they had already sold all of them to raise money.

CHAPTER 25

The Nazis Murder Eva's Father

In August 1942, my grandfather Natan heard word that the ghetto was about to be liquidated and sent my Mom, Babcia, and Regina out of the ghetto and told them to go the home of a gentile family they were friends with. The plan was for him join them later. The three of them knocked on the door, but no one answered. My mother thought they were afraid to help Jews, even though her family had thought them to be friends and they apparently were home. Instead, the trio found shelter with other Jews by hiding in a potato cellar during the liquidation. Then some more Jews entered their hiding place. Those in the shelter learned that the action was going on. They heard Germans passing back and forth, with dogs barking, shouts in German and shooting. In the middle of the night, others there led the three to a place where the Słucz River wasn't very deep, and the group waded to the other side. It was summer and the water wasn't very cold. Someone must have carried five-year-old Regina. They entered the forest. Thus began my mother's long chapter of hiding in the woods.

Soon after entering the forest, they met someone who had survived the mass grave on the outskirts of Ludwipol.[1] They learned from him that Natan had gone to the friends outside the ghetto to look for his family, but he too got no response. So Natan went back to their apartment in the ghetto and hid under a bed. He survived the liquidation of the ghetto, but at night some Poles or Ukrainians went to the apartment to loot it, found him and turned him in to the Germans.[2] The Germans took him to a mass grave and shot him.

The mass murder of the people in the ghetto was even worse than I had imagined. The German police and Ukrainian auxiliary police prevented people from leaving their homes. (Fortunately, my mother, Babcia and Regina had already fled. Unfortunately, my grandfather hadn't.) Then, Lohnert, the Nazi commissar, accompanied by Judenrat members, went house to house

180 | The Pessimist's Son

ordering everyone out, after which the Jewish ghetto inmates were marched across a bridge to what had been the Polish military barracks on the far side of the river.[3] At that point, my grandfather was hiding in his apartment. Survivor Yehuda Raber continues:

> On the way to the murder site, many elderly people became tired, since they were exhausted anyway, and they fell down. The murderers beat the laggards who were walking slowly with their rifle butts, until they fell—and then we, the young men, were ordered to carry them upon our shoulders. . . . The courtyard was packed with men, women, and children, and it was about 10 AM on Elul 12, 5702 [August 25, 1942]. I saw all the Zionist activists there. . . . They were all sitting, wondering aloud what would happen to them. . . . For instance, Yitzhak Raber said that it was impossible for all of us to be annihilated, and that a selection would probably be carried out, and the majority would be allowed to return home. Shichne Shemesh told us that our Lord in heaven wouldn't let [the Germans and Ukrainians] . . . commit such a massacre of Jews. . . . [Some] completely righteous people, however, shouted that there was no God in the heavens because He would not permit [such acts of cruelty to be carried out.] Old Khaim Shlein was standing, surrounded by his large family: his daughters, sons, and their children were embracing each other and crying loudly. By contrast, some other families were sitting together in deathly silence, as though petrified. Once again, there were some individuals, especially young ones, who tried to bribe the guards to turn a blind eye to their attempt to break through the fence. . . .
>
> [T]he murderer [commissar] proceeded to explain . . . that, at 5 AM on the next morning, all [the Jews] would be shot dead. The wails and cries of the women and the children did not move him, and he went on to announce . . . that the children would be given their last bread ration and [some kind of] hot food, and that was all. And thus, when we had heard the whole truth about our fate, a group was organized whose members decided to break through the fence and run away as soon as the opportunity arose. . . .[4]

The Nazis Murder Eva's Father | 181

With the help of a man who let Raber climb on his back to get over the fence, Raber barely escaped while the Nazis and their accomplices were shooting at him and others. He adds:

> I suffered pangs of remorse for not bidding farewell to my loved ones, and for failing to stay by their side. But the will to flee and the prospect of survival didn't leave me much time to think. When I felt that I was free [on the other side of the fence], I began to run as fast as I could. I had to cross the plot of land where the Polish army used to conduct horse races. . . . I reached the forest and found a ditch. . . .[5]

Before finding this testimony and that of Mordechai Volman, I had clung to the hope that the Germans hadn't forced my grandfather to strip naked before murdering him, a dehumanizing and humiliating act they usually performed before committing mass murder of Jews.[6] Partly, the Nazis did this to obtain the clothes of those they murdered, *sans* blood stains and bullet holes. The Nazis had slave labor sort the belongings of the people they had murdered. They sometimes rewarded their Ukrainian or other collaborators who carried out the actual shooting of Jews with the clothes of their victims.[7] I had thought that Natan may not have been forced to strip because the person who had climbed out of the mass grave and reported Natan's death was, I assume, himself dressed when he made the report. But presuming Natan was murdered with the rest of the Jews on August 26—my birthday, it so happens[8]—it seems highly unlikely he was spared this final insult. Volman writes:

> On the next day, [the Jews] were awakened and ordered to strip naked and go in groups toward the pits. Three pits had been dug by non-Jewish residents of the surrounding villages: for the men, the women, and the children. Each group was forced to stand on a plank; they were then shot, and fell into [the pit]; a second [group] would then approach. . . . The machine guns of the SS men, who were drunk on wine and blood, kept firing, killing the innocent people one by one, the old and the young alike, all of them full of dreams for the future. These dreams were drowned in torrents of blood—their own blood and that of their loved ones, their

relatives and brothers. This bloodbath went on throughout Wednesday, and some 1,500 people were apparently killed in the course of that day. . . . My father was among those who were put to death at the Polish barracks. He and his friends went [to their deaths] asking each other for forgiveness. . . .[9]

If the thought of the Nazis sadistically forcing her father to strip naked before being murdered ever occurred to my mother, she never mentioned it, and I like to think she never contemplated it.

CHAPTER 26

Into the Woods

Hiding in the forests was more common than I realized. According to Allan Levine:

> [As] the Nazi assault on Europe ended, approximately 25,000 Jews, entire families in some instances, walked out of the forests of Poland, Belorussia, Lithuania, the Ukraine and Russia.... The fugitives emerging from the forests had harrowing tales to tell.[1]

Indeed, he writes that "by about 1942, the forest emerged as the Jews' final haven, their last chance for survival."[2] It is perhaps fitting that my mother, whose father had made his living connected with wood from forests, would find shelter in the woods with her mother and sister.

My Mom, Babcia, and Regina lived in the forests with the original group from the root cellar and other groups of Jews, on and off, for about two years. That they were with Ludwipol natives who presumably knew the woods probably helped them survive. In the forest, my Babcia found one of her six brothers, Mordechai (Motek). The Germans were afraid of partisans in the forest, my mother said, though she doesn't recall seeing partisans in the woods early on. By contrast, Gutman, who was presumably not with my mother, writes that, "In the forests [soon after escaping the liquidation of the ghetto] we walked around free, because we were among partisans, whose numbers constantly grew from day to day."[3]

My mother's group built a shelter. There was a fire in the middle, around which people huddled, and a hole at the top for smoke to vent. The group picked berries and probably mushrooms, sometimes ventured into neighboring villages to beg for food and sometimes stole potatoes and other crops from fields to survive. (Jack Glotzer also mentions eating rabbit when he was

184 | The Pessimist's Son

hiding in the forests near Łopuszna.[4] It is possible my mother's group did this too, but she never mentioned it.) My mother never named the forests they were in (as a child, she may never have known their names). Gutman writes that, "The majority of Ludvipol Jews settled in the forests of Levatshes . . . ," which I've been unable to find on the map. Whatever their name, my mother lived in the forests across the Słucz River, between Ludwipol (now, Sosnove) and Mochulyanka.

It was the "attitude and actions of Polish, Lithuanian, Ukrainian and Belorussian peasants that determined the immediate fate of countless Jewish fugitives when they first arrived in forest areas."[5] It was dangerous to hide or help Jews, and some peasants seized Jews and turned them over to the Germans. Unsurprisingly, the theft of peasants' crops did not endear the fugitives to the locals near the woods.[6] In addition, the Germans rewarded Poles who captured Jews with 200 zlotys plus the clothes and shoes of the Jew after he or she was executed. Peasants were promised salt, sugar, and money for turning in Jews, and "Jew hunts" became a daily occurrence.[7] In Volhynia, where my mother was hiding, the Germans gave informers three liters of vodka per denounced Jew.[8]

In his memoir, Aharon Appelfeld recalls seeing a terrifying hunt:

> The small figure was no more than a child, and those pursuing him, peasants. There were many peasants, with axes and scythes in their hands, pressing forward, determined to catch him. Now I saw the child's figure very clearly; he was breathing heavily and turning his head every few moments. It was clear that he wouldn't escape them. He couldn't escape. They were many and they could outrun him; soon they would be blocking his path.[9]

Snyder asserts that some Polish peasants participated in hunts because their village leaders could, in principle, be executed by the Nazis if a Jew who had been known to be hiding in their village remained free.[10] Gross, however, focuses on greed. He writes that the "direct motive to commit the majority of murders and denunciations of Jews in the countryside was the desire to plunder them, to take over their belongings, which were imagined to be considerable."[11] To make matters worse, Polish peasants often tortured Jews they found hiding, raped Jewish women, and killed Jews, including young children.[12] An ethnomusicologist enamored of Polish village life and its culture found painful "a universal sense of triumph [among peasants] because [Jews] are no longer there."[13] These facts suggest a deep hatred, and undercut arguments that peasants acted out of more benign motives. Regardless of motivation, however, local people joining in the hunts was a "ubiquitous phenomenon."[14] Other peasants, sometimes for payment and sometimes out of kindness, helped Jews survive. Yosef Gitterman writes of Polish and Ukrainian villagers who took pity on his family and sheltered them and brought food to them when they were back in the forest.[15] In fact, he says that one villager even built them a bunker in the forests.[16] Gitterman also writes of a General "Kolpaks" who led partisans, including Jewish ones, in the forests in May 1943.[17] He must have been referring to General Kovpak, who was discussed in Chapter 18 in connection with the raid on Skalat.

There was a labor shortage in Eastern Europe because the Nazis were bringing millions of Poles, Ukrainians, Belarussians and Russians to work in Germany (to make up for its men being away), and some peasants harbored Jewish children in exchange for their labor. Hundreds of mostly orphaned Jewish children, maybe a few thousand, survived this way.[18] My mother, though not an orphan, may have benefited from the labor shortage. At one point, for three or four months, my mother stayed with a peasant family, working as a nanny for their blind child.

It must have been difficult and anxiety-provoking for Babcia to decide to entrust the lives of her young two daughters to strangers. Such stays were dangerous because, as Grabowski writes, "There is no question that the great majority of Jews in hiding perished because of betrayal. They were denounced or simply seized, tied up, and delivered by the locals to the nearest station of the Polish police, or to the German gendarmerie."[19] But remaining in the forest meant hunger, exposure to the elements and the fear of being found by Germans, hostile peasants or hostile partisans like the Banderites. Though the timing is unclear, my grandmother also found some Poles or Ukrainians who took Regina in. Regina was with them from two to four weeks, but she developed an infectious disease, and the people Regina was staying with asked my grandmother to take her back. They had a close call on the way back to the forest when a German soldier found them and asked, "*Jude?*" Fortunately, Regina spoke in Polish to my grandmother, and the soldier let them go, apparently thinking they were Poles. During this period, my mother also got a job of sorts taking care of cows, taking them to the pasture and back.

After a while, my mother and her family would change locations because the Germans were getting close. My grandmother found people who let them hide in their barns and haystacks. The peasants would bring them food once a day, in the evening. For fear of being caught, the three of them could not venture out of the haystacks until nighttime, even to relieve themselves. (In her testimony, my mother isn't sure whether her uncle was with them then.) Then, while moving from one part of the forest to another, they would find hay stacked in fields and at night they would hollow out spaces to sleep in. My mother remembers the hay as being very warm, which helped them survive the cold.

Browning highlights the dangers of hiding in the forests during the winter:

> The winter weather made life in the forests increasingly difficult and precarious; any movement in the snow left tracks, and on at least one occasion frozen feces gave away a Jewish hiding place carved out within a haystack. Thus, when it appeared that the deportations had come to an end, many Jews calculated they stood a much better chance of survival within one of the permitted ghettos than as hunted prey in the forests.[20]

Babcia met a Polish man in a village who let the four of them (including her brother Motek) use a small room in his parents' room. The man was married but wanted my grandmother to sleep with him. Such "payments in kind" were often seen by gentiles who aided Jews for money "as part of the deal, or as an added bonus to it."[21] My grandmother kept giving the man excuses and eventually he kicked them out, though the timing is unclear. My mother also thought that Babcia was paying the man, using money she'd gotten from the sale of furs. My grandmother hid whatever money she had sewn in a corset, which she wore every day.

In addition to being demeaning—my mother couldn't bring herself to beg, though my grandmother did—begging was dangerous. Again, Jews were often detained and dragged to the nearest Polish police station, where they were killed or forcibly escorted to the nearest German police station (and *then* killed).[22] Around this time, while begging for food one day, Babcia went to the local priest's house. The priest's housekeeper was kind and would give my grandmother some food. The priest also had found out about them and was, in my mother's words, a "human being." He began helping them. In doing so, the priest was extraordinary. Other people in the village may have known about them but tolerated their presence because of the priest's influence.[23]

The exact sequence of events isn't clear, but, around this time, my mother contracted rheumatic fever. For six months, she couldn't walk or use her hands. She was in a home, but she didn't remember whose home. Around this time, too, my mother's mother and uncle came down with typhus, a common problem in both ghettos and woods. Life as forest fugitives led to many different medical problems.[24] At some point, the kind village priest sent a Polish doctor from the village to treat my mother and, later, my grandmother and her brother. This presumably involved multiple visits. Also around this time, they would hear rumors sometimes that Germans were coming to the village, and they would flee to the forest. (Presumably, someone had to carry my mother.) She thought the original group with which they had fled Ludwipol built a winter shelter large enough for about twenty people, again with an opening in the roof or top for smoke from their fires.[25]

While in the forest, my grandmother ran into a man named Goldman, who had been good friends with my grandfather.[26] Like them, he had been in the Ludwipol Ghetto. He told my grandmother that he and some other people were being hidden by a Polish family named Korkush (English phonetic) and that he could arrange for them to be hidden by that family too. So, from then on, they were hidden by the Korkushes, who were very kind to them. My grandmother used some more of the proceeds of the fur sales to pay the Korkushes something. Presumably, the money went toward food her family consumed and similar expenses. My mother learned to knit. She knit socks for the family and helped with weaving and work around the house.

The Korkushes were an older couple and they had two daughters, one of whom was newly married and had a bedroom for herself and her husband. Otherwise, everyone slept wherever there was space and there was no privacy whatever. My mother remembers they had a big wooden bowl with boiled potatoes. When there were rumors that Germans were coming to the village, all the Jews fled to the forest. My mother said that most of the villages they stayed at were more Polish than Ukrainian, and the Ukrainians who were there wanted to integrate into the Polish communities. She contrasted these Ukrainians with the Banderites, whom she called "merciless."

CHAPTER 27

Liberation . . . Then Bitter Tears

My mother didn't recall getting any news from the west (Poland), but they were hearing that the eastern (Soviet) front was getting closer and they were very excited by this news. This went on for quite a few months, as they anticipated being liberated. My mother thought they were hearing about this from partisans, with whom Motek may have been in touch. Fights between Ukrainian partisans and Poles intensified. Raver says that Jews rejoiced at the deaths of Ukrainian murderers but that their hearts ached for Polish families, and they feared getting in the middle of their "war."[1] Apparently, some Ukrainian villages were deserted, and Jews would raid their fields and take potatoes and groceries left by their previous owners. "We had no morality," Raver writes,[2] being overly hard on himself. Jews from the forest were now able to recover some of the valuables they had left with their Christian neighbors (many had refused to return them earlier[3]), and the Jews began bartering for salt, wheat (which they would grind) and butter.[4]

My mother was in the village of Mochulyanka, near Ludwipol, when they were liberated, around January 9, 1944.[5] People were jubilant, crying and shouting—all the pent-up emotions poured out. Arriving Red Army soldiers tossed biscuits and cigarettes to the welcoming Jews. Jews wanted to know what the Russians would do next and they also started giving the names of the people who had participated in the killings.[6] The Soviets required young men to go before a medical committee and began drafting them into the army, which many didn't expect.[7] The Soviets set up administrative offices, but at least one survivor found them not interested in prosecuting gentiles who had informed on Jews. When Raver tried to give names to the NKVD, the NKVD man smiled and said, "Maybe you can tell me what they did against the Soviet government and then they will be punished."[8] In addition, all of the accused now denied any wrongdoing and claimed—with more than a little *chutzpah*—that they had actually *saved* Jews. Glotzer had a similar experience in Rohatyn, having to tell the NKVD that a man who had betrayed hiding Jews had killed Russian soldiers in order to get the Soviets to deport the man to Siberia.[9] Hader Rock, however, writes that she was able to able to report fifty farmers and a doctor to the NKVD in Rohatyn, which jailed the doctor for twenty years and shot many of the others.[10]

One of the first things my mother did was ask someone to take her to the mass grave in Ludwipol. She sat there crying bitterly. Today, though my mother probably didn't know about it, there is a monument at the site of the mass grave.[11]

My mother, grandmother, and aunt moved to Stara Huta, where my grandmother got a job working in a hospital. While working there, she met Mieczysław (pronounced "MYEH-chih-suave") Engelberg, a Jewish doctor originally from Łódź. Eventually, they married, and they remained in Stara Huta until the war ended in 1945. While in Stara Huta (and my mother remembers living on a top floor of the hospital), a Bandera group shot its way into the hospital, killing many people, in order to free a wounded Banderite prisoner it feared would be executed by the Soviets. My mother attended school in Stara Huta and remembers being taught Soviet propaganda. Jews, though, tried to resume normal lives despite Soviet Communism. In the summer of 1945, my mother, Babcia, Regina, and Mieczysław took a Russian transport back to Poland (Łódź). The ride took two weeks in a cattle car.

CHAPTER 28

Some Reunions in Łódź: "Everyone's Been Killed"

Łódź (pronounced "Woodge") sits about eighty-five miles southwest of Warsaw and is Poland's third-largest city. It had the second-largest Jewish community in prewar Poland, after Warsaw. The Germans annexed Łódź on September 1, 1939, established a Jewish ghetto in April 1940, and used Jews for slave labor in textile and other factories there.[1] The Łódź Ghetto's Judenrat was headed by Chaim Rumkowski, who used his position to enrich himself—Ringelblum sarcastically referred to him as "King Rumkowski."[2] Rumkowski infamously gave a speech, in September 1942, asking ghetto inmates to deliver 20,000 children to the Nazis.[3] Among the many horrors perpetrated by the Germans in that city, on the occasion of a visit by Goebbels on October 8, 1939, a pogrom was organized, during which several Jews were murdered and SS men tossed children from windows onto the streets. Between November 11 and 15, 1939, the Germans burned about ten synagogues to the ground in Łódź,[4] including the Great Synagogue.

After the wave of deportations to the Chełmno death camp beginning in early 1942, the Germans transported the remaining population to Auschwitz and Chełmno, where most were murdered upon arrival. During 1942, the Germans also deported about 4,200 Roma and Sinti to Chełmno. From May 6, 1941, to August 15, 1943, about 60,000 Łódź Ghetto residents—approximately a third of the population—starved to death.[5] A total of 210,000 Jews passed through the ghetto; but only 877 remained hidden and alive when the Soviet Red Army arrived. About 10,000 Jews from Łódź survived the war outside of the city, including my mother's stepfather, Mieczysław.

From 1945 to 1950, Łódź was the major urban center of Jewish population in Poland.[6] In Łódź, Babcia learned that her sister-in-law and two of her daughters had survived the war and were living there. The two daughters were my mother's first cousins, Sarah (Weinwurzel) Menk and Saba (Weinwurzel) Singer (with her husband, Moshe).[7] Their brother, Shmuel ("Shmulek") Weinwurzel, would survive Auschwitz. (All three cousins of my mother were much older than she.)

According to registration records circa 1946, my mother's family lived at no. 6 Cegielniana Street,[8] in the southern part of the city. Babcia and Mieczysław went by themselves to western Poland to find housing, where apartments on land that had been ceded from Germany to Poland were available for the taking. My mother said that people were "throwing out the Germans" and "taking whatever was the Germans."[9] They found an apartment in the city of Legnica ("Leg-KNEE-tsa"; formerly, Liegnitz, Germany) and came back for my mother and Regina.[10] In the meantime, my mother was attending school in Łódź for about two months. My mom stayed for a short time with her aunt Chaja and a cousin, but then stayed with Regina in a small room in someone's house.

As a mature fourteen-year-old girl, having lived through the war, my mother traveled by herself to Radom because she had heard that Fela, Babcia's then-unmarried sister, had survived. My mother had been very close to this aunt (who had bought my mom her first pair of ice skates) and wanted to see her. It was right after the war, and the trains were a "complete mess" in terms of schedules and the train cars overflowing with people. "People were hanging on . . ." It took my mother a whole day of travel to Radom—a distance of 100 miles. She spent a day there and it took a whole day to return to Łódź.

In Łódź, my mother learned from Chaja that "everyone [in their family] had been killed." Because this aunt was the sister of mother's father, she was presumably speaking of family in Ostrowiec. My mother's father, Natan, had had five sisters (including Chaja) and a brother. Chaja and Saba had been in a camp, and Chaja's oldest daughter, Sarah, had survived under a Polish name while working in Warsaw passing as a Polish maid.[11] Chaja and her daughter Saba may have worked as cooks in a labor camp.[12]

Ukrainian and Baltic (Latvian and/or Lithuianian) auxiliary units had assisted the Germans in *Judenrein* actions in the Radom district.[13] In Ostrowiec, which was also in the Radom district, Ukrainians, Lithuanians, and Latvians had helped the Germans murder Jews.

For example, on October 10, 1942, 15,000 people from Ostrowiec were sent to the Treblinka death camp for extermination. *Sefer Ostrovtsah* paints this scene:

> [The Germans] chased all the Jews with their wives and children together in one place and held them there for a few days, without food, without water. The German, Lithuanian, Latvian and Ukrainian murderers sat with rifles over their heads and shot them for any small infraction.
>
> [H]ere the murderers spilled blood with particular pleasure, gruesomely beating and laughing about it, making jokes.[14]

Of the Polish Jews who managed to flee their ghettos before, or at, liquidation, about two-thirds died, and in most cases their Christian neighbors contributed to their deaths in various degrees.[15] My parents were in both in the lucky third. In Łódź, my mother also learned that her uncle, Henri (originally, Henryk) Goldstein, Babcia's brother, had survived Auschwitz. He had worked in the infirmary there as a doctor.[16] He had been finishing his medical studies before the war in Paris because Jews could not study medicine in Poland, but was arrested by French police, imprisoned in two camps in France, and then, in July 1942, sent to Auschwitz. Jews like Henri, without French citizenship, were ten times more likely to get sent to Auschwitz than Jews with French citizenship.[17] It was presumably in January 1945 that Henri was evacuated from Auschwitz-Birkenau to Buchenwald, the first concentration camp in Germany. He probably was on a death march to the camp. In April 1945, he and the camp were liberated by the US army. Henri would settle in France, one of only 2,500 deportees to do so.[18]

Many survivors visited Aunt Chaja's home in Łódź, and my mother would hear stories from survivors about what had happened to them during the war. Naturally, my mother was very interested in what had transpired in her hometown of Radom.

CHAPTER 29

The Destruction of Jewish Radom

As a general matter, the Germans' sadism cannot be overstated: Among other things, they made games of shooting Jews, buried Jews—including children—alive, burned Jews alive, tormented invalids in front of their families (who were powerless to intervene), and murdered children in front of their parents before killing the parents. Wives and children were forced to watch their husbands and fathers suffer beatings conducted with canes, truncheons, and electrical rods, which were often deliberately applied to the genitals.[1] Husbands and sons were forced to watch their wives, daughters, and sisters being raped.[2] German soldiers "photographed themselves laughing heartily as terrified Jews cut each other's beards or performed other humiliating exercises."[3] Two SS men played a "game" where one tossed Jewish babies out an upper story window and one on the ground tried to "catch"—that is, spear—the falling baby on his sharp bayonet.[4] At the arrival platform of Auschwitz in July 1944, an SS man also speared a young infant, threw the baby up in the air, and speared him or her again. Instinctively, the baby's mother lunged at the SS man and "popped his eyeballs like two little eggs" with her fingers, after which she was killed.[5]

The Nazis sadistically beat, tortured, and humiliated the Jews of Radom. In addition, per their standard practice, they forbade Jews to pray in their synagogues, which the Germans turned into stables and the like.[6] They demanded payments of large sums as ransom from the Jewish community and confiscated Jewish valuables.[7] (As can be seen from Nazis' actions in the Ludwipol and Podhajce Ghettos, this was standard operating procedure for the Germans.) The Nazis ordered the establishment of a Judenrat, a temporary one in late September 1939 and a permanent one in December.[8] Prior to the establishment of the permanent Judenrat, and perhaps because they lacked a Ukrainian militia to do it for them, unlike in Rohatyn, the Germans themselves caught Jews on the street and forced them to do humiliating menial labor.[9] As noted, the Nazis burned the beards on Jewish men's faces, mostly just on one side, and then made them pose in grotesque positions.[10] These assaults, at least in part, were done to show that Jews had no rights and could be assaulted with impunity by anyone, not only by Nazi soldiers.[11]

In the fall of 1939, *Volksdeutsche* from neighboring towns and Poles from the (annexed) Poznań region moved to Radom, taking over the best homes after expelling the Jews living in them. There also was an influx of Jewish refugees from German-annexed western Poland, including from cities like Łódź.[12] Of course, this created terrible overcrowding.

In November 1939, my mother's cousin, Yechiel ("Chilek") Goldstein, an older brother of Philip (né Fishel) Goldstein, fled Radom for Lwów to avoid being arrested by the Nazis. Until January 1940, he was homeless in Lwów, "surviving," as he put it, in a former prison. Having no money, he worked on a construction site in the cold winter for a few pennies just to buy bread each day.[13]

Nazi demand for Jewish slave labor began to spike around July 1940.[14] In August 1940, almost all able-bodied Jewish males in Radom were ordered to report for shipment to forced labor camps on the German-Soviet border, in the Lublin district of the General Government, to dig anti-tank fortifications.[15] The Radom Judenrat worked to send these workers food and clothing, but nearly all the workers perished.[16] At Philip Goldstein's camp, Cieszanów, the SS would shoot inmates at random and bury the bodies in the woods.[17] At the end of October, the surviving inmates were transferred to Krasnik, southeast of Lublin, at which point my cousin was able to slip away and make his way back to Radom.

In March 1941, the Germans ordered the creation of a ghetto in Radom. A week earlier the Jewish ghetto police had been formed by the new Nazi administration. About 33,000 Jews were placed in the ghetto there; 27,000 at the main ghetto, and about 5,000 at a smaller ghetto in the suburb. Most of the ghetto area was not walled and the exits were manned by Jewish and Polish police. The "large ghetto" was set up at Wałowa Street, and the "small ghetto" in the Glinice District. Jews were not allowed to use the main streets.[18]

The Destruction of Jewish Radom | 197

The Polish police helped Germans during Nazi actions.[19] Transformed by the Germans in occupied Poland, after Germany had destroyed the Polish state, the Polish police, also known as the Blue Police because of the color of their uniforms, became an integral part of the Nazi oppression and extermination of Jews in ghettos in the General Government:

> [T]he evolution from murderers' apprentices to murderers in their own right was, in the case of the Polish policemen, rather swift. One can even venture to say that the policemen proved to be very diligent pupils who, in many cases, surpassed their German teachers even before the end of 1942.[20]

In the first months of 1942, the Germans carried out several actions in Radom, arresting or summarily executing various leaders of the Jewish community. These were part of an operation the Nazis carried out throughout the General Government.[21] This included my cousin, Moshe Goldstein, a brother of Philip and Chilek. The Germans murdered Moshe on April 28, 1942.[22] He had been very active in the underground Hashomer Hatzair movement in Radom, and their home became the contact place for couriers from Warsaw. It so happened that Mordechai Anielewicz, who was to lead the Warsaw Ghetto Uprising in the spring of 1943, was the Goldsteins' guest for the first and second Passover seders in 1941.[23]

The day after Moshe's murder, Philip was shipped out to Auschwitz-Birkenau with other Jews from the ghetto.[24] The Germans began to liquidate the Radom Ghetto in earnest, starting in August 1942 as part of Operation Reinhard, the code name of the secret German plan to exterminate Polish Jews in the General Government.[25] After three years of persecution, on the nights of August 4, 16, and 17, 1942, the Germans deported 30,000 Jews from Radom, primarily to the death camp of Treblinka.[26] By the end of August, approximately 2,000 Jews remained in Radom.[27] Two hundred Jews were given the task of sorting the belongings of the Jews the SS either murdered outright or deported to Treblinka, some of which were sold or distributed for free to (non-Jewish) Polish residents of Radom.[28] Sometime in early 1942, the Germans executed my mother's Aunt Sabina, for trying to buy food, it seems.[29]

In fourteen weeks, between August 4, 1942, and mid-November, at least 310,000 Jews of the Radom district (including most of my cousin Philip's family) were gassed to death at Treblinka.[30] They were murdered immediately upon arrival at the death camp.[31] There was, however, about a two-week pause in deportations from the Radom district beginning at the end of August because the Germans had exceeded the killing capacity of Treblinka: "[T]he number of Jews waiting to be killed and the number of corpses that could not be disposed of quickly enough piled up."[32]

On January 13, 1943, another 1600 Jews were loaded aboard freight cars bound for Treblinka.[33] They were people whose names had appeared on a list of those requesting a visa to Palestine or who received permits for *aliyah* (emigration) to Palestine.[34] The Nazis likely tricked these people into registering with the Germans, as the Nazis did elsewhere.[35] A considerable number succeeded in jumping off the train and returning to the ghetto. Many others were shot by the SS guards or ground to death under the train wheels.[36] Peasants would flock to the Treblinka train station when trains arrived, bribe guards to get access to them and then sell cups of water at extortionate prices to the severely parched and condemned prisoners inside.[37] Polish railroad employees also would extort money from desperate Jews before they were led to the gas chambers.[38]

The remnants of the Radom Ghetto were turned into a temporary labor camp. Among them was Azriel Goldstein, Philip's oldest brother. (Philip had three brothers and a sister.) Azriel had been doing forced labor for the Wehrmacht as a doctor and thus had escaped being sent to Treblinka with his parents and sister.[39] (Philip was already in Auschwitz-Birkenau.) The last Radom Jews were evicted in July 1944, when on July 26 they were deported to Auschwitz.[40] Azriel probably was in that transport. He had been informed that Philip was dead, so the brothers had an especially emotional reunion in Birkenau. In the camp, Azriel worked alongside his cousin, Henri Goldstein, as a physician. As longtime survivors of the camp, Henri and Philip helped Azriel adjust to life in the camp. Azriel worked there for about three months.

By the early fall of 1945, my cousin Philip had survived Auschwitz-Birkenau, a death march from Birkenau, the concentration camp of Gross-Rosen in Lower Silesia, as well as a death march from there, the Flossenburg labor camp, and two satellite camps of Dachau.[41] Philip's survival in Birkenau for nearly three years is especially remarkable given that the average life expectancy of an Auschwitz inmate selected for labor was just three *months*.[42] Philip later learned that Azriel had been at Flossenburg in April 1945—about a month after Philip left there. There was no further news of Azriel, and Philip was heartbroken that his oldest brother had apparently died just days before liberation. Philip didn't know how Azriel perished. Philip speculated that it may have been from starvation or during a death march.

The Destruction of Jewish Radom | 199

Philip eventually found himself in a Displaced Persons camp in Stuttgart, Germany. It was there he received news that his brother Chilek had survived the war in the Soviet Union. In July 1940, Chilek had been forcibly transported by the Soviets from Lwów, where he was a refugee from Radom to a northern labor camp in the USSR, hundreds of kilometers north of Archangelsk. As in Podhajce, many Jews in Soviet-annexed Poland, hoping to return to their homes in Poland after the war, had declined Soviet citizenship; as a result, they were sent to the labor camps.[43] Chilek hadn't wanted to accept Soviet citizenship because that would have laid the groundwork for him to be drafted into the Red Army.[44] North of the Arctic Circle, he was put to hard labor chopping down trees.

Abe Zukerman, a Jew from Wierzbnik (whose mother happened to hail from nearby Radom), also was deported by the Soviets from Lwów to the same or a very similar camp:

> [F]rom [Lwów] "Stalinist Saviours" sent me to a camp in Archangelsk. It was far away beyond, "the hills of darkness" where there was not the slightest trace of a human footstep to be found and no sign of human civilization.
>
> There in the virgin forests, under the constant surveillance of the N.K.V.D. with their trained dogs and rifles at the ready, I quickly became an expert woodsman to the extent that I knew how to escape a falling tree. It often happened that out of ignorance, people ran in the wrong direction and were crushed by falling trees.
>
> Working from early morning until late at night in the deep, dense forests, and enduring so many hardships, I imagined that if I survived and returned home, I would have much to tell about the harsh conditions of my wrongful exile. Even in Siberia, aside from fear, the surroundings were cultivated and not as incomprehensibly primitive and uncivilized as in Archangelsk. Apart from forests I saw nothing, not even a bird. In these faraway forests in the middle of nowhere, we who were able-bodied did the work not only of machines, but also of horses and oxen. Besides the daily physical toll of hard work, hunger and cold, at night, lying on bare boards we anguished over the question "why".

Not knowing that worse could exist, that the devil could be even more terrible and take on more gruesome forms, we were constantly tormented by thoughts about justice that broke our spirit, and undermined our general health more than the heavy physical work. If we heard someone preaching equal rights, we understood it to be the propaganda of the "Russian paradise", that in reality it was the opposite! . . .

On my return to Poland, when I crossed the former Russian-Polish border and discovered the Holocaust, there was no point in relating my experiences. I soon realized that pain and suffering had no limits, and that everything I had endured had been child's play compared to the torture and humiliation my relatives must have suffered up to the final moments of their lives. . . .

My fervent hope that someone from my family had survived turned out to be an empty dream, sheer fantasy. I am utterly incapable of expressing in words how devastating it was for me to make this discovery and come to terms with the fact that not a single member of my entire family had survived. They had all perished. Even my sister Gitshe, may she rest in peace, who had been on a visit to Poland from Palestine, was also destined never to return. I was now certain that I could no longer remain on Polish soil. The tragic disappearance of all who were dear to me convinced me that the strong ties that bound me to my place of birth had been severed. I decided to leave Poland forever.[45]

After the outbreak of the German-Soviet war in July 1941, Poland's government-in-exile resumed diplomatic relations with the USSR. As a result, in September 1941, the Soviets declared an "amnesty" and freed Chilek as one of about 30,000 prisoners from Poland. (In this regard, Chilek was fortunate because not all prisoners were released.[46]) The Soviet Union encouraged the freed prisoners to move to the Caucasian republics. Even if it had been possible, returning to Nazi-occupied Poland would not have been wise, so Chilek ended up in Osh, a city in Kyrgyzstan near the border with Uzbekistan. He worked there in all kinds of jobs, including managing a home for seniors. He married his wife in Osh in 1944.

The Destruction of Jewish Radom | 201

Although my mother didn't know it when she was in Łódz, her cousin, Lutka, also survived. When the Germans occupied Łuck, Lutka lost her job and was forced into the Łuck Ghetto. Luckily, it turned out she had a relative in the Judenrat, who helped her escape. A Polish woman, Janina Vlaska, took her in without telling her husband that Lutka was Jewish, and Lutka lived with them for a time, masquerading as a Pole. She moved to Kyiv, which was under German occupation, registered as a Pole of German origin and got a job. She then moved to Odesa. After the war ended, she made her way to Łódź, where she found her Aunt Chaja and her daughters.[47]

Lutka then traveled to Radom to see it. Polish neighbors occupied an apartment in a house that belonged to her family and had taken their furniture, claiming to have bought it. No relatives from her large family (which included Natan, Babcia, my mom, and Regina) remained. She and her brother, Didek, were able to book passage on a ship to Palestine.[48] Their brother, Mietek, separately visited Radom and ran into a childhood acquaintance living there under a false Polish identity. She warned him against greeting two old prewar schoolmates he saw on the street, telling him they were members of the Home Army and antisemitic killers. He returned to Łódź upset.[49]

CHAPTER 30

"Radom-in-Exile" and Motek's Murder

Philip said that the Stuttgart DP camp had become "Radom in exile, attracting Radom survivors from all over Germany, as well as some who came out of Poland."[1] Indeed, about 2,600 Radomer refugees organized a "Radom Centre" in the camp to provide for the refugees' educational, occupational training, social help, religious and cultural needs. It was here that work on *Sefer Radom* began.[2] In *Sefer Radom*, survivor Yakov Vayngort writes of six Jewish returnees who were murdered in Radom during robberies—or what were labeled robberies—in 1945.[3] Anti-Jewish flyers advising Jews to quit Radom and Radom County appeared two weeks before some of the murders, in July.[4] As a result of these murders and warnings, virtually all returnees, including Vayngort himself, quit their hometown.[5] (Vayngort wrote his account in Stuttgart, and it was originally published in "Radom Centre," so he presumably was in the DP camp there too.) These murders were part of what the historian Jan Gross calls "[t]he Unwelcoming of Jewish Survivors." Gross estimates that about 1,500 Polish Jews were killed in Poland from 1944 to 1946.[6]

In "The Terrible Disappointment of the 'Liberated' Jews of Ostrovtse [Ostrowiec]," the *Sefer Ostrovtsah* excerpts a September 1945 letter by Ostrowiec Jews who returned to their town after surviving the Holocaust. It reads in part: "Many Jews who were miraculously saved from the crematorium ovens and barely survived to see the end of the war were murdered by Polish 'patriots' after they returned to Ostrovtse." (My mother's Aunt Chaja apparently returned briefly to Ostrowiec after liberation because her husband was there.) Thorne similarly writes that, upon reaching the town of his birth after being liberated, it was clear that "[w]e had to leave Schodnica [a village near Drohobycz], for we could tell from the ugly, sullen faces of the

204 | The Pessimist's Son

townsmen that even if the Germans did not return to kill us, the Poles would do so with pleasure."[7] I don't know whether any other relatives on my maternal grandfather's side returned to Ostrowiec, even briefly.

On June 12, 1945, a year before the infamous Kielce pogrom (which I discuss below), some Poles in the large city of Rzeszów (pronounced "ZHEH-shoove") placed the mutilated body of a child in the basement of a building that served as the residence of Rabbi Leon Thorne and of Jews transiting through the city, in order to blame the child's murder on the Jews as an excuse for a pogrom.[8] Polish police and other Poles went on a rampage, rounding up and beating Jews—including ones they had dragged off trains passing through the city. No one was killed because some Russian Jewish military officers intervened. According to Thorne, the rabbi at the center of these events (though he was away when they occurred), all but one of the city's Jews then fled town.

Thorne writes that what happened in Rzeszów shouldn't have surprised anyone. Gross, however, takes a somewhat different view. He writes, "That Jews were vulnerable to assaults in small towns and villages was accepted at the time as a matter of course," but he suggests that such large-scale collective anti-Jewish violence in a large Polish city, the purpose of which was to make the city *Judenrein*, was surprising. Two months later, on August 11, 1945, however, scores of Poles in the former Polish capital of Kraków, including soldiers and militia, killed between one to five Jews and grievously wounded dozens. According to Gross, "many of the best representatives of the Polish intelligentsia reacted with disbelief and unmitigated despair" to this event.[9] This may have been their genuine reaction, but Thorne notes that the adverse effect that the publicized Kraków pogrom had on the world's opinion of Poland made the Polish press, for the first time, deem it "necessary to come out in open condemnation of the pogroms and the rabble-rousers who had instigated them."[10]

Some Polish intelligentsia may have reacted with disbelief to this violent "welcome home," but it was foreseen by some, as in this excerpt of an internal Polish Government-in-Exile memo from August 1943:

> Among our national problems there is also the Jewish problem. . . . A very considerable number of Jews will certainly survive, and their repatriation after the end of the war may force us to take into account a Jewish population of one or two million. . . .[11] At this moment, Christian compassion for the

tormented Jews is predominant in the Homeland; at the same time, however, a very strong animus prevails against Jews in the eastern part of Poland. This is the aftermath of the period of Bolshevik occupation. *In the Homeland as a whole . . . the position is such that the return of the Jews to their jobs and workshops is completely out of the question, even if the number of Jews were greatly reduced.* The non-Jewish population has filled the places of the Jews in the towns and cities; in a large part of Poland this is a fundamental change, final in character. *The return of masses of Jews would be experienced by the population not as restitution but as an invasion against which they would defend themselves, even with physical means.* Thus *it would be a really tragic thing for our policies if, in the moment of settling our frontiers, securing credits, concluding pacts or forming federations, Poland were to be pilloried by world opinion as a country of militant anti-Semitism.*[12]

Consistent with Thorne's view regarding the 1945 pogrom in Kraków, the Polish officials' focused concern in 1943 was about the international opinion of Poland.[13]

In 1945, my mother's uncle Motek, who had survived the war with my mother, Babcia, and Regina, was murdered during a robbery in Wrocław. In her testimony, however, my mother doesn't suggest that Motek was killed because he was a Jew. This seems somewhat less likely to have happened because he was in formerly German territory (that is, not attempting to reclaim pre-war property in Poland). There also was a lot of banditry in Poland in wake of the war.[14] But it is quite possible that antisemitism was involved. According to Gross and Grudzinska Gross, "Some variation of the line 'We'll have to put up a monument to Hitler for having gotten rid of the Jews' was overheard in private conversations all over Poland."[15]

On July 4, 1946, Polish soldiers, police officers, and civilians engaged in a murderous pogrom in the city of Kielce. (Years before the infamous pogrom, Ringelblum wrote that Kielce Province was known for its "exuberant anti-Semitism."[16]) Based on a blood libel, the Poles attacked a community center's gathering of Holocaust survivor refugees. Forty-two Jews were killed and more than forty were wounded. Some were shot, many had their skulls crushed by Poles wielding iron bars and the like, and some were flung off balconies to be finished off by the crowd below.[17] Among other things, the crowd

206 | The Pessimist's Son

shouted, "Death to the Jews!" and "We'll finish Hilter's work!"[18] To add insult to (literal) injury, Kielce's bishop formed a commission ostensibly to study what had happened there. It erroneously found that Jews had shot first into the crowd and it concluded that "Jews are disliked, even hated, on the entire territory of Poland" because they "are the main propagators of Communism in Poland . . . ," which was "being imposed on the Polish nation by force."[19] Indeed, a week after the pogrom, then-Bishop of Lublin, Stefan Wyszyński—later Poland's primate and mentor to Karol Wojtyła (who would become Pope John Paul II)—refused to speak out on behalf of Jews and suggested that they "just clear out of Poland. . . ."[20] The only leader of the Polish church to speak up was Teodor Kubina, the bishop of Częstochowa. He denounced the blood libel as a lie, and he appealed to Poles not to "debase themselves" by engaging in antisemitic violence.[21] Outside of the church, the infamous Kielce pogrom met with approbation by many in Radom, Ostrowiec, and elsewhere in Poland.[22]

The events in Kielce convinced many Polish Jews who had miraculously survived the war that they had no future in the country of their birth. My mother's cousins, Sarah Weinwurzel, together with Mietek and Józia Steinman and their young daughter, Milochka (later renamed Batami), were among them.[23] The *Bricha* organization smuggled them to Czechoslovakia and then via Vienna to Germany. Sarah's brother Shmulek Weinwurzel and his wife Pela were living in Munich with a German family, and Sarah parted with the Steinmans to live with them.[24] The Steinmans ultimately moved to Stuttgart, where Mietek's father and his new wife were living in the DP camp. While living in Stuttgart, the Steinmans were visited by my mother's Aunt Chaja, en route to Palestine to join her daughters, Shoshana (born Róża) and Esther. Her other two daughters, Roma and Sarah, came later when Israel was declared a state.[25] Joseph Steinman and Mietek's family also moved to Israel. Shmulek and Pela would later move to New York, and our families were close throughout my childhood and teenage years. Their older son, Henry, now lives in Israel, while their younger son, Bob, lives in New Jersey.

After returning from the USSR to Poland in January 1946, Chilek and his wife moved to Szczecin, a city on the Baltic Sea that was formerly German territory. On May 10, 1946, Philip left on a US troopship from Bremerhaven, Germany, for New York, unaware that his brother was back in Poland. Philip was part of the first group of displaced persons arriving in the United States after the war, and the pier in New York City was filled with newspaper reporters and photographers.[26] Motivated at least in part by what had happened in

Kielce, Chilek and his pregnant wife left Szczecin in August 1946 illegally for Berlin, where they lived two years in a United Nations refugee camp established in the city's American sector. Memoirist Margulies Chernoff and her mother also went to Szczecin in June 1946 (albeit just for several days), from where they too were smuggled into the American Zone in Berlin. She noted the irony that, given the presence of Allied forces in Germany after the war, the birthplace of Nazism "was a far more hospitable place for Jews than Polish cities. . . ."[27] In 1948, Chilek and his wife moved into an apartment. Chilek got a job and opened a clothing shop in the 1950s. He raised a family in Berlin and remained there until his death in 2004, at the age of eighty-eight. He and Philip remained very close.

CHAPTER 31

Antisemitism: From Łódź to Legnica

In Łódź, my mother attended public school under her family name, Najnudel, which identified her as Jewish, as did her appearance. There were a few other Jewish kids there and the Polish students started bullying them.[1] Antisemitism had existed in Polish public schools before the war too,[2] but my mother had been in a private Jewish school in Radom. The Soviet schools she had been in since fleeing Radom most likely did not tolerate overt antisemitism. Moreover, antisemitism against survivors immediately after the Shoah must have been especially devastating. It really got to my mother, and she decided "not to be a Jew because she didn't want anyone picking" on her.[3] She "went to Religion" and prayed in class with Polish Catholic students to try to make herself seem less Jewish. She did this until the Jewish holiday of Rosh Hashanah. My mother said her aunt was religious and made my mother stay home from school on Rosh Hashanah. When her teacher asked her where she had been the previous day, my mother said she had been sick. In front of the entire class, the teacher asked, "Wasn't there a Jewish holiday yesterday?" and my mother answered, yes. It seems that was it in terms of her denying her Jewishness in that school.

In Legnica, the same thing happened. Polish students called the Jewish students names and bullied them. My mother said that "as much as I wanted to be myself, I couldn't take it." She started going to church and to religion classes in school. (From 1945, religion was taught for many years in Polish public schools.) My mother decided to attend religious education, which was Catholic, which presumably most Jewish students did not do.[4] She began being ashamed of being Jewish. From 1945 until 1951—about six years— she denied her Jewishness. When it came time to register and get their Polish identification papers (akin to internal passports), my mother pressured

210 | The Pessimist's Son

Babcia to change her parents' last names, so that they wouldn't sound too Jewish. She made her mother observe Catholic holidays too. Her stepfather had grown up in a very secular, assimilated home—not coincidentally, he had a very Polish first name, Mieczysław—so this may not have bothered him as much as it did Babcia.[5] My mother stopped associating with Jews and associated only with Poles. My sister and I having been raised by both our parents to be proud Jews all our lives, I find this part of my mother's story shocking. But, of course, her father had been murdered for being Jewish and she and her remaining family had been hunted like animals because they were Jewish, so it is understandable.

Against this, my grandmother tried to persuade my mother to associate with Jews. Pointing to a woman who had converted years earlier to Catholicism, my grandmother said that neither Jews nor Poles were interested in marrying this woman, and the woman told my mother the same thing. In his memoir, Ben-Zion Gold makes a similar point: "Assimilationists spoke only Polish, but Poles continued to view them as Jews despite their efforts to become part of Polish culture and society. Religious Jews looked on assimilationists with a mixture of pity and contempt."[6] Unsurprisingly, the contempt probably was more strongly felt in the shtetls. (A contributor to *Sefer Podhajce* calls the few converts there "heretics" and notes, perhaps with some *schadenfreude*, that they too were killed by the Nazis.) My mother felt she couldn't return to being openly Jewish while living in Legnica but told my grandmother she would do so when she went to university in Wrocław.

My mother was in Wrocław from 1951 until 1955. She became good friends with a classmate from Legnica with whom she wasn't friendly in high school because the woman was Jewish. The woman and her future husband brought my mom into a Jewish circle of friends. My mother was no longer hiding her identity and, as a result, she felt better about herself. Some of her Polish friends were very nice, and she didn't recall antisemitic incidents. The main problems then were political because Stalin had a "terrible grip on Poland," and everyone was afraid of his or her own shadow—people feared that they would be denounced as anti-Communist. Generally, however, they were happy days of my mother's life. In Wrocław, she was introduced by a mutual friend to my father. Their first date was supposed to be at a theater. My mother showed up a little late after having her hair done, but my father left after waiting only a short time. Fortunately for my sister and me, our mother agreed to give him a second chance.

PART 3

ALEXANDER AND EVA KIMEL

CHAPTER 32

1956: Quitting Poland for Israel: A Knife in Eva's Heart

Antisemitism was on the rise in 1956. Among other things, amid the general upheaval and condemnation of earlier government policies, "some people started blaming Jews for many, if not most, of the crimes and absurdities of the Stalin era," playing into the Judeo-Communism myth.[1] Władyłsaw Gomułka had become the prime minister. As the head of the Communist party, he allowed Jews to leave Poland for Israel. This became known as the "Gomułka Aliyah." (*Aliyah* is the Hebrew word used to describe emigrating to Israel. For example, people say, "so-and-so made *aliyah*.")

Ever since 1948, my dad had wanted to leave Poland. By 1956, he had family in the United States and no family left in Poland. "Citizen" (*obywatel*) Aleksandr Kimel also completed his Master's degree that year.[2] Although he wasn't particularly observant, he wanted to live a full Jewish life and didn't see Poland as particularly hospitable to Jews. He also saw better economic opportunities outside of Poland. He wasn't alone in wanting to leave. Polish historian Dariusz Stola writes about "emigration fever" circulating especially among Jews in Lower Silesia, where most Polish Jews (including my parents and my mother's family) lived.[3]

Before marrying, my father told my mother he wouldn't remain in Poland under any circumstances, and he made her choose between staying in Poland and marrying him. My mother was in a tough spot because her mother, sister, and stepfather still lived in Poland (Legnica), and she didn't want to leave them. Her sister, Regina, had just started studying medicine in college. Ultimately, my mother decided to marry my dad and quit Poland. My parents were married in 1956 in Legnica, by the closest thing to a rabbi there—a kosher butcher. In August 1956, my dad received a visa from the

Israeli consulate in Warsaw allowing him to live permanently in Israel, which I found in his papers. (See photo.) I assume my mom got one at the same time. (My dad was not the sentimental sort, so the fact that he saved the document shows its significance to him.) When my grandmother and stepfather saw that my parents really were going to leave Poland, they too applied for exit visas and eventually received them. My mother was very close with Babcia, and, in her testimony, my mother remembered the physical pain she felt at their parting. She said it was as if someone had "taken a knife and cut [out] my heart." The Polish government made my parents renounce their Polish citizenship as a condition for their departure—a sort of farewell present, I guess. This added insult to injury for my mother, because the Polish Communist government was essentially telling her and my dad that it didn't want them coming back—ever—and it was forcing her to burn her bridges behind her. This would later create problems for her.

The transition to life in Israel, where my parents needed to start all over again as immigrants, was "tough," with difficult economic conditions, my dad said. My mother noted that this was during the Sinai War (Suez Crisis) of 1956 and that the economic situation in Israel was "very tough." Back home, my mother's stepfather was very assimilated, and he didn't want to leave Poland. Israel was very far away—a strange and alien place to him. At the time, my mother was writing letters to her mother describing how difficult the conditions were in Israel. My mother thinks that, based in large part on those letters, her mother and stepfather changed their minds and decided to remain in Poland. From her testimony, it is clear my mother regretted writing those letters.

For at least part of the time they lived in Israel, they lived in Holon, south of Tel Aviv. Polish Jews had played an important role in the founding of Israel and its development. Many of Israel's early prime ministers hailed from Poland. As another example, in 1923, immigrants from Łódź had started large textile factory named Lodzia in Holon. (Coincidentally, there is now a monument to the victims from tiny Ludwipol in the Holon cemetery.) In Israel, my mother learned Hebrew at an *ulpan* (an intensive language school) for six months and then got a job as an economist at an Israeli firm. (She didn't have an advanced degree in economics, so I'm not sure what this work entailed.) Although she missed her mother, stepfather, and sister terribly, after about six months to a year, my mom got acclimated to life in Israel. They had a very nice apartment, my mother had a lot of family there on her father's side, and, little by little, friends from Poland migrated there. (About 50,000 Jews, typically those actively expressing Jewish identity like my parents, left Poland in 1957–1959, under Gomułka and with his government's encouragement.[4]) My parents had a very full social life. My dad worked as an engineer but was unhappy with his professional prospects in Israel. He couldn't advance commensurate with his abilities. He had been let go the day before he would have gotten certain employment rights and, being an excellent engineer, this stung him. Having his father, sister, and her family in New York probably added to his desire to leave Israel. He begged my mom to move to the United States, and she ultimately agreed, but—again—she didn't want to leave the country she was in.

CHAPTER 33

Starting over yet Again in a New Country: Israel to America

After living in Israel for over two years, my parents emigrated to the United States in 1959. My dad's father sponsored them, and they started off living with him in his apartment in the Bronx (a New York City borough). My mother said her English upon arriving in the United States was "practically nil."

While my dad was reunited with his father, sister, and brother-in-law, along with Luba's children, Harold and Paula, my mom wouldn't see her mother or sister for years because they remained in Poland, making them part of only about 50,000 or fewer Jews in Poland after 1960. (Some estimates are even lower.) I was born in 1960, the first grandchild of Babcia. In 1961, when I was ten months old, my mother took me to Poland so that my grandmother, aunt, and stepfather could meet me. (See the photo of my one-year-birthday celebration in Legnica.) My sister, Pamela, was born in 1963. In 1965, we moved from the Bronx to Teaneck, NJ, where Pam and I grew up.

My parents picked Teaneck for its proximity to Manhattan, where my dad had his engineering firm, and its large Jewish population. It was about forty percent Jewish and the public schools were closed two days each year for Rosh Hashanah. We joined a conservative synagogue, where my sister Pam and I attended Hebrew School until we had our respective bat and bar mitzvahs. Both our parents felt a powerful connection to the Jewish people, whose continuation was very important to them. Jewish culture, we were taught, with its traditions, emphasis on learning, long, rich history and ethical worldview, was something to cherish and propagate.

We attended shul on major holidays, even though my dad doubted the existence of God. He couldn't see how God, if he existed, could have allowed Auschwitz (as a stand-in, or metonym, for the Shoah).[1] I don't recall ever discussing the question with my mother. In his foreword to a version of Thorne's book published in 1961, the Nobel laureate Isaac Bashevis Singer writes, "Every Jew has asked the same question: Why did God allow this? And the answer is always the same: What do we know of the ways of God?"[2] That may satisfy the devout, who cannot even conceive that God doesn't exist, but it falls short for many who can. Yehuda Bauer lays out some of the problems with this answer,[3] as does philosopher Berel Lang.[4]

Another explanation holds that the souls of the Jewish martyrs of the Holocaust survived and will receive their reward in the afterlife. As one Hasidic writer put it, "The precise number of years they lived in this world must be viewed in the context of the [eternal] continuum of the soul."[5] In other words, a martyr's suffering and the length of anyone's life in this world are but a blink of an eye compared with the eternal afterlife. As my dad notes, however, the afterlife is not a concept stressed in most streams of Jewish theology. The late Rabbi Menachem Schneerson, the former leader of the Lubavitcher Hasidic movement who is (still) regarded as the Messiah by many of his followers, also said that Jews killed in the Shoah died for *Kiddush Hashem*—that is, as martyrs, which he deemed the highest religious privilege.[6] Bauer points out various problems with this explanation and with Orthodox Judaism's inability to explain why nearly a million innocent children perished. While such attempts at explanation did not satisfy my dad either, he found some level of Jewish religious observance important in maintaining a connection to his heritage and the Jewish people. He also found some Jewish rituals meaningful and helpful in celebrating or coping with life events.

It is interesting how different Shoah survivors reacted when it came to Jewish observance. One cousin who survived Auschwitz was fairly observant and one of his sons is Orthodox and has a very religious family. His other son is less so but made *aliyah* many years ago. Another cousin who survived Auschwitz was culturally extremely Jewish but became completely non-observant and raised his children that way. A third cousin, whose father survived Auschwitz, also identifies as Jewish, but was raised by her family in a completely non-observant way and raised her children that way. Among the many survivors I knew who weren't in Auschwitz, most I would say were moderately observant, celebrating the major Jewish holidays and life events and so on. Some kept kosher homes, but most didn't. This applied to both Israelis and Americans. Among survivors, Bauer says, there was "no significant movement from religion to the rejection of religion, or the other way around."[7] He doesn't cite any authority, however, and my sample size isn't large enough to draw any firm conclusions. I know only about my own parents and some relatives.

CHAPTER 34

1967: Poland Denies Eva's Request to Attend Her Stepfather's Funeral

1967 was not a good year for my family.

In September 1967, my grandfather, Leon Kimel, died. He was seventy-two, and I had just turned seven. It was one of the few times in my life I saw my dad cry. I remember going to shul (synagogue) with my grandfather (whom I called Grandpa), but I have few clear memories of him. My cousin Paula tells me our grandfather didn't smile very often. He isn't smiling in any of the few family photos I have, though there may have been the beginnings of a smile in a photo taken at my cousin Harold's bar mitzvah celebration. Unrelated to that, I'm told he loved watching professional wrestling on TV.

People generally don't consider pessimism a good trait, but Grandpa's pessimism helped most of his family members survive the Holocaust when so few Jews did. Fearing the worst, he started converting Polish zlotys into hard currency as he saw storm clouds gather. He then left the money in the care of family friends, the Goralniks, who safeguarded it. Sometimes, it's unclear whether his pessimistic actions helped or not. For instance, his concern that the Soviets were going to deport his family to Siberia led him to bribe a contact in Rohatyn and move his family there. We'll never know whether they would have been deported. The chances are that even deportation would have been better for them but, as my mother said, who knows? If they had remained in Podhajce and been forced into its ghetto, that may have proved worse than the Rohatyn Ghetto but, again, we don't know. This being the Holocaust, Grandpa's pessimism may have led to some still-bad-but-less-horrible outcomes. By not sending his wife to the ghetto's supposed typhus hospital, he enabled her to die peacefully. Had my grandmother gone to the "hospital," she may well have been murdered there—like the young son of Mechele the *Stolar*.

In August 1967, my mother's stepfather also passed away. Unfortunately for my mother, this was two months after Israel won the Six-Day War over Arab states equipped militarily by the Soviet Union. As a result of that victory, a "tsunami of purges with strong anti-Semitic overtones [took place] throughout the Polish Communist military and Party establishments in 1967 and 1968."[1] Once again, historical events outside their control directly affected my parents. Because my mother had emigrated from Poland to Israel—the *only* country Poland had *allowed* Jews to emigrate to in 1956 (as part of the "Gomułka Aliyah")—she was denied a visa in 1967 to attend her stepfather's funeral. She needed a visa because Poland had forced her, in 1956, to renounce her Polish citizenship as a condition of leaving Poland. She was not allowed to see her stepfather laid to rest or to be with her mother to comfort her.

In 1968, the Communist government declared Jews "enemies of socialist Poland" and persecuted them, leading to a mass emigration of Polish Jews. The situation was so bad that a joke circulated among Jews in Poland: "How does a smart Jew talk to a stupid one? By phone from Vienna."[2] We encountered this personally when, in 1968 or 1969, a young Jewish couple from Legnica who had just left Poland stayed with us in Teaneck for a time until they could get settled in this country. Like my parents in 1956, Jews leaving Poland in 1968 were forced to renounce their Polish citizenship.[3]

Some 25,000 Jews left Poland during the 1968–1970 period, leaving only between 5,000 and 10,000 Jews in the entire country.[4] As noted earlier, before the war, over three *million* Jews lived in Poland. Hence, my aunt and grandmother were two of only a tiny remnant of Polish Jews still living in Poland. For Babcia, who had lost her first husband in the Holocaust and who had lived it through it herself with her young daughters, the government's overt hostility towards Jews must have brought back terrible memories and been very frightening. Being newly widowed must have just amplified her anxiety. Babcia was torn between her two daughters—one in America, one in Poland, and she didn't speak any English, so she remained in Poland.

My aunt married a Catholic Pole and had two girls, who were raised as Catholics and live in Legnica where they raised their children.[5] Regina was a pediatrician and she assimilated successfully. Tragically, she died very young from cancer. When I was growing up, out of all my many Jewish relatives from Poland and all of my parents' many Polish-Jewish friends, we were, with one exception, the only ones I knew of who still had (and have) family in Poland.

CHAPTER 35

The "Refugees" Achieve the American Dream—Awe and Gratitude from the Next Generation

In New York, my dad passed his licensing exams in 1963 on his first try to become a "professional engineer," and started his own consulting engineering firm in Manhattan, doing electrical and HVAC design for buildings. My mom stayed at home for about eleven years with my sister and me and got an accounting degree at Fairleigh Dickinson University. She then worked as an accountant for large companies, including Vornado Inc. and Sony.

In an effort to raise us in an "Americanized way," my mother observed what American-born parents did in terms of child rearing and generally tried to do the same. As noted in the Foreword, I, however, always liked that I came from a different background and always took pride in it. My paternal grandfather's brothers and sisters emigrated here at the start of the twentieth century. My mother said they were aloof. "They had no interest in refugees, which is how they viewed us," she said. "The whole family treated us as the 'greeners,'" a derogatory term for newcomers. By "whole family," I believe my mother was including the American-born children of my grandfather's siblings. My mother said that when we lived in the Bronx, people in the building were friendly. But she said that when our family went to a Catskills, New York, bungalow colony for a vacation, not many Jewish people there wanted to associate with us. She noted that very few of her European friends in the United States have American-born friends, suggesting that they had met with a similarly frosty reception.

My parents had a very tight-knit circle of friends, almost all of whom were from Poland, many of whom were also survivors. Maybe because of their shared experiences, which Americans back then (including American Jews) were generally not interested in hearing about, this may have been common. In the Afterword to his book, Thorne's children note that they grew up in an Orthodox community, nearly all of whose members were survivors.

My parents and their friends rarely talked about those experiences among themselves, but they shared a special bond. Having come from Poland provided another special connection. Their conversations would switch back and forth between Polish and English, with the occasional joke in Yiddish tossed in. They enjoyed socializing together and loved to dance, especially at *simchas*—joyous events. (My bar mitzvah was especially meaningful to my dad because, he told me, he never expected during the war to live long enough to have a son become a bar mitzvah.) My parents also enjoyed playing bridge, attending the theater, and skiing. They kept in touch with relatives and friends in Poland, France, Israel, Germany, Canada, Australia, and elsewhere. My parents loved to travel and did so extensively. They remained extremely close with their friends and relatives in Israel. Whenever they went to Israel for a vacation, they were, in my mother's words, "treated like royalty." My wife, Miriam, and I got a taste of this when we visited Israel in 1998 before we got engaged, where we couldn't have been treated any more warmly by these relatives and family friends. (They all advised me to propose to Miriam because they knew a gem when they saw one.)

Far from the "broken" people that survivors are often portrayed as by some children and grandchildren nowadays, the vast majority of the survivors I knew—which basically included all my living relatives of my parents' generation—were pretty well adjusted.[1] There is an understandable impulse for historians to make well-intentioned, blanket statements like this one: "And what haunted these child survivors [who had lost one or both parents] for the rest of their lives, *what they were unable to overcome*, were memories not only of their own physical suffering but that of a parent or sibling."[2] My mother and father each lost a parent during the war. While that may have haunted them in ways, they each overcame it. They, along with the vast majority of survivors I knew, had gone through hell, survived, and worked hard to achieve the American dream (or the analog of whatever country they settled in), which they all did. They demonstrated amazing bravery and resilience throughout their lives, coming to America (or other countries) with little to no money and often, like my mother, not speaking the local language.

They sacrificed a lot to give their children and grandchildren the best lives possible, and, like me, many of my fellow children of survivors (the children of my parent's friends or relatives) regard their parents with awe and gratitude. (Of course, like adolescents everywhere, growing up, we didn't always express this to our parents.) Like our parents, we were also grateful the United States had let them in.

There is a widespread notion today that we children of survivors were almost all traumatized by being raised by survivor parents.[3] That is not, however, consistent with my personal experience of having grown up with many fellow "second generationers."[4] For instance, I know of no one who felt he or she had to "parent their parents" or "could never express unhappiness or pain" because it might upset a parent or because no unhappiness or pain could compare to what the first generation experienced.[5] Nor do I know of any families where the dead were "almost more 'present'" than living family members.[6] Instead, I agree with Menachem Rosensaft, who said, "I firmly believe that most of us [children of survivors] look upon our parents and grandparents as role models and a source of strength."[7] Moreover, viewing everything through the lens of trauma can lead people to misinterpret motivations. For example, Fulbrook acknowledges that some survivors, like my parents, wanted their children to marry Jews to continue the Jewish people, whom Hitler had wanted to completely wipe off the face of the Earth. But then she adds, without citing any support, that this view was "undoubtedly strengthened by heightened fear and mistrust of gentiles."[8]

With respect to the *third* generation, different survivors handle trauma differently, but I personally don't know of *any* grandchildren of Holocaust survivors who have somehow "inherited" post-traumatic stress disorder from their grandparents, as some third-generation members are now claiming. I think it does survivors' memories a disservice to claim or suggest that this is a common occurrence.[9]

In April 2022, I moderated a panel discussion for Yom HaShoah (Holocaust Remembrance Day) at my government agency, which was webcast to all my agency's offices across the country. The panel consisted of one other Second Genner and three Third Genners. In preparing, I wanted to discover any differences in how the two generations learned about their loved ones' Holocaust experiences or differences in how they had processed that knowledge. Did the children know more than *their* children? Probably, I think, but it was impossible to get a clear read without both generations present. Then it hit me: The largest difference I observed involved emotions.

226 | The Pessimist's Son

The grandchildren spoke of their grandparents in the adoring, worshipful tones typical of grandchildren. Having been raised by my parents, I related to my dad far differently than my children related to my dad. (Unfortunately, my children were very little when my mom died.) I loved my parents dearly but, of course, I knew their strengths and shortcomings in a way my children never did.

If I have one regret as a child of immigrants, it is that my parents stopped speaking Polish to me when I was very young. The story is that I was playing with another child in the Bronx, and I didn't understand what he was saying because he was speaking to me in English, at which point my parents switched to 100 percent English with me. Back then, there also was a lot of social pressure on immigrants to assimilate, and ethnic pride wasn't yet a thing in America. I was exposed to a lot of spoken Polish in my house, so I picked up a little, in the same way that my mother picked up Yiddish when her parents wanted to speak privately (though she doubtless picked up more Yiddish than I did Polish).

When my grandmother came for extended visits, communication with her for me was very difficult because she spoke only Yiddish and Polish, and my Polish was broken and extremely limited. Babcia was very lonely because my parents both worked outside of the house (there was no telework back then) and she was dependent on them. She couldn't speak with Americans, including other seniors at our Jewish community center, who either didn't speak Yiddish or didn't want to speak it. When I later wanted to study Polish in college, my dad dissuaded me, noting that there was only one country in the world where Polish was spoken (and it was a closed-off Communist country, to boot, at the time). It made sense but, looking back, I regret that I took that advice.

When I visited my Babcia, cousins and uncle in Communist Poland in the summer of 1983, it certainly would have been good if my Polish had been better. My uncle and first cousins spoke no English whatever. I happened to be visiting the country when Poland was under martial law (*stan wojenny*). The Solidarity movement had taken off and Wojciech Jaruzelski, Poland's leader, had declared martial law in an attempt to crush the movement before the Soviet army invaded Poland to do the job, à la Hungary in 1956 and Czechoslovakia in 1968.

The Polish economy was a mess, and food and other basic goods were rationed. Store shelves were empty. You didn't order from a menu in a restaurant, you asked the waiter what food they had. The airport in Wrocław we

The "Refugees" Achieve the American Dream | 227

used to fly to Warsaw was dingy, and anti-Reagan posters greeted travelers. *Zomo* (special paramilitary squads) seemed to be omnipresent in Warsaw, but people found clever ways to protest lawfully. There was a large cross made of flowers as a protest. I especially admired the silent protest of a name plate on an apartment door with the family's name written in the style of Solidarity's red logo. On my train leaving Poland for East Germany and Paris, a border guard grilled a middle-aged woman about how much currency she was carrying out of the country. The poor woman, traveling to East Berlin, became very distressed. She nervously opened a jar of her cold cream and quickly scooped out its entire contents with her hand to show the border guard that there was no money hidden inside the jar. The incident gave me a greater gut-level appreciation of what my parents had gone through in Communist Poland and when they were under direct Soviet rule.

Later, in the mid-to-late 1990s, I took evening classes in Polish. Had I learned Polish as a young child, I would now have a perfect accent and would not have had to struggle with the language's notoriously difficult grammar. (Why on Earth invent a language that has at least seventeen grammatical forms of the number "two"?!) Despite that, my Polish has been useful in speaking and corresponding with my cousins in Legnica and when I visit Poland. Fortunately, too, many of my Polish cousins now speak English. Unlike many Second Genners, Poland for me was not an alien place I visited one time to discover family history. It is a place where I have ongoing familial ties, a place where I attended my Babcia's funeral in 1993 and where my mother returned for her high school reunion in 2005. I joined my parents in Poland during that trip.

My 2005 trip to Poland was great. Encouraged by my wife, I left her and my two then-young children to meet my parents in Kraków. It was great being in Poland with them again. Among other things, we took in a Chopin recital. We also dined one evening in a "Jewish"-themed restaurant in the touristy Jewish Kazimierz District, which was about as real as Disneyland. You could say it was Poland's take on Judaism without Jews. There, you could buy little figurines of hook-nosed Jews.

I did some more sightseeing on my own, including a pilgrimage to Auschwitz-Birkenau. (My parents had been to Auschwitz decades earlier and had no desire to return.) In my tour group, I befriended a mother and her adult daughter from Israel who had been speaking Hebrew. At the end of the tour, I mentioned to our Auschwitz-Birkenau Memorial and Museum-employed tour guide that I had relatives who had been inmates there, and she asked me whether they were Jewish or Christian. We chatted a few minutes in Polish, and I thanked her for a great tour. I was happy to see that she, a Polish Catholic, viewed her job as more than a paycheck. The next day, I visited the Wieliczka salt mine to see its amazing carvings (its wartime history went unmentioned), and later took a train to Wrocław, where my parents and cousins picked me up. We spent time in that city's large and beautiful *rynek*. From there we went to Legnica to see the rest of our family. It was a wonderful trip—and the last time my parents would ever be in the land of their birth. One night in Kraków, my mother experienced excruciating back pain. It was gone the next day, so nothing was done about it. It turned out to be her first sign of pancreatic cancer. As a tough woman, my mother got through the pain and saw no reason to interrupt her limited time in Poland with a visit to the ER. During the trip, we reconnected with our Legnica cousins, which was very special. Three of them—Iwona (Regina's youngest daughter), her husband, Grzegorz, and their daughter Zuzia—visited us the next summer.

I took my family to Poland in the summer of 2018, and we all couldn't have had a better time. It was my family's first time in Poland and meeting many of our Polish family. I was stunned by what a modern European city Warsaw had become—how much it had changed since 1993! We did a whirlwind tour of Kraków, and my family was especially impressed with Wieliczka. In 2023, Miriam and I also had a blast attending the Polish wedding of Zuzia. I love my cousins there, who have always welcomed us warmly. The sounds of Polish make me nostalgic. And having been in Poland during Communist times, I continue to marvel at what a beautiful, modern country it has become—for example, the dark and dingy Wrocław airport (with its anti-Reagan posters in 1983) has been replaced by a bright, modern one. Nevertheless, I have an ambivalent relationship with Poland. While I have never experienced any overt antisemitism there, I have seen signs on occasion. I also can't forget Poland's history with respect to Jews generally or my parents' history, specifically. Finally, I have read too much not to know that antisemitism is fairly widespread in Poland today. (It is also more widespread in America than many of us thought.)

Late in life, after repeated tries, my dad finally qualified for a modest German pension until his death because of the slave labor he had performed in the Rohatyn Ghetto. This was the result of Germany's Ghetto Pensions Law passed only in 2002—nearly sixty years after the war's end. At this point, virtually half of all survivors were over eighty.[10] To add insult to injury, in the first five years of the program, only about five percent of the roughly

70,000 claims filed had been approved.[11] I don't remember precisely how old my dad was when he started receiving his pension, but he probably was close to eighty. He used to receive letters from the German government periodically asking him to attest that he was still alive, so that his benefits would continue. To the best of my recollection, my mother received no compensation from Germany, even though the Germans murdered her father and despite all that she herself endured. In any event, she died in 2008.

My parents were devoted grandparents to my children, David and Sarah, and to my sister's sons, Jonathan, Robbie, and Matthew. Unfortunately, my children were very young when my mother passed away at the age of seventy-six from pancreatic cancer. Even after being struck by this horrible disease, my mom demonstrated great courage and served as an inspiration to her family and many friends. My dad bore tremendous stress as he worked hard to take care of her at home, under extremely difficult conditions.

My mom died on the second day of Passover (April 2008), which was her favorite holiday and which we always celebrated with big family seders and delicious homemade gefilte fish that she prepared. We think that she willed herself to live until the holiday. When I was growing up, my dad and other men of his generation, including my Uncle Sunio and cousin Shmulek, would sit around the table and chant the Haggadah in Yiddish-inflected Hebrew, with melodies from their childhood seders in prewar Poland. No Passover seder was complete without a shot of *shlivovitz*, high-proof plum brandy from the old country. Lacking at least a few people with fluency in Hebrew and knowledge of those melodies, however, we have not been able to replicate those seders of my youth.

My dad died in 2018, at the age of ninety-one. He lived long enough to see his grandchildren mature, which, sadly, my mom did not. He always maintained a positive attitude towards life, but Parkinson's disease diminished his short-term recall and cognitive ability in his later years. My dad recognized this and, having been a brilliant man, it bothered him in his old age. There is a rhyming Polish saying, "*starość nie radość*"—old age isn't joy. Fortunately, however, my parents had a lot of joy in their lives—before and after the Holocaust. And, in his later years, my dad would always accept things he couldn't change with his trademark phrase, "*C'est la vie.*"

We Will Never Forget—Auschwitz

By Alexander Kimel

We will never forget the selections at Auschwitz,
Where Black Jackals condemned millions to gas
Right—death, left—life, right death . . . death . . . death.
The black finger, surrounded with barking dogs,
Works like the Angel of Death, creating living hell.

Children are torn apart from the tender embrace
Of mothers, clinging to their treasures.
Babies wailing from hunger,
Parents parting tearfully with their children.
Fathers shaken with helpless rage.
The condemned form a column of trembling fear.

Soon the mass of fainting humanity
Is led to the clean foyer of death.
Disrobe quickly, take a shower and you will be fed.
Food! Food! The hungry mass of disoriented humanity
Awakens, runs and fights to get into the chamber of gas.

The heavy door closes and the Zyklon dropped.
 Soon the parents choke and tum blue,
Later the children tum rigid with death
The people become a twisted load,
Of intertwined limbs and heads glued with blood.

When the human pulp is ready for the works,
Sondercommando quickly pulls
The bodies apart, peels the gold from the mouths.
And the remains are taken to the open pit,
Where the bones are cleaned with fire,
And the fat drained for human soap.

Six days a week the Jackals drink beer
And rejoice doing the Devil's work.
Sunday is the day of rest, the day
When the Jackals ride to the Church,
to praise God
And ensure the Salvation of their pious souls.

Deutschland, Deutschland Über Alles!
In this Kingdom of Evil,
There is no peace for the Righteous.
It is the wicked that inherited
This tortured World, engulfed
In the red, milky, cry-absorbing fog,
Guarding the wilted conscience of man.

Holocaust Lamentations

By Alexander Kimel

PRAYER
Praised be O God, Ruler of the Universe, who made us captives of Hope.
Guard me, O Lord, from hating man, my brother.
Guard me from recalling what he did to me.
Even when all the stars in the sky are quenched,
Even when my soul becomes mute,
When I am overcome by disaster,
Let me not lay his guilt bare.

When the barbed wire fence is locked,
Darkness over the nation reclines,
And we are drained of love and rejected,
I am bound to my rock—O Lord
Permit me to see in my brother a spark,
The spark of humanity still shining,
That I may know that in me, myself,
Not all is extinguished yet.

Relatives Known to Have Perished in the Holocaust

Alex's Side:

Pesia Lehrer Kimel (1942?) (mother)
Chaim Lehrer (1941) (grandfather)
Roncia Milch Lehrer (1942) (grandmother)
Abraham Milch (1907–1942) (uncle)
Ethel Lehrer (1904–1942) (aunt)
Zysio Lehrer (1942) (uncle)
Regina Fogel Lehrer (aunt)
Pinchas Lehrer (cousin)
Sura Lehrer (cousin)
Jozef Koren (cousin)
Jonata Koren (cousin)
Elke Rubler (1943) (cousin)
Libby Rubler Jupiter (1943) (cousin)
Mottel (Melche) Jupiter (1943) (cousin by marriage)

Eva's Side:

Eliezer (Lejzor) Najnudel (1868–?) (grandfather)
Natan Najnudel (1902?–1942) (father)
Abraham Najnudel (1908–?) (uncle)
Masha Najnudel Zilberstein (aunt)
Sabina Najnudel Steinman (aunt)
Moshe Goldstein (1919–1942) (uncle)
Simcha Goldstein (1917–1942) (uncle)
Yechiel Goldstein (1910–1942) (uncle)
Fela Goldstein (1910–1942) (cousin)
Azriel Goldstein (1912–1945) (cousin)
Moshe Meir Goldstein (1915–1942) (cousin)
Mayer Goldstein (1942) (cousin)
Feiga Goldstein (1942) (cousin)

Roma Najnudel Zabner (aunt)
Inka Zabner (cousin)
Margalit Nayhaus Goldstein (1942) (grandmother)
Jeremiasz Goldstein (1882–1942) (grandfather)
Mordechai Goldstein (1886–1941) (great-uncle)
Sarah Goldstein (1895–1942) (great-aunt)
Leah Goldstein (maiden name) (1890s–1942) (great-aunt)
Yechiel Goldstein (1899–1942) (great-uncle)
Buchek Steinman (cousin)
Deborah Zylberszpic (1942) (great–aunt)

Endnotes

Foreword

1 My dad refers to his father as "father." To avoid possible confusion, I will generally refer to my father as "dad."

2 *German Crimes in Poland*, Central Commission for the Investigation of German Crimes in Poland (New York: Howard Fertig, 1982), 134.

3 I fully support Ukraine in its defensive war against Russia and condemn Vladimir Putin's and the Russian military's unjust and barbaric attacks on Russia's sovereign neighbor. I refer to "the Polish Ukraine" instead of simply "Ukraine" because Ukraine did not exist as a country immediately before or during World War II. The usage is important for a few reasons. First, Jews like my father were under Polish sovereignty growing up (prior to Polish independence, however, Podhajce was part of Austria-Hungary) and never considered themselves to be "Ukrainian Jews." Second, Ukrainian nationalism proved to have very significant negative repercussions for Jews during the Holocaust, and this point may be obscured if one mistakenly speaks of Ukraine as an already existing state in the prewar and war periods. Third, not keeping the status of Ukraine clear has led some journalists to make erroneous statements such as that Ukraine was the European country with the largest prewar Jewish population when it was Poland that had the largest prewar Jewish population in Europe.

4 Eric J. Sterling, ed., *Life in the Ghettos during the Holocaust* (Syracuse, NY: Syracuse University Press, 2005).

5 For a discussion of *yizkor* books, see my "Co-Author's Note on the Use of *Yizkor* Books and Rohatyn Memoirs."

6 The Yale historian Timothy Snyder has written, "[W]hile Auschwitz has been remembered, most of the Holocaust has been largely forgotten." Timothy Snyder, *Black Earth: The Holocaust as Warning and History* (New York: Crown, 2015), 207. See also Martin Kimel, "We Must Remember the Holocaust Beyond Auschwitz," *Baltimore Sun* (January 26, 2025). This book certainly touches on Auschwitz, but it remembers the Holocaust beyond that one terrible place.

Co-Author's Note on the Use of *Yizkor* Books and Rohatyn Memoirs

1 Christopher R. Browning, *Remembering Survival: Inside a Nazi Slave-Labor Camp* (New York: Norton, 2010), 7.

2 Omer Bartov, *Genocide, the Holocaust and Israel-Palestine: First-Person History in Times of Crisis* (London: Bloomsbury Academic, 2023), 63–64. See also Shimon Redlich, *Life in Transit: Jews in Postwar Lodz, 1945–1950* (Boston: Academic Studies Press, 2010), x. ("I am convinced now even more than in the past that individual voices are highly significant in the writing of history, no less than the more conventional and traditional sources.")

238 | The Pessimist's Son

3 See Jack Kugelmass and Jonathan Boyarin, eds., *From a Ruined Garden: The Memorial Books of Polish Jewry* (Bloomington: Indiana University Press, 2nd edition, 1998), 1.
4 Sefer Radom [The book of Radom; the story of a Jewish community in Poland destroyed by the Nazis (Radom, Poland)], ed. Y. Perlow and Alfred Lipson (Tel Aviv: n.p., 1961), trans. for JewishGen, https://www.jewishgen.org/yizkor/radom/radom.html (hereafter Sefer Radom),

Part 1

Chapter 1

1 Podhajce was about sixty percent Jewish.
2 Steven T. Katz, ed., *The Shtetl: New Evaluations* (New York: NYU Press, 2007), 6.
3 Baruch Milch, "Experiences and Figures from the Recent Past," in Me'ir Shimon Geshouri, ed., *Sefer Podhajce* [The memorial book of Podhajce (Pidhaytsi, Ukraine)] (Tel Aviv: Podhajce Society, 1972), 243–244. I will refer to this English translation as *Sefer Podhajce*.
4 Galicia is a historic region spanning what is now southeastern Poland and western Ukraine. While western Galicia was predominantly Polish, eastern Galicia (home to Podhajce) was predominantly Ukrainian. It was the birthplace or breeding ground of several spiritual and political movements including the Haskalah (the Jewish Enlightenment), Hasidism, Zionism, and Ukrainian nationalism. Omer Bartov, *Erased: Vanishing Traces of Jewish Galicia in Present-Day Ukraine* (Princeton, NJ: Princeton University Press, 2007), 26–27.
5 In his video testimony, my father said there were about ten to fifteen *melameds* in a *cheder*. Jewish boys and girls were taught separately. The girls learned colloquial Hebrew, while the boys learned the *loyshen koddish*, as the holy Hebrew of the liturgy was known in Yiddish.
6 Sociologist Celia Heller, herself born in Poland, puts this point strongly: "The Jews were . . . treated as foreigners in Poland. Like their inferiority, their basic foreignness was assumed to be everlasting. . . . [Poles] regarded the Jews as intruders whose presence in Poland was due only to Polish good will." Celia S. Heller, *On the Edge of Destruction: Jews of Poland between the Two World Wars* (Detroit, MI: Wayne State University Press, 1994), 62–63. Indeed, after the death of Jozef Pilsudski in 1935, responsibility for Jewish affairs was transferred from Poland's ministry of internal affairs to the ministry of foreign affairs. Snyder, *Black Earth*, 58.
7 Henia Shourz, "A Path Full of Obstacles and Suffering," trans. Jerrold Landau, in *Sefer Podhajce*, 327. I am not including M.'s full name.

Chapter 2

1 Heller also stresses the traditional Polish Jews' emphasis on community: "[T]he traditional Jew's sense of responsibility was supposed to extend beyond himself—to the family and the Jewish community. At the center of his beliefs was that all Jews are mutually accountable to each other." *Edge of Destruction*, 170. Many writers in *Sefer Podhjace* talk about the town's various charitable institutions, including credit institutions that made interest-free loans to merchants and tradesmen. See, for example, *Sefer Podhajce*, 141 and

Endnotes | 239

278. I don't know what percentage of the Podhajce *kehilla*'s budget was devoted to charity and help to struggling businesses but, in the city of Kielce (which was not in Galicia), about one-third of the *kehilla*'s budget was so earmarked in the early 1930s. Sara Bender, *In Enemy Land: The Jews of Kielce and the Region, 1939–1946* (Boston: Academic Studies Press, 2018), 26–27.

2 Martyr's death; literally, "Sanctification of the [Divine] Name."

3 The *Maftir aliyah* refers to the last person called to the Torah on Shabbat and holiday mornings.

4 This is commented on by many people in *Sefer Podhjace*.

5 Omer Bartov, *Tales from the Borderlands: Making and Unmaking the Galician Past* (New Haven, CT: Yale University Press, 2022), 26–27. See also Katz, *The Shtetl: New Evaluations*, 3 ("In the Ukraine, especially, the Jews would find themselves resented as the agents of the hated Polish nobility").

6 Bartov, *Borderlands*, 27 (citations omitted).

7 Ibid., 62. As an example of the latter, Bartov cites *Taras Bulba*, by the great nineteenth-century Russian-language writer Nikolai Gogol. *Borderlands*, 63–71.

8 Lucy S. Dawidowicz, *The War against the Jews, 1933–45* (New York: Rinehart and Winston, 1975), 295 and 296.

9 Bartov, *Genocide, the Holocaust and Israel-Palestine*, 28.

10 Jan Grabowski, "The Polish Police Collaboration in the Holocaust," Ina Levine Annual Lecture, Center for Advanced Holocaust Studies, United States Holocaust Memorial Museum, November 17, 2016, 26, https://www.ushmm.org/m/pdfs/20170502-Grabowski_OP.pdf. It is often stated that ten percent of Poland's Jews survived. That is a misleading statistic, however, because most of the Polish Jews who survived had been deported to the USSR proper (for example, to Siberia).

11 Dara Horn, "The U.S. and the Holocaust Reveals the Dark Limits of Democracy," *The Atlantic*, September 16, 2022.

12 Heller, *Edge of Destruction*, 181.

13 Ringelblum, Emmanuel, *Notes from the Warsaw Ghetto: The Journal of Emmanuel Ringelblum*, ed. and trans. Jacob Sloan (Berkeley: ibooks inc., 2006), 103.

14 Christopher R. Browning, *Ordinary Men: Reserve Police Battalion 101 and the Final Solution in Poland* (New York: Harper Perennial, 2017), 136–137.

Chapter 3

1 About 25,000 German Jews took refuge in Poland. Jeremy Black, *The Holocaust: History and Memory* (Bloomington: Indiana University Press, 2016), 48.

2 The camp was established by Pilsudski.

3 The Przytyk pogrom occurred between the Polish and Jewish communities in Przytyk, Radom County, on March 9, 1936. A boycott of Jewish shops was organized, and it escalated into a wave of violent attacks on Jewish shops, which resulted in the creation of a Jewish self-defense group. The boycott later devolved into riots in which three people were killed and more than twenty injured. On June 26 that year, eleven Jews were sentenced to prison terms of six months to eight years, while thirty-nine Poles received sentences of six months to a year. The accused Jews claimed they had acted in self-defense, but the court rejected those arguments. The verdict outraged the Jewish community. See Martin Gilbert, *The Holocaust: The Human Tragedy* (New York: Rosetta Books, 2014), 69; and David Vital, *A People Apart: The Jews in Europe,*

1789–1939 (Oxford: Oxford University Press, 1999), 793–794. Heller writes that Jewish self-defense in Poland in the 1930s existed but was "de facto illegal and was treated as defiance of authority." In "The Town is Burning: Thirty Years since the Disturbances and Self-Defense in Przytyk," in *Sefer Przytyk* [Przytyk memorial book], ed. David Shtokfish (Tel Aviv: Przytyk Societies in Israel, France and the USA, 1973), 157, trans. for JewishGen, https://www.jewishgen.org/yizkor/przytyk/przytyk.html, Shtokfish argues that Jewish self-defense in 1936 Przytyk inspired Jewish resistance during the Shoah. Yehoshua R., in "The Przytyk Events," in *Sefer Radom*, 93, notes that, "Even the youth from such a small town . . . demonstrated that they were prepared to sacrifice themselves for Jewish honor, and that Jewish blood and possessions are not in a state of free-for-all." He also concludes that: "The verdict, no less than the events, left a frightening impression on the entire Jewish world. It demonstrated the situation of lack or rights in which the Jews of Poland found themselves under the rule of the Sanacja regime." The Sanacja regime was established after the 1926 coup by Pilsudski. It became more authoritarian after his death. Jan T. Gross, *Fear: Anti-Semitism in Poland after Auschwitz* (New York: Random House, 2006), 198.

4   Indeed, Heller argues that at a time when Poland could have harnessed the entrepreneurial spirit of its Jewish citizens to help lift the country from its economic woes, it did exactly the opposite by persecuting them and engaging in their "economic strangulation." *Edge of Destruction*, 95–100. Jews had been encouraged to settle in Poland by medieval Polish princes to help develop the country economically, ibid., 14–15, and the tension between Poles hostile to Jewish entrepreneurship (mainly, Jewish shop owners and artisans) and the fact that Jews contributed disproportionately to economic development in Polish towns was nothing new. For example, in 1841, a Polish merchants' association in Kielce successfully urged the Russian authorities to ban all Jews from Kielce. After Jews started returning around 1863, they developed local stone, lime, brick, tile, glass, and lumber industries. Bender, *Enemy Land*, xv–xviii.

5   My father may have been thinking of *Mały Dziennik* (The Little Journal). During the war, however, the Nazi government published Polish-language newspapers such as *Nowy kurier warszawski* (The new Warsaw courier). Emmanuel Ringelblum, *Polish-Jewish Relations during the Second World War*, trans. Dafna Allon, Danuta Dabrowska, and Dana Keren (Evanston, IL: Northwestern University Press, 1992), 192.

6   The idea of settling Madagascar with Poles was first raised in 1926. The idea resurfaced in 1936 when, after Pilsudski's death, Poland's foreign minister proposed the emigration of Polish Jews to the French colony of Madagascar to France's (Jewish) prime minister, Leon Blum. The inhabitants of the island, however, rejected any settlement from Poland. In 1938, Hitler suggested it to Warsaw as part of his unsuccessful attempt to convince Poland to ally itself with Germany and help Germany defeat the USSR. Although the Polish leadership wanted to be rid of most Polish Jews, it didn't want to go to war with the Soviet Union and it, rightly, thought Hitler's plan impractical. Snyder, *Black Earth*, 74–76. In the early years of the war, Alfred Rosenberg, the rabidly antisemitic Nazi ideologue whom Hitler appointed Reich Minister for the Occupied Eastern Territories in July 1941, was a "stubborn advocate" of a murderous plan to brutally remove Jews from Europe and dump them on the tropical island, where they would have a hard time surviving. Richard J. Evans, *Hitler's People: The Faces of the Third Reich* (New York: Penguin Press, 2024), 216.

7   Though it had long been hostile to Jews, Romania was neutral at the start of the war. It later would become Nazi Germany's military ally.

Endnotes | 241

8   Ben-Zion Gold, *The Life of Jews in Poland before the Holocaust* (Lincoln: University of Nebraska Press, 2007), 75–77. The government lent more than moral support to boycotts of Jews. For example, in August 1936, the Ministry of Commerce ordered that signs on stores and establishments display the name of the owners as they appeared on their birth certificates, thus flagging whom to boycott. Heller, *Edge of Destruction*, 104.

9   See Szymon Rudnicki, "Economic Struggle or Antisemitism?," in *Polin: Studies in Polish Jewry*, vol. 30: *Jewish Education in Eastern Europe*, ed. Eliyana R. Adler and Antony Polonsky (Oxford: Littman, 2018), 397–398. Writing about the effects of the boycotts, one survivor from Podhajce notes that antisemitism increased in Poland after Hitler came to power and then says:

> There were calls for an economic boycott against the Jews. Political machinations of the government also increased, both from the political parties and the incited masses. . . . The Jew felt impoverished, abandoned and alone. . . . People began to look for the possibility to leave Poland. However, the world was locked to Jewish immigrants. Even the gates of Palestine were locked [to] Jews. Only a fortunate few were able to go there.

Nachman Blumethal, "From the Past: History of the Jews of Podhajce," *Sefer Podhajce*, 142–143.

10 See Rudnicki, "Economic Struggle or Antisemitism?," 397 and 401. See also Anna Landau-Czajka, "The Jewish Question in Poland: Views Expressed in the Catholic Press between the Two World Wars," in *Polin: Studies in Polish Jewry*, vol. 11: *Focusing on Aspects and Experiences of Religion*, ed. Antony Polonsky (Oxford: Littman, 1998), 263; Heller, *Edge of Destruction*, 111 (the Catholic press "persistently poured out anti-Semitic venom . . ."); and Bender, *Enemy Land*, 46 (the Church's view of the Jew as a "dangerous alien" was "manifested in various ways in all ecclesiastical newspapers, including those meant for the lower classes and the clergy").

11 Heller, *Edge of Destruction*, 44. "Polish nation" was understood to mean Polish Catholics only.

12 Bender, *Enemy Land*, 5–6.

13 Pilsudski told Polish Jewish leaders he had ordered the army to intervene on the behalf of Jews but he refused to make the order public, saying he was not an "autocrat." Joshua D. Zimmerman, *Jozef Pilsudski: Founding Father of Modern Poland* (Cambridge, MA: Harvard University Press, 2022), 298.

14 Paul Hanebrink, *A Specter Haunting Europe: The Myth of Judeo-Bolshevism* (Cambridge, MA: Belknap Press, 2018), 60.

15 Vital, *A People Apart*, 748.

16 Jeffrey Veidlinger, *In the Midst of Civilized Europe: The Pogroms of 1918–1921 and the Onset of the Holocaust* (New York: Metropolitan Books 2021), 236. Like the Nazis, Dmowski regarded Jews as a distinct, parasitic race, and he came to admire Hitler. Yehuda Bauer, *The Death of the Shtetl* (New Haven, CT: Yale University Press, 2009), 15. He also viewed Jews as Bolshevik enemies of Poland. In early 1923, Endecja made a national hero of a supporter who assassinated the newly elected President Gabriel Narutowicz as the creator of "Judeo-Poland" because he had been elected with support of Polish minorities. Zimmerman, *Jozef Pilsudski*, 382–387.

17 Allan Levine, *Fugitives of the Forest: The Heroic Story of Jewish Resistance and Survival during the Second World War* (Guilford: Lyons Press, 1998), xxiv; and Bauer, *The Death of the Shtetl*, 17. In the early 1920s, Romanian nationalist students similarly demanded that limits be placed on Jewish enrollment and forcibly expelled Jewish students from their dormitories. See Hanebrink, *Specter*, 65.

242 | The Pessimist's Son

18 Snyder, *Black Earth*, 69–70. See also Ringelblum, *Polish-Jewish Relations*, 16 & n. 7. See also ibid., 18 ("Exponents of racialist 'doctrine' [against Jews] . . . were hospitably entertained in the [Polish] colleges"). In Warsaw, Polish university students belonging to Endecja would go out in groups to attack Jews in the streets, and the police would arrest Jews who fought back. Harry Lenga and Scott Lenga, *The Watchmakers: A Story of Brotherhood, Survival, and Hope Amid the Holocaust* (New York: Citadel Press, 2022), 65. In fact, Jewish college students were attacked across Poland and a few were even killed. Heller, *Edge of Destruction*, 119–124.

19 Snyder, *Black Earth*, 47. *See also* Hanebrink, *Specter*, 60. At the same time, Endecja accused the Jews of trying to take over the world through capitalism. Rudnicki, "Economic Struggle or Antisemitism?," 398.

20 Mary Fulbrook, *Reckonings: Legacies of Nazi Persecution and the Quest for Justice* (Oxford: Oxford University Press, 2018), 487.

21 See Jonathan Huener, *Auschwitz, Poland, and the Politics of Commemoration, 1945–1979* (Athens, OH: Ohio University Press, 2003), 212–217.

Chapter 4

1 When negotiating the Molotov-Ribbentrop "nonaggression" pact before the war, the two countries secretly signed a codicil in which they agreed to invade Poland and divide the country between them. The USSR invaded Poland on September 17.

2 Timothy Snyder notes that "eastern Poland was generally a very poor area, though its society was far more prosperous than that of the Soviet Union to which it was to be leveled." Snyder, *Black Earth*, 128.

3 Batya Hakman, a survivor from Ludwipol (where my mother was in a ghetto, as discussed in Part 2), also notes songs of praise for Stalin coming from the local school after the Red Army invaded Ludwipol. "There Once Was a Shtetl Ludvipol," in *Sefer Ludvipol*, 167, trans. Yocheved Klausner for JewishGen, https://www.jewishgen.org/yizkor/ludvipol/lud163.html#Page167 (hereafter *Sefer Ludvipol*). Similarly, Yehuda Raber, also of Ludwipol, writes, "The Soviets came to us in 1939 and then all public, Zionist and cultural life was silenced. . . . With great pain we saw our dear school turn into a propaganda club for the theory of Communism. . . ." "In the Valley of Death," in *Ludvipol (Wolyn); Sefer zikaron le-kehilat Ludvipol (Slisht Gadol)* [In memory of the Jewish community, Ludwipol (Sosnove, Ukraine)], ed. N. Ayalon (Tel Aviv: Irgun yots'e Ludvipol be-Yiśra'el uva-tefutsot [Ludvipol Relief Society of Israel], 1965), 98 (Hebrew) (hereafter *Sefer Ludvipol*).

4 Timothy Snyder, *Bloodlands: Europe Between Hitler and Stalin* (New York: Basic Books, 2010), 128–129; and Dora Gold Shwarzstein, ed., *Remembering Rohatyn and Its Environs* (N.p.: Meyer Shwarzstein, 2019), 300. (Hereafter, I will refer to Shwarzstein's book as *Remembering Rohatyn.*)

5 The Katyn massacre was a series of mass executions of nearly 22,000 Polish military officers and intelligentsia carried out by the Soviet Union, specifically the NKVD (the Soviet secret police) in April and May 1940. Though the killings also occurred elsewhere, the massacre is named after the Katyn Forest, where some of the mass graves were first discovered by German forces. The Nazi government announced the discovery of the mass graves in April 1943—and, of course, blamed Jewish Bolsheviks. The Soviet Union blamed Germany and continued to do so until the Soviet Union acknowledged responsibility in 1990.

Endnotes | 243

6 Some men had left their families and fled east alone on the notion that the Germans would leave women and children unharmed. Unknown to my father then, his future wife and her family had fled to the Polish Ukraine from Radom, Poland. I discuss this in Part 2.

7 I am not providing Yossel's full name.

8 *Sefer Podhajce*, 376–377.

9 See Snyder, *Black Earth*, 137. For more on the Soviet occupation, see ibid., 120–128.

10 In the interwar period, the number of Jewish Communists was small. Jews were, however, overrepresented in the Communist Party because, other than the Polish Socialist Party, it was the only Polish political party to take a decisive and continuous stand against anti-semitism. That Polish antisemitism was "the main cause of overrepresentation of people of Jewish origin in the Communist Party of Poland was overlooked. . . ." Heller, *Edge of Destruction*, 254–255.

11 Gross, *Fear*, 176–177.

12 Levine, *Fugitives*, 14–16. These were not Karski's personal views. He smuggled microfilm from the Jewish resistance in the Warsaw Ghetto out of Poland and reported to the Polish, US, and British governments on the Nazi extermination of Jews in German-occupied Poland. Ibid. Israel made him an honorary citizen. For more on Karski, see Timothy Snyder, "Biographical Essay of Jan Karski," in Jan Karski, *Story of a Secret State: My Report to the World* (Washington: Georgetown University Press, 2013), xxv–xxxi.

13 Hanebrink, *Specter*, 4 and 10. In the interwar period, Germany had the "largest and most successful Communist Party outside the Soviet Union," from which it took orders. It was "above all the party of the unemployed, whose ranks had swollen in Germany since the mid-1920s. . . ." Benjamin Carter Hett, *The Death of Democracy: Hitler's Rise to Power and the Downfall of the Weimar Republic* (New York: St. Martin's Griffin, 2018), 12–13. The belief that Communism was a tool of the Jews was prevalent among the far right in Germany after the First World War. Evans, *Hitler's People*, 205.

14 *See* Snyder, *Black Earth*, 153. See also Saul Friedlander, *The Years of Extermination: Nazi Germany and the Jews, 1939–1945* (New York: HarperCollins, 2007), 239 ("[F]or Hitler the destruction of Soviet power could not but mean the destruction of Jewish power; the struggle was one and the same").

15 Snyder, *Black Earth*, 151 ("In 1941, in the doubly occupied lands [lands occupied by the Soviets and then the Germans], Germans directed the experience of Soviet occupation against Jewish neighbors") and 152. See also Anatoly Podolsky, "Collaboration in Ukraine during the Holocaust: Aspects of Historiography and Research," paper presented at the conference "The Holocaust in Ukraine: New Sources and Perspectives," Center for Advanced Holocaust Studies, United States Holocaust Memorial Museum, 2013, www.ushmm.org/m/pdfs/20130500-holocaust-in-ukraine.pdf, 190 (most Nazi propaganda in the Ukraine was directed at blaming the Jews for Bolshevism and the crimes of the NKVD; the regime and the authorities in Ukraine were labeled "Jewish" or "Jewish-Bolshevik." This was an "open call to kill Jews as representatives of Bolshevik ideology and practice, following which the liberation under the aegis of the Greater German Reich would take place"). Podolsky goes on to say, "The belief that Jews, qua Jews, participated in Bolshevik crimes became the principal motive for collaboration [with the Nazis], particularly in western Ukraine (Galicia)." Ibid. Historian Paul Hanebrink says the Nazis made the Judeo-Bolshevik myth "a crucial element in the origins of the Holocaust." *Specter*, 4 and 136. Snyder goes even further, calling the Judeo-Bolshevik myth "a major source of the Second World War. . . ." *Black Earth*, 22. The United States was not wholly uninfected by the myth. Henry Ford was spreading it in 1920, and some have argued that fear of the Jewish Bolshevik "menace" caused the United States and other countries in the 1920s to close their doors to Jewish immigration. See Veidlinger, *Civilized Europe*, 8–9.

In the 1930s, antisemites in the United States such as Father Charles Coughlin, whose political radio program was heard by tens of millions of Americans, also assailed "the Jews" as Communists.

16 Hanebrink, *Specter*, 58. Among the Jews that the Polish soldiers lined up and executed in Pinsk were women and children. Zimmerman, *Jozef Pilsudski*, 343 (citations omitted). Ignacy Paderewski, the Polish prime minister and famous pianist, defended the shooting of Jews in Pinsk as a "matter of pure Bolshevism." *Specter*, 79–80.

17 Zimmerman, *Jozef Pilsudski*, 347.

18 Hanebrink, *Specter*, 81–82. The weak League of Nations, however, failed to enforce the treaty and the "existence of the Treaty only angered the Poles. . . ." Heller, *Edge of Destruction*, 78.

19 Zimmerman, *Jozef Pilsudski*, 366–367.

20 Hanebrink, *Specter*, 27.

21 See, for example, Gross, *Fear*, chapter 6 ("Żydokomuna"); and ibid., 243 ("Rather than bringing Communism to Poland, as facile historiography of this period maintains, after a millennial presence in these lands, Jews as a matter of political expediency were finally driven out of Poland under the Communist regime").

22 See, for example, Antony Polonsky and Joanna B. Michlic, eds., *The Neighbors Respond: The Controversy over the Jedwabne Massacre in Poland* (Princeton, NJ: Princeton University Press, 2004); and Irena Grudzinska Gross, "The Eternal Jew Hatred," Project Syndicate, July 5, 2019, https://www.project-syndicate.org/onpoint/the-eternal-jew-hatred-by-irena-grudzinska-gross-2019-07. See also Jan Grabowski, *Hunt for the Jews: Betrayal and Murder in German-Occupied Poland* (Bloomington: Indiana University Press, 2013), 31 (in Poland, the "Jew-Communist" still persists in the literature, not only in popular accounts, or in the media, but in academic circles as well); Genevieve Zubrzycki, *Resurrecting the Jew: Nationalism, Philosemitism, and Poland's Jewish Revival* (Princeton, NJ: Princeton University Press, 2022), 6 (opinions such as, "The Jews had it coming after all, since they collaborated with the Soviets," are frequently heard in Polish newspaper editorials, academic panels, public roundtables and church sermons); and Hanebrink, *Specter*, 2 (in Poland and Romania, right-wing extremists blame "Jewish Communists" for promoting homosexuality and multiculturalism).

23 Gross, *Fear*, xiii.

24 A report from the Polish Catholic Church to the Polish Government in Exile from the Summer of 1942 stated:

> As far as the Jewish question is concerned, it must be seen as a singular dispensation of Divine Providence that the Germans have already made a good start, quite irrespective of all the wrongs they have done and continue to do to our country. . . . [T]he Jews wreak incalculable damage on our entire religious and national life. . . . [T]hey bear a major responsibility for houses of prostitution, for trafficking in white slaves, and for pornography. They make our people into inveterate drinkers. . . . They infiltrate immoral and un-Catholic ideas into our literature, arts and public opinion.

Yisrael Gutman and Shmuel Krakowski, *Unequal Victims: Poles and Jews during World War II* (New York: Holocaust Library, 1986), 53 (citation omitted). The statement bears a close similarity to a statement about "the Jews" made by Poland's primate, Cardinal Hlond, in early 1936. See Bauer, *The Death of the Shtetl*, 22–23; and Heller, *Edge of Destruction*, 112–113.

Endnotes | 245

25 *The Yad Vashem Encyclopedia of the Ghettos during the Holocaust*, vol. 2, ed. Guy Miron and Shlomit Shulhani (Jerusalem: Yad Vashem, 2009), 920; and Snyder, *Black Earth*, 269–271. Żegota had members from both the Polish Socialist Party and the antisemitic right. Snyder writes that the antisemitic rescuers of the right "tended to dislike Jews and wanted them out of Poland, but nonetheless regarded them as humans and capable of suffering." He adds: "In some cases, antisemites who rescued Jews thought of themselves as protecting Polish sovereignty by resisting German policy. . . ." *Black Earth*, 270. Snyder, however, seems to look for the positive when writing about Poles during the Shoah. By contrast, Friedlander notes that the right-wing Catholic movement quit Żegota in July 1943 because it "could not, at length, countenance the assistance given to the Jews" and that this was consistent with the positions taken by much of the Polish Catholic Church. Friedlander, *The Years of Extermination*, 877 (citation omitted). And Ringelblum argues that the activity of Żegota was limited by a "lack of funds and lack of help from the government [in exile]." *Polish-Jewish Relations*, 212–213.
26 Ringelblum, *Polish-Jewish Relations*, 235.
27 Jan Grabowski and Barbara Engelking, eds., *Night without End: The Fate of Jews in German-Occupied Poland* (Bloomington: Indiana University Press, 2022), xxxi. For example, many Poles known as *szmalzowniki* blackmailed Jews who were living outside of ghettos as "Aryans," and denounced Jews who couldn't meet their financial demands. Ringelblum, *Polish-Jewish Relations*, 42.
28 More subtly, historian Lukasz Krzyzanowski argues, "The German occupation broke Polish society into two almost completely disconnected groups: Polish Jews and Christian Poles. That distance that had existed between the before the war became an abyss." Lukasz Krzyzanowski, *Ghost Citizens: Jewish Return to a Postwar City*, trans. Madeline G. Levine (Cambridge, MA: Harvard University Press, 2020), 34.

Chapter 5

1 Avraham's full name was Adolph Abraham Milch. It is unclear whether Zysio left Podhajce or where he and his wife went if they did. They may have gone to Stanisławów (now Ivano-Frankivsk), which was a relatively big city about thirty-six miles south of Rohatyn. Zysio Lehrer perished in 1942 and his wife Regina (Fogel), perished at an unknown date during the Shoah.
2 As discussed later, my father's aunt Ethel fled to a town named Mikulince. According to the Yad Vashem testimony of Leon-Leib Milch (January 5, 1989), https://collections. yadvashem.org/en/documents/3559163, my father's first cousin, Ethel and Avraham too were worried about being deported to the USSR. Conditions in Mikulince do not appear to have been better than in Podhajce generally. According to Leon's testimony, my father's maternal grandfather and grandmother went with them to Mikulince but later returned to Podhajce.
3 Veidlinger, *Civilized Europe*, 58–61.
4 Vital, *A People Apart*, 717. Vital notes the true number of dead could easily be twice as high and refers to the "many tens of thousands of heavily wounded and mutilated men, women, children, and infants who survived and the untold thousands of women and girls of all ages who had been raped. . . ."
5 See ibid., 717–718.
6 Hanebrink, *Specter*, 49.
7 Ibid., 47–48.

246   The Pessimist's Son

8   Veidlinger, *Civilized Europe*, 153. It is oddly fitting that Proskuriv was renamed Khmelnytskyi in 1954.
9   Ibid., 263–264.
10   Vital, *A People Apart*, 718.
11   Hanebrink, *Specter*, 59–60.
12   Veidlinger, *Civilized Europe*, 10. The "normalization of mass murder in the previous conflict emboldened the Germans in their genocidal ambitions." Ibid., 356. Veidlinger provides graphic accounts of many major pogroms of this period in his book. See also Vital, *A People Apart*, 716–717 (describing the horrific pogrom in Proskuriv in February 1919).

Chapter 6

1   Snyder, *Black Earth*, 133.
2   Gilbert, *The Holocaust*, 205. Nazi Germany's allies—Slovakia, Romania, Hungary, Italy, Spain and Finland—also participated in Operation Barbarossa.
3   Ibid.
4   Wendy Lower, *The Ravine: A Family, a Photograph, a Holocaust Massacre Revealed* (Mariner Books, 2021), 39–40. See also Black, *History and Memory*, 81 ("From August [1941], the killing, which initially focused on male Jews, escalated to include large numbers of women and children, again in response to instructions from Himmler and Heydrich ..."). See also ibid., 80 ("in early July 1941, Ukrainian nationalists and the Waffen-SS massacred hundreds of Jewish men, women and children in Złoczów, north of Podhajce"). Himmler may have given an order after he toured the conquered territories in late July and early August 1941 and met with commanders. Veidlinger, *Civilized Europe*, 366. According to Bauer, the Einsatzgruppen primarily killed male intellectual Jews in the early days of Barbarossa. *The Death of the Shtetl*, 63.
5   Delphine Bechtel, "The 1941 Pogroms as Represented in Western Ukrainian Historiography and Memorial Culture," paper presented at the conference "The Holocaust in Ukraine: New Sources and Perspectives," Center for Advanced Holocaust Studies, United States Holocaust Memorial Museum, 2013, https://www.ushmm.org/m/pdfs/20130500-holocaust-in-ukraine.pdf, 2.
6   Friedlander, *The Years of Extermination*, 367.
7   Bechtel, "The 1941 Pogroms," 2.
8   See also Wendy Lower, "Anti-Jewish Violence in Western Ukraine, Summer 1941: Varied Histories and Explanations," paper presented at the conference "The Holocaust in Ukraine: New Sources and Perspectives," Center for Advanced Holocaust Studies, United States Holocaust Memorial Museum, 2013, www.ushmm.org/m/pdfs/20130500-holocaust-in-ukraine.pdf, 146 ("The Soviets pursued a policy of mass murder of Ukrainian prisoners during the retreat, and the Germans and their Ukrainian allies used this policy to organize antisemitic 'retaliation' campaigns. The fact that Jews, Russians, and Poles also were victims of NKVD atrocities in Galicia and Volhynia was conveniently suppressed"). In eastern Galicia (home to Podhajce and Rohatyn), the NKVD murdered at least 5,387 prisoners. Hanebrink, *Specter*, 134. (As discussed in Part 2, my mother's family fled to Volhynia when the war broke out.)
9   Edmund Kessler, *The Wartime Diary of Edmund Kessler, Lwow, Poland, 1942–1944*, ed., Regina Kessler (Boston, MA: Academic Studies Press, 2010), 36–40.
10   Bechtel, "The Holocaust in Ukraine," 2.
11   Gilbert, *The Holocaust*, 230–231.

Endnotes | 247

12 For example, in the Galician town of Buczacz, German soldiers led by Ukrainians broke into Jewish houses and raped young Jewish girls. Omer Bartov, *Anatomy of a Genocide: The Life and Death of a Town Called Buczacz* (New York: Simon & Schuster Paperbacks, 2018), 167. (The title is very similar to my father's, except my dad's book is *Anatomy of Genocide*—there is no article before "genocide.") Kessler writes: "On [Petliura Day], most of the Jewish intelligentsia were murdered. From the windows one could see horrible sights: Groups of teenagers armed with cudgels, knives, and shovels rampaged through the half-deserted streets, hitting indiscriminately any passerby who looked Jewish. Thousands of dwellings in the Jewish quarter were plundered and destroyed." Kessler, *Wartime Diary*, 48.

13 Bechtel, "The 1941 Pogroms," 2. Lower notes that the involvement of Ukrainians in anti-Jewish violence cut across class, educational, generational, and political lines. Thus, she writes, "one finds among the participants in the violence and destruction in Galicia fanatical nationalists, devout Christians, secular professionals, youth, elderly, civic leaders, and rural farmers." "Anti-Jewish Violence," 147. Reports the Germans sent back to Berlin "expressed approval of the enthusiasm that locals in Galicia and western Volhynia displayed in attacking Jews on their own initiative." Veidlinger, *Civilized Europe*, 361–362. Snyder says that a pogrom in Lwów on July 25 was organized by the Germans with the help of local Ukrainian nationalists, and that it provided political cover for Ukrainians who had been Communists or collaborators with the Soviet Union. *Black Earth*, 155–156.

14 Bechtel, "The 1941 Pogroms," 3.

15 Aryeh and Cyla Blech, "Rohatyn during the Occupation Years," in *Remembering Rohatyn*, 300.

16 Sylvia Lederman writes that "The Germans began move to move from house to house, hunting down whatever Jews they could find searching attics and dragging their victims away." Whoever opposed them was "beaten to the raw and pulled by the arms through the streets over the rough cobblestones. The gutters ran with blood." *Sheva's Promise: Chronicle of Escape from a Nazi Ghetto* (Syracuse, NY: Syracuse University Press, 2013), 4. She also notes that a Rabbi Liezer was dragged out of his house and thrown into the public latrines, where he sank in the sewage. Ibid. There are several other similar accounts in *Remembering Rohatyn*. While similar, they are not identical, and each is worth reading.

17 See Abraham Sterzer, "How Rohatyn Died," in *Remembering Rohatyn*, 440 ("The plan was to drive them all [into the synagogue] after taking away their valuables, to lock them in and then to set the building on fire"). See also Jack Glotzer, *I Survived the German Holocaust against All Odds: A Unique and Unforgettable Story of a Struggle for Life*, Rohatyn Jewish Heritage, 2022, https://rohatynjewishheritage.org/en/memoir/glotzer/e00/, 10 ("The plan was to set the synagogue on fire [with the Jewish people in it] after taking all their valuables"); Lederman, *Sheva's Promise* (distraught women "tried to petition the Germans to release the prisoners, but were told that the synagogue would be burned down—with all the Jews in it"). In a letter dated January 24, 1943, Genia Messing writes to her sister and brother, "On returning home, I learned that they [Ukrainian militiamen] will set the synagogue on fire with the people inside. Women collected gold, silver, money, and in this way we succeeded in rescuing 600 Jews from a terrible death. This was the Germans' greeting to us"), "Letter from Beyond the Grave," in *Remembering Rohatyn*, 504.

18 Bartov, *Erased*, 153. Tarnopol is about fifty-four miles east of Rohatyn. My uncle (by marriage) hailed from Tarnopol.

19 *Pinkas Hakehillot Polin* [Encyclopedia of Jewish communities, Poland], vol. 2 (Jerusalem: Yad Vashem, n.d.), 440–442, https://www.jewishgen.org/yizkor/pinkas_poland/pol2_00506.html#:~:text=%E2%80%9CRohatyn%E2%80%9D%20%2D%20

Encyclopedia%20of,MM.YYYYReturn; and Lower, "Anti-Jewish Violence," 145. *Pinkas Hakehillot Polin* notes that all synagogues in the town were burned down. There were, however, some positive acts by Ukrainian elites. In Buczacz, Ukrainian Greek Catholic priests strongly protested the destruction of Torah scrolls by hooligans and even offered to safeguard any scrolls brought by Jews to their monastery. Bartov, *Anatomy of a Genocide*, 168–169.

20 Snyder, *Bloodlands*, 195.

21 Ibid. According to Gilbert, at least 800 people were locked into the synagogue before it was set ablaze. *The Holocaust*, 214. According to a cousin of my mother, the Germans, aided by local Poles, killed about 1,200 more Jews that day. See Josefa Steinman, *Lost World* (2d ed., 2013, unpublished), 201–202.

22 *German Crimes in Poland*, vol. 1, 140–141. In his memoir, Henryk Schonker describes the Jewish reaction to the Germans' torching of the Great Synagogue in the town of Oświęcim (where the Auschwitz concentration camp would be built). Henryk Schonker, *The Touch of an Angel*, trans. Scotia Gilroy (Bloomington: Indiana University Press, 2020), 35–36. The Germans' "cultural aggression" included destroying synagogues and plowing over ancient Jewish cemeteries because the Nazis wished to obliterate any traces that Jews had ever lived in Europe. Alexander Kimel, *Anatomy of Genocide* (unpublished, available in the US Holocaust Memorial Museum), 123. Russia's pillaging of Ukrainian museums as an attack on Ukrainian identity is somewhat analogous, albeit less extreme. See Jefferey Gettleman and Oleksandra Mykolyshyn, "As Russians Steal Ukraine's Art, They Attack Its Identity, Too," *New York Times*, January 14, 2023.

23 The Gestapo were the secret police in Nazi Germany and German-occupied Europe.

24 Jan T. Gross, *Neighbors: The Destruction of the Jewish Community in Jedwabne, Poland* (Princeton, NJ: Princeton University Press, 2001).

25 Jan Tomasz Gross with Irena Grudzinska Gross, *Golden Harvest: Events at the Periphery of the Holocaust* (Oxford: Oxford University Press, 2012), 42.

26 Browning, *Ordinary Men*, 9–10; and Snyder, *Black Earth*, 106. They also participated fully in other aspects of the Nazi genocide against Jews.

27 Snyder, *Black Earth*, 41. See also Lower, *The Ravine*, 39 (German police "served as the foot soldiers of the Holocaust").

28 Snyder, *Black Earth*, 147–148; and Yohanan Petrovsky-Shtern and Antony Polonsky, eds., *Polin: Studies in Polish Jewry*, vol. 26: *Jews and Ukrainians* (Oxford: Littman, 2014), 43.

29 *Yad Vashem Encyclopedia of the Ghettos*, 560.

Chapter 7

1 My dad is referring to regular German soldiers, not SS or Gestapo men. That said, regular soldiers in the German army, the Wehrmacht, participated widely in the crimes of the Shoah. See generally The Hamburg Institute for Social Research, *The German Army and Genocide: Crimes Against War Prisoners, Jews, and Other Civilians in the East, 1939–1944* (New York: The New Press, 1999). See also Frank Trentmann, *Out of the Darkness: The Germans 1942–2022* (New York: Knopf, 2024), 23 ("war crimes were an integral feature of German warfare [during World War II], not an aberration"). Among other things, the Wehrmacht "systematically cooperated with the Einsatzgruppen and the police forces in the destruction of Jewish communities." Snyder, *Bloodlands*, 200–201. See also Trentmann, *Out of the Darkness*, 55 (the sheer scale of the killings in Shoah "was only possible because of more or less direct support from regular troops . . ."). For a chilling account of the Wehrmacht aiding an Einsatzkommando in the slaughter of young children, see Friedlander, *The Years*

of Extermination, 370–371. Even without the Einsatzgruppen or the SS, Wehrmacht soldiers took part in mass shootings of Jews in Soviet Belarus. Snyder, *Black Earth,* 189.

2   My dad doesn't say how the members of the Rohatyn Judenrat were chosen. It was done in various ways in different ghettos. See Isaiah Trunk, *Judenrat: The Jewish Councils in Eastern Europe under Nazi Occupation* (Lincoln: University of Nebraska Press, 1996), 21–26.

3   See Yehuda Bauer, *Rethinking the Holocaust* (New Haven, CT: Yale University Press, 2001), 170–171.

4   Tsvi Wohl, in "The Destruction of Rohatyn," in *Remembering Rohatyn,* 301–308, writes that the Jewish community had fourteen days to raise the money. He then says: "Fortunately, we were permitted to pay this ransom in old Polish money and in Russian rubles. The Judenrat assembled the demanded sum assiduously from the surrounding shtetls (towns) as well as from ours. The imposed ransom was paid on time." The Blechs write that the Germans threatened to "burn all the Jews of Rohatyn" if they didn't receive their ransom money. "Rohatyn during the Occupation Years," 300.

5   Snyder, *Black Earth,* 110. There also was a decree two months earlier by Heydrich, chief of the Security Police, that a Council of Jewish Elders be set up in every Jewish community. Trunk, *Judenrat,* 1–2. Germany divided the area of Poland it occupied prior to attacking the Soviet Union into two areas: the western part that it annexed and the so-called General Government, which it completely controlled, and which Frank governed. The General Government itself had four districts. Germany added Galicia as a fifth district after the Germans attacked the Soviet Union. (Note: I am using "Judenrats" instead of the German plural.)

6   Browning, "*Remembering Survival,* 34.

7   Trunk, *Judenrat,* 317. Avoiding membership in the councils was dangerous. Members who managed to escape (with or without their families) usually did so at the early stages of the occupation before ghettos were established. Ibid.

8   Fulbrook, *Reckonings,* 74.

9   Snyder, *Black Earth,* 113.

10   Leon Thorne, *It Will Yet Be Heard: A Polish Rabbi's Witness of the Shoah and Survival,* ed. Daniel Magilow and Emmanuel Thorne (New Brunswick, NJ: Rutgers University Press, 2019), 29.

11   Sending ghetto inmates to the Judenrat's jails for failure to deliver furs and other goods or money was also practiced in Częstochowa, Będzin, Chmielnik, and Radom (which was my mother's hometown). Trunk, *Judenrat,* 483.

12   *Sefer Ostrovtsah: le-zikaron ule-'edut* [Ostrowiec; A monument on the ruins of an annihilated Jewish community (Ostrowiec Świętokrzyski, Poland)], ed. Gershon Silberberg and Meir Shimon Geshuri (Tel Aviv: Society of Ostrovtser Jews in Israel, 1971), 47, trans. for JewishGen, https://www.jewishgen.org/yizkor/ostrowiec/oste046.html#Page47.

13   Thorne, *It Will Yet Be Heard,* 29.

14   Sima Weisman, "Baptists Save Jewish Refugees," in *Sefer Podhajce,* 373.

15   "Tarnopol," Holocaust Historical Society, https://www.holocausthistoricalsociety.org.uk/contents/ghettoss-z/tarnopol.html.

Chapter 8

1   It is ironic my dad chose this simile, because in Exodus the Jews were fleeing *from* slavery, whereas here they were heading *into* slavery.

2   Aryeh and Cyla Blech say 13,000 Jews were crowded into a small area and that it meant ten people to a room. "Rohatyn during the Occupation Years," 301. Jack Glotzer also says some houses had several families to a room. *I Survived,* 11.

250 | The Pessimist's Son

3 My dad doesn't provide a first name for Bloch. It could be the father of his friend, Willie (who is discussed later).

4 As noted earlier, Shiko (spelling from the Polish slightly changed) was my dad's nickname at the time. In the United States, only his father and Luba's family called him that. His Polish nickname was Olek.

5 The town is near Tarnopol, and many people in the town had connections to Podhajce. Nusia Schweizer Horowitz, writing in Mikulince's *yizkor* book, relates the horrors that befell the town. *Mikulince; sefer yizkor* [Mikulince Yizkor Book (Mikulintsy, Ukraine)], ed. Haim Preshel (N.p.: Organization of Mikulincean Survivors in Israel and the USA, 1985), 49–77, trans. for JewishGen, https://www.jewishgen.org/yizkor/Mikulintsy/mik049.html.

6 Awrumce is a diminuitive form of Abraham in Yiddish. His full name was Adolph Abraham Milch.

7 Dawidowicz, *War*, 277.

8 Snyder, *Black Earth*, 109.

9 Ringelblum, *Polish-Jewish Relations*, 60 n. 4.

10 *German Crimes in Poland*, vol. 1, 146 (citing the Nuremberg trials). Frank was Hitler's personal lawyer. Snyder, *Black Earth*, 6 and 145.

11 Fulbrook, *Reckonings*, 78 (quoting a girl's diary from the Łódż Ghetto). Also in the Łódż Ghetto, Josef Zelkowicz wrote: "The gravest [crime committed in the ghetto] was the transformation of people who had worked for decades to maintain their culture and ways, the fruits of millennia of effort, into predatory beasts after half a year of life under inhuman conditions." Michal Unger, ed., *In Those Terrible Days: Writings from the Lodz Ghetto*, trans. Naftali Greenwood (Jerusalem: Yad Vashem Publications, 2003), 131.

12 Dawidowicz, *War*, 271.

13 Lazar Kahan, "The Slaughter of the Jews of Chelm," *Yisker-bukh Chelm* [Commemoration Book Chełm (Poland)], ed. M. Bakalczuk (Johannesburg: Former Residents of Chelm, 1954), 505, trans. Gloria Berkenstat Freund for JewishGen, https://www.jewishgen.org/yizkor/chelm/Che505.html.

14 Yitzhak Weisbard, "The German Army Arrives," in *Sefer Radom*, 278. This was also done in some other places. *See* Browning, *Remembering Survival*, 32; and Ringelblum, *Polish-Jewish Relations*, 47–48.

15 In 1920, during the Polish-Soviet War, Polish solders had similarly publicly humiliated Jews in Kyiv in a show of dominance, cutting men's beards and forcing them to dance and sing for the crowds' amusement. Veidlinger, *Civilized Europe*, 290–291.

Chapter 9

1 Ringelblum writes that, in the Warsaw Ghetto, wealthier Jews paid bribes to the Judenrat to keep their sons out of work camps or bribed Jewish doctors to give their sons medical exemptions. *Notes from the Warsaw Ghetto*, 159. This apparently also happened in the town of Buczacz. Bartov, *Anatomy of a Genocide*, 171. I don't know whether this also happened in Rohatyn, though it seems likely. At this point, however, most of my grandparents' money probably was still in Podhajce. As my dad also mentions, his family were considered refugees in Rohatyn, which didn't help them in terms of assignments.

Endnotes | 251

2   Chaim Bronshtain, ed., *Skalat: Kovets zikaron lekehila sheharva bashoah* [Skalat: A memorial anthology for a community destroyed in the Holocaust (Ukraine)] (Tel Aviv: Bet ha-sefer 'al shem Ya'aḳov Ḳarol ye-'Irgun Yehude Sḳalaṭ be-Yiśra'el, 1971), trans. for JewishGen, https://www.jewishgen.org/yizkor/skalat/skalat.html (hereafter *Skalat Yizkor Book*).

3   Shlomo Teicher, "In the Borki Wielki Work Camp," in *Sefer Podhajce*, 376–377.

4   Thorne, *It Will Yet be Heard*, 48. Kessler, who was in Lwów in whose suburbs the Janowska camp was located, similarly writes that labor camps were "simply places for torturing, tormenting and finally executing Jews" and that few prisoners came back alive. Kessler, *Wartime Diary*, 58.

5   Thorne, *It Will Yet be Heard*, 50.

6   Wendy Lower, "Facilitating Genocide: Nazi Ghettoization Practices in Occupied Ukraine, 1941–42," in *Life in the Ghettos during the Holocaust*, ed. Eric J. Sterling (Syracuse, NY: Syracuse University Press, 2005), 133. Rasch had two doctorate degrees and accordingly was known as "Dr. Dr. Rasch." He was later indicted for war crimes, but the proceedings were discontinued for medical reasons. He died in custody, in 1948. Ibid.

7   *The German Crimes in Poland*, vol. 1, 136.

8   Browning, *Remembering Survival*, 133.

9   Fullbrook, *Reckonings*, 94.

10   Ibid., 96.

Chapter 10

1   Gilbert, *The Holocaust*, 383. There is also evidence that it was decided earlier.

2   William Samelson, "Piotrków Trybunalski: *My Ancestral Home*," in *Life in the Ghettos during the Holocaust*, ed. Eric J. Sterling (Syracuse, NY: Syracuse University Press, 2005), 11. Hitler and Himmler also created an *Einsatzgruppe* that was prepared to go to North Africa in 1942 in the event of a German military victory there in order to extend the Final Solution to include the approximately one million Jews living in North Africa and the Middle East. Jeffrey Herf, "Nazi Antisemitism & Islamist Hate," *Tablet Magazine*, July 6, 2022.

3   *Aktion* in German, *akcja* in Polish. In actions, the Germans, often aided by Jewish police and Ukrainians, would round up Jews for mass killing, which would be carried out either in or around the ghettos or by shipping the captives to death camps.

4   This is according to the Blechs, "Rohatyn during the Occupation Years," 302. Sterzer says that the elderly, the sick, and the old were assembled in the market square with others, and then taken to the mass grave to be murdered. "How Rohatyn Died," 444. Glotzer says that the Germans lined some people up outside their homes—including "little children, old people and pregnant women"—and shot them. *I Survived*, 12.

5   Wohl, "The Destruction of Rohatyn," in *Remembering Rohatyn*, 309.

6   *Remembering Rohatyn*, 288.

7   Sterzer, "How Rohatyn Died," 444.

8   *Bursztyn* means "amber" in Polish.

Chapter 11

1 My father used the name "Neil," and I'm not sure what name he had to translate to get to it, so I am using the name Naftali (which is also my Hebrew name and that of my maternal grandfather).

2 Based on *yizkor* books and my father's *Anatomy of Genocide*, it seems that Jews often referred to the Nazis in Yiddish as *de rotschim* ("the killers" or "the murderers").

Chapter 12

1 Rachel and Moshe NasHofer, "The Community of Rohatyn Destroyed," *Remembering Rohatyn*, 287.

2 Normally, there would be *Kol Nidre* services the eve of Yom Kippur, but my father doesn't say anything about them, probably because of events the next day. As noted earlier, a family named Orenstein were neighbors of my father in Podhajce. I didn't find any Orensteins listed as martyrs in *Remembering Rohatyn*. While the martyrologies in *yizkor* books generally aren't complete, it is quite possible that my father incorrectly recalled the name of the family in Rohatyn in whose home the services were held.

3 This is consistent with Snyder's statement, with respect to German ghetto actions, that "[t]he Germans were aiming for daily quotas to fill trains and would sometimes pass on quotas to the Jewish police who were responsible (at the risk of their own positions and thus lives) for filling them." *Bloodlands*, 260.

4 *Remembering Rohatyn*, 304.

5 Snyder, *Bloodlands*, 260. About 700–1000 Jews were kept alive at any one time to do work like cleaning the freight cars, sorting confiscated property, emptying the gas chambers and so on. "Belzec," *Odot hashoah*, Yad Vashem, https://www.yadvashem.org/yv/pdf-drupal/de/education/Belzec.pdf.

6 Operation Reinhard is often described as the plan to murder every Jew in the General Government, but the Germans also planned the mass murder of Jews in the western part of Poland annexed by Germany (including Łódź) and Jews outside of Poland. See, for example, Browning, *Ordinary Men*, 50 ("Preparations for gassing began at three locations in the fall of 1941: Auschwitz/Brikenau near Katowice in Silesia and Chełmno near Łódź in the Warthegau, both in the incorporated territories, and Bełżec in Globocnik's Lublin district").

7 Fulbrook, *Reckonings*, 114–115 (citations omitted).

8 Browning cites the lower number. *Ordinary Men*, 52. Fulbrook cites the figure of about half a million. Some have put the number as high as 650,000.

9 Snyder, *Bloodlands*, 254–256. Browning says that the so-called Trawnikis were recruited Ukrainians, Lithuanians and Latvians who were screened "on the basis of their anti-Communist (and hence almost invariably anti-Semitic) sentiments. . . ." Browning, *Ordinary Men*, 52. Snyder focuses more on demoralized Soviet prisoners of war having been willing to do anything to get out of Nazi "starvation camps." *Black Earth*, 200. Most camp guards, however, were not reluctant enforcers of German rules. Rather, "those manning the camps were often extremely violent thugs and there were no restraints on their cruelty and arbitrariness." Black, *History and Memory*, 124.

10 *Remembering Rohatyn*, 288.

11 See, for example, Bauer, *Rethinking the Holocaust*, 144. ("Collaborating Jewish police were hated and despised—the few exceptions were admired and noted—and this finds its echo in the many thousands of testimonies of survivors.")

12 Browning, *Remembering Survival*, 236–237. By coincidence, Harry Lenga speaks of Jeremiah Wilczek, his stepmother's brother (his "Uncle Yirmia"), who was the chief of the Jewish police in Starachowice and hated by the Jewish prisoners, including Lenga. Lenga and Lenga, *The Watchmakers*, 182–183 and 194. Wilczek and his son were strangled to death by rivals from Lublin *en route* from Starachowice to Auschwitz. Ibid., 388–389.

Chapter 13

1 See Sterzer, "How Rohatyn Died," 443. There were two times that surviving Jews from the surrounding towns arrived in Rohatyn. The first one occurred after the March action, as my father says. The second was after the Yom Kippur actions. See, for example, Yaakov Feldman, *Remembering Rohatyn*, 353–354; and Leon Schreier, "Zurow and Bukaczowce," in *Remembering Rohatyn*, 366.

2 In information he provided to Yad Vashem, my father refers to Mechel as Mottel, and his last name is Jupiter.

3 Sterzer, "How Rohatyn Died," 450. Jack Glotzer writes that over 1,000 Jews were sent to Bełżec.

4 Thorne, *It Will Yet Be Heard*, 154–155.

5 Ibid., 157.

6 Of course, the Nazis carried out severe reprisals for resistance. For example, on the eve of Rosh Hashanah 1942, Meir Berliner, an Argentinian Jew in Treblinka, fatally stabbed a German guard. Ukrainian guards shot dozens of people, and the Germans shot an additional 160 people as punishment. Yitzhak Arad, *The Operation Reinhard Death Camps: Belzec, Sobibor, Treblinka* (Bloomington: Indiana University Press, 2018), 273.

Chapter 14

1 It isn't indicated how advanced Ania's pregnancy was at this point. Abortions were apparently somewhat common in ghettos. In his Warsaw chronicle, Ringelblum wrote that news from the Łódź Ghetto was that "Łódź Jews had been prohibited from marrying and having children" and that "women pregnant up to three months had to have an abortion." Ringelblum, *Notes from the Warsaw Ghetto*, 230. In addition, David Patterson quotes Vilna (Vilnius) Ghetto diarist Herman Kruk, writing on February 5, 1942, "Today the Gestapo summoned two members of the Judenrat and notified them: No more Jewish children are to be born. The order came from Berlin." In July 1942, Kovno (Kaunas) Ghetto diarist Avraham Tory wrote, "From September on, giving birth is strictly forbidden. Pregnant women will be put to death." David Patterson, "Death and Ghetto Death," in *Life in the Ghettos during the Holocaust*, ed. Eric J. Sterling (Syracuse, NY: Syracuse University Press, 2005), 164 (citations omitted). See also Lower, *The Ravine*, 115 (several Nazi decrees forbade pregnancies and births in the ghettos of Lithuania).

2 Soviet forces launched a counteroffensive against the Germans arrayed at Stalingrad in mid-November 1942. They quickly encircled an entire German army, more than 220,000 soldiers. In February 1943, after months of fierce fighting and heavy casualties, the surviv-

254 | The Pessimist's Son

ing German forces—only about 91,000 soldiers—surrendered. The Nazi response to the loss at Stalingrad was to call publicly for the extermination of the Jews (Trentmann, *Out of the Darkness*, 38), though, of course, by then the Germans had already exterminated most of the Jews in Europe.

3   A *shako* is a tall, cylindrical military cap, usually with a visor, and sometimes tapered at the top. It is usually adorned with an ornamental plate or badge on the front, metallic or otherwise; and often has a feather, plume or pompom attached at the top.

4   Kolomyja is south of Rohatyn and the rail lines from there to Bełżec passed very close to Rohatyn. See Gilbert, *The Holocaust*, 413.

5   In Ukrainian, as well as in Polish and Russian, the name derives from the word "love." Of course, it also was the name of my father's sister.

Chapter 16

1   *Sefer Podhajce* lists at least eight Goralnicks (sometimes transliterated as "Goralnick") who perished. See *Sefer Podhajce*, 459. It is "at least" eight because some of the entries refer, for example, to "Hirsh and his family." Given that the vast majority of Jews in Podhajce, as in other towns, died at the hands of, or because of, the Nazis, it is probable that most if not all my father's family friends perished.

2   For reasons that will become apparent, I am not using his name or real first initial.

3   Schonker also refers to this. Schonker, *The Touch of an Angel*, 207.

4   *Stolar* means "carpenter" in Yiddish.

5   According to Abraham Sterzer, a physician, pharmacists on the Aryan side of town "refused to sell the Jews any medicines." "How Rohatyn Died," 442.

6   Ibid.; and Lederman, *Sheva's Promise*, 38.

7   Gilbert, *The Holocaust*, 609.

8   Yochanan Fein, *Boy with a Violin: A Story of Survival* (Bloomington: Indiana University Press, 2022), 27; and Meri-Jane Rochelson, *Eli's Story: A Twentieth-Century Jewish Life* (Detroit, MI: Wayne State University Press, 2018), 137.

9   Thorne, *It Will Yet Be Heard*, 110–111.

10   "The Evacuation of the Jewish Hospital, Orphanage and Old-Peoples' Home," in *Sefer Radom*, 311.

11   Bartov, *Anatomy of a Genocide*, 176–177.

12   Schonker, *The Touch of an Angel*, 107; and *Yad Vashem Encyclopedia of the Ghettos*, 927. It isn't clear whether any of the doctors and nurses were non-Jews.

13   *Remembering Rohatyn*, 446.

14   See, for example, Bartov, *Anatomy of a Genocide*, 177.

15   See *Bloodlands*, 253 and 263. See also Browning, *Remembering Survival*, 84–87 ("The systematic killing of the elderly, the handicapped, and those who did not follow orders was clearly standard operating procedure for the ghetto-clearers"; and noting that some families were forced to decide whether to abandon aged and infirm family members in their homes because they would not be able to make it to the market square within the fifteen minutes the Nazis allotted or to stay with those family members and be shot together).

16   Browning, *Remembering Survival*, 126–127.

17   Ibid., 132.

18   "The Janowska Concentration Camp: What We Know and Don't Know," Ukrainian Jewish Encounter, July 31, 2020, https://ukrainianjewishencounter.org/en/the-janowska-con-

centration-camp-what-we-know-and-dont-know/. In addition, some Jewish citizens of foreign enemy states were prisoners in the Vittel internment camp in occupied France, near the German border, living under conditions far better than those of other German camps. Himmler agreed that Jews with strong ties to enemy states could be exempt from the "Final Solution" and traded as hostages for German citizens interned in those countries. Some Jewish internees were exchanged with the United States and the United Kingdom in 1944, but most of the internees were deported to Auschwitz that year and murdered.

19 Schonker, *The Touch of an Angel*, 212–214.

20 See, for example, Snyder, *Black Earth*, 219 ("American and British Jews were safe, not just in their home countries but everywhere. The Germans did not contemplate murdering Jews who held American and British passports, and, with few exceptions, did not do so"). In France, about three-quarters of French Jews survived, whereas Jewish residents of France who lacked citizenship there, like my cousin Henri (born Henryk) Goldstein, were deported to Auschwitz. His story is discussed in Part 2.

Chapter 18

1 When the final ghetto liquidation began, Warsaw Ghetto inhabitants managed to hold off the far-superior German forces for nearly four weeks—from April 19 to May 16, 1943. They put up massive resistance, killing about sixteen Germans and causing about eighty-five injuries. *Yad Vashem Encyclopedia of the Ghettos*, 920. See also Fulbrook, *Reckonings*, 168.

2 By the end of the war, "not a single one of the approximately three hundred Jewish ghettos established by the Nazis [had] escaped liquidation." Gutman and Krakowski, *Unequal Victims*, 350; and Friedlander, *The Years of Extermination*, 858. There were, however, several rebellions that are less known than that of the Warsaw Ghetto. These too tended to take place when it became clear the ghettos were going to be liquidated. For example, during the final major deportation push by the Nazis in August 1943, the Jewish Combat Organization (*Żydowska Organizacja Bojowa* or *ZOB*) in the Sosnowiec and nearby Będzin Ghettos staged an uprising. "Sosnowiec," Holocaust Historical Society, https://www.holocausthistoricalsociety.org.uk/contents/ghettoss-z/sosnowice.html. See also Mary Fulbrook, *A Small Town Near Auschwitz: Ordinary Nazis and the Holocaust* (Oxford: Oxford University Press, 2012), 6. (Sosnowiec happens to have been the home-town of Vladek Spiegelman, the survivor whose story is told in his son Art Spiegelman's Holocaust classic, *Maus*.) In Białystok, the underground staged an uprising just before the final destruction of the ghetto in September 1943. "Jewish Uprisings in Ghetto and Camps, 1941–44," *Holocaust Encyclopedia*, https://encyclopedia.ushmm.org/content/en/article/jewish-uprisings-in-ghettos-and-camps-1941-44. Before this, somewhat akin to the burning of furs discussed in Chapter 7, some Jews in the Białystok Ghetto had also sabotaged German industrial establishments there, such that many "Białystok boots" made by ghetto labor and used by German soldiers fell apart during the winter offensive against the Soviet Union. Daniel Feierstein, "The Jewish Resistance Movements in the Ghettos of Eastern Europe," trans. Stephen A. Sadow, in *Life in the Ghettos during the Holocaust*, ed. Eric J. Sterling (Syracuse, NY: Syracuse University Press, 2005), 226.

   Northeast of Rohatyn, in Brody, Jews resisting deportation killed four Ukrainians and several Germans. Several hundred people managed to escape the cattle cars, though many were killed attempting to do so. Gilbert, *The Holocaust*, 803. In Turzysk, in the Volhynia region of the Ukraine, according to one account, a young man named Berish

Segal grabbed a German's submachine gun and wounded several policemen before he was fatally shot. *Yad Vashem Encyclopedia of the Ghettos*, 853. In another Volhynian ghetto, Sarny, a small number of Jews escaped being massacred when their ghettos were liquidated, in late August 1942, and fled to the forests. Nearly all the local Poles and Ukrainians participated in killing many of the escapees in Jew hunts, but some were not caught, and some of them joined a partisan group led by an NKVD officer. Yehuda Bauer, "Sarny and Rokitno in the Holocaust: A Case Study of Two Townships in Wolyn (Volhynia)," in *The Shtetl: New Evaluations*, ed. Steven T. Katz (New York: NYU Press, 2007), 268–269. But Jewish escapees from the nearby shtetl of Rokitno who made it to three Polish villages received a friendlier welcome, especially by the local Catholic priest and a local schoolteacher. Ibid., 272–273. In these villages, Polish peasants helped escaping Jews (ibid.), which was extraordinary.

3   The last action was something the Germans actually did to Jews.

4   My dad doesn't say where the money came from, though it is possible that some of it came from his father because my father says in this video testimony that my grandfather contributed money to resistance groups.

5   Levine, *Fugitives of the Forest*, xxxv–xxxvi, 149, and 183–185.

6   In "Partisans, Heroes, and Martyrs," in *Sefer Radom*, L. Richtman cites antisemitism of the Polish *Armia Krajowa* (Home Army) as one reason it was hard for Jews to engage in effective partisan activity. In March 1943, members of the Home Army abruptly turned on seventeen young Jewish men who had escaped from the Ostrowiec Ghetto and whom they had been training as fighters, killing twelve and injuring the rest. *Yad Vashem Encyclopedia of the Ghettos*, 561. Snyder acknowledges that the Home Army sometimes attacked Jewish partisan groups and sometimes robbed and killed Jews (it cited the Judeo-Bolshevik myth to justify its conduct), but argues the Home Army was not generally antisemitic. He notes that the Home Army had a Jewish section that supplied information to foreign media beginning in early 1942 and that it issued death sentences to some Poles who were blackmailing Jews. Snyder, *Black Earth*, 275–276. Ringelblum, however, says that the Jewish section was confined to collecting documentary material from the Warsaw Ghetto in mid-1942 and that it was only at the end of 1942 that it "began to concern itself with providing some aid to the Jews. . . ." Ringelblum, *Polish-Jewish Relations*, 163. The Home Army also supplied some arms to the Warsaw Ghetto rebels, Fulbrook, *Reckonings*, 168, but enabling ghetto residents to fight Nazis was not inconsistent with antisemitism because it was in the Home Army's interest (and the Jewish resisters were unlikely to survive). In addition, radical nationalists within the Home Army consistently described the Warsaw Ghetto as a Communist base and later welcomed its destruction. Hanebrink, *Specter*, 155. The general perception of the Home Army among Jewish survivors is more aligned with Richtman's views than Snyder's more nuanced understanding. See, for example, Dina Porat, *Nakam: The Holocaust Survivors Who Sought Full-Scale Revenge* (Stanford: Stanford University Press, 2023), 83.

7   Bauer, *Rethinking the Holocaust*, 138.

8   Shmuel Gutman, "The Death of a Brave Partisan," in *Sefer Radom*.

9   Levine, *Fugitives*, 184. See also Bauer, *The Death of the Shtetl*, 130. The precise timing is unclear to me because the labor camp was liquidated sometime in June 1943.

10 Baruch Amitz, "With the Kovpak Men to the Carpathian Mountains," in *Skalat Yizkor Book*, 90, https://www.jewishgen.org/yizkor/skalat/ska089.html#Page90.

11 See Blechs, "Rohatyn during the Occupation Years," 304; and Gilbert, *The Holocaust*, 802.

Chapter 19

1. In his testimony, my father suggested that Luba thought there would be more time before the ghetto was liquidated and that she belonged to a resistance group, which didn't want to abandon the ghetto before it was necessary so as not to panic or dishearten other Jews.

2. *Tefillin* are a set of small black leather boxes with leather straps containing scrolls of parchment inscribed with verses from the Torah. *Tefillin* are traditionally worn by Jewish men during weekday morning prayers. I don't know how often my father used them in Podhajce or Rohatyn. Given his anger at God, I suspect he didn't use them often in Rohatyn.

3. Prof. Daniel Feierstein notes this was a general issue: "In forming a resistance strategy, the issue arose concerning whether to send contingents to the forests to support the partisan brigades in guerrilla warfare against the Nazis or to remain in the ghetto. [E]migrating to the forests would signify the abandonment of the greater part of the ghetto population to its passive extermination." Feierstein, "The Jewish Resistance Movements," 251.

4. It makes sense that my grandfather, a well-known pessimist, would have had this view of the resistance. My father nowhere says why his father gave some money to that cause. Perhaps he was pressured to do so or maybe he earlier thought it was worth a try.

5. I am not using the person's name or real first initial. Given that it is unclear whether V. betrayed the group, it seems unfair to his memory to name him and suggest that he may have done so.

6. The Germans discovered the Jewish police's resistance plans. On June 6, all the Jewish police were gathered together and shot. Their bodies were mutilated and hanged in public as a warning. See the Blechs, "Rohatyn during the Occupation Years," 305; and Gilbert, *The Holocaust*, 802.

7. "The Shoah in Rohatyn," Rohatyn Jewish Heritage, https://rohatynjewishheritage.org/en/history/timeline-shoah/.

8. *Remembering Rohatyn*, 445.

9. The latter was consistent with common Nazi protocol not to "waste . . . bullets on Jewish children. They were instead to be crushed by the weight of their kin and suffocated in blood and the soil heaped over the bodies." Lower, *The Ravine*, 8–9.

10. *Pinkas Hakehillot Polin*, vol. 2. My dad mentions the Sevastopol "mega bunker" in his autobiographical notes in in *Life in the Ghettos during the Holocaust*, ed. Eric J. Sterling (Syracuse, NY: Syracuse University Press, 2005).

11. "Belzec," *Holocaust Encyclopedia*, https://encyclopedia.ushmm.org/content/en/article/belzec.

12. Ibid. For more on this, see Gross with Grudzinska Gross, *Golden Harvest*.

13. See Fulbrook, *Reckonings*, 117.

14. Ibid., 491.

Chapter 20

1. The Battles of the Isonzo were a series of twelve battles between the Austro-Hungarian and Italian armies in World War I, mostly on the territory of present-day Slovenia and the remainder in Italy, along the Isonzo River on the eastern sector of the Italian Front between June 1915 and November 1917.

2 Throughout the war, Nazi propaganda referred to the sub-human, Jewish Bolshevik "Asiatic" threat. See Hanebrink, *Specter*, 146 and 147. It specifically did so regarding Katyn in falsely blaming "Jewish Bolshevik murderers" for having executed the captured Poles. Ibid., 153–154.

3 Generals Georgy Zhukov, Ivan Konev, and Konstantin Rokossovsky were top Soviet military commanders.

4 Snyder, *Black Earth*, 316–318.

5 See Gross and Grudzinska Gross, *Golden Harvest*, 98; and Grabowski, *Hunt for the Jews*, 289.

6 Steinman, *Lost World*, 226.

7 Gross and Grudzinska Gross, *Golden Harvest*, 97–98. See also Bender, *Enemy Land*, 253–254 ("Polish police who discovered Polish protectors of Jews, beat them, destroyed their property, murdered the Jews in the protectors' yards, and ordered the Polish benefactors to bury them—often without bothering to report this to the Germans.").

8 Grabowski, *Hunt for the Jews*, 153. In Part 3 of Kessler's *Wartime Diary*, Kazimierz Kalwinski, a Pole whose family sheltered Kessler and other Jews from Lwów on their farm, provides his perspective. He recounts that when thirty-four Jews were discovered by a Ukrainian policeman on a neighboring farm in December 1943, the Germans hanged them along with the two Polish sons of that farm's owner. Kessler, *Wartime Diary*, 114.

9 Grabowski, *Hunt for the Jews*, 138.

10 Ibid., 163.

11 See Snyder, *Bloodlands*, 25–27.

12 Ibid., 78–87.

13 Ibid., 86.

14 Glotzer, *I Survived*, 23–26.

15 Podolsky, "The Holocaust in Ukraine," 194.

16 Petrovsky-Shtern and Polonsky, *Polin: Studies in Polish Jewry*, vol. 26: *Jews and Ukrainians*, 46.

17 Friedlander, *The Years of Extermination*, 365. This extremely dark side of Ukrainian nationalism is often forgotten or not well known today. See, for example, "Canada's House Speaker Anthony Rota Sorry for Honoring Nazi Veteran," *Washington Post*, September 25, 2023. (In the article, the speaker apologizes for honoring a Ukrainian member of the Waffen-SS, who was declared a "Canadian hero" and received a standing ovation in parliament for having fought for Ukrainian independence and supporting Ukraine today.)

18 Petrovsky-Shtern and Polonsky, *Polin: Studies in Polish Jewry*, vol. 26: *Jews and Ukrainians*, 50. Since Ukraine gained independence from the Soviet Union in 1991, streets have been named after Bandera and monuments erected to him in western Ukraine. In Drohobych (Drohobycz, in Polish), a memorial to Bandera stands in the middle of a park that extends over the perimeter of the former ghetto, which is left unmarked. Bechtel, "The 1941 Pogroms," 6–7. According to Bechtel, Bandera has "long been the object of a particular cult in Galicia, constituting a provocation for Ukraine's central and eastern provinces, where the anniversary of the Great Patriotic War and the engagement of the Soviet partisans against Nazi Germany still symbolizes local heroism, and where the Banderivtsi, Bandera's partisans, are considered war criminals" (ibid.). Bereżany (Brzeżany, in Polish) similarly erected a monument with a bust of Bandera to celebrate the town's 630th anniversary. Bartov, *Erased*, 162. Bartov also notes that popular Jewish opinion views a direct line running from Khmelnytskyi to Petliura to Bandera. *Borderlands*, 37. Indeed, Jews sometimes use the same term to refer to both the Khmelnytskyi massacres and the Shoah—*khurboynes*

Endnotes | 259

(catastrophes), and the first modern memorial books emerged as a response to Petliura-era pogroms. See Kugelmass and Boyarin, *From a Ruined Garden*, 18.
19 Hanebrink, *Specter*, 143–144.
20 Bauer, *The Death of the Shtetl*, 99.

Chapter 21

1   This was quite a different greeting from the one Yochanan Fein received when he was liberated near Kaunas, Lithuania. A Russian soldier pulled Fein out of a pit he had been hiding in and exclaimed, "My brother, you are free!" Fein, *Boy with a Violin*, 145. My father doesn't provide a date for his liberation, but nearby Tarnopol was liberated by the Red Army on April 13, 1944, so it must have been not long after that. For video on the liberation of Tarnopol, see "The Fall of Tarnopol (1944)," British Pathé, YouTube, April 13, 2024, https://www.youtube.com/watch?v=RtRWKAtNwYU.

Chapter 22

1   Snyder makes the point repeatedly that the Jews of eastern Poland—where my father was born and where my mother and her family fled to—suffered to an especially great degree. For example, he writes:

> [T]he impact of multiple continuous occupation was most dramatic in the lands that Hitler conceded to Stalin in the secret protocol to the nonaggression pact of 1939, then took from him in the first days of the invasion of 1941, then lost to him again in 1944. Before the Second World War, these lands were: independent Estonia, Lativia, Lithuania, and eastern Poland. . . . The region was the heartland of Jewish settlement in Europe, and its Jews were trapped when the Germans invaded the newly extended Soviet Union in 1941. Almost all of the Jews native to the region were killed.

Bloodlands, 393. Snyder puts the number of Jews killed in this region, in which I would count my paternal grandmother, at 1.6 million.

2   As mentioned, Jack Glotzer writes about surviving in the forests of Łopuszna. See Glotzer, *I Survived*, 26–27.

3   Many Jewish families placed their children with convents, orphanages, and foster families during the war in an effort to save them. After the war, surviving families often engaged in difficult, protracted searches to find their children. Often the children didn't remember their biological parents when they were reunited and were reluctant to go with them. "Hidden Children: Quest for Family," *Holocaust Encyclopedia*, https://encyclopedia. ushmm.org/content/en/article/hidden-children-quest-for-family. When a project to place a few hundred Jewish children with convents was discussed during the war, according to Ringelblum, some Orthodox Jews protested that the children would be lost to Judaism and that future generations would say that any such children should have been taught *Kiddush Hashem* (i.e., to die as martyrs). *Polish-Jewish Relations*, 150–151.

4   Glotzer also discusses his being drafted into the Red Army, in July 1944. He suggests that Jewish survivors were able to legally decline serving but indicates that many decided

The Pessimist's Son

to join the army because they wanted revenge for "what the German animals did to our people." *I Survived*, 33. Yehuda Raber, a survivor from Ludwipol, however, had a different experience, telling how a young Jewish man who tried to dodge the draft was shot dead by the Soviets. *Sefer Ludvipol*, 148–149 (Hebrew). It isn't clear from the Hebrew character *bet or vet* whether Yehuda's last name was Raver or Raber. The transliterations into English are inconsistent. I will use "Raver" unless using a direct quote that employs a "b."

5   I don't know how Roncia was killed. Ethel's husband, Abraham, was murdered in Bełżec. My father's first cousins, Leon and Barry Milch, survived the war and eventually emigrated to Australia, where they were raised by their uncle.

6   *Sefer Ludvipol*, 150 (Hebrew).

7   Yehuda Grussgott, "Meir Mass, the Hero of Our Town," in *Sefer Podhjace*, 217.

8   Nachum Pushteig, "The Destruction of our City," in *Sefer Podhajce*, 336.

9   See, for example, Henia Schourz, "Four Years of War and Destruction," in *Sefer Podhajce*, 302 (the Nazis' murder of the Judenrat "was the payment for their faithful service of providing silver, gold, money, precious stones and anything that the murderous Nazis desired . . . as well for providing people for the aktions against the Jews in Podhajce and in other places . . ."); Yehoshua Weiss, "The Annihilation: A Letter from Hell," ibid., 367 ("The Judenrat was an institution that had a bloodthirsty spirit for Jewish blood. It went way beyond the bounds. . . . It has Jewish tears and indescribable agony on its conscience"); and Weisman, "Baptists Save Jewish Refugees," 373 (the Judenrat officials "often behaved immorally and filled their own pocket with money. "[They] religiously carri[ed] out all orders of the authorities . . ."). Compare, for example, Sterzer:

> To this very day I cannot understand the Jews who were members of the Judenrat and were active in it. They put themselves at the disposal of the Germans. I have the impression that they didn't grasp the Hilterite aims. Perhaps they hoped that the Judenrat members and their families would escape danger and would not have to pay fines or go to the concentration camps. . . . But I also marveled at the iron nerves of the Judenrat members. To sit and wait for the arrival of the Gestapo, or to be called to Gestapo headquarters without knowing for what purpose or aim, was not a small display of courage.

"How Rohatyn Died," 442.

10   Shoshana Haber, "The Campaign of Annihilation and Destruction in Podhajce," in *Sefer Podhajce*, 353.

11   Pushteig, "The Destruction of Our City," 336.

12   Leah Feldberg, "Podhajce under German Occupation," in *Sefer Podhajce*, 379.

13   Haber, "The Campaign of Annihilation," 354.

14   See, for example, Feldberg, "Podhajce under German Occupation,"379.

15   Pushteig, "The Destruction of Our City," 336–337.

16   Genia Shourz, "Four Years of War and Destruction," in *Sefer Podhajce*, 369. (Genia appears to have been the daughter of Henia Shourz, who wrote a separate entry for *Sefer Podhajce*.)

17   Pushteig, "The Destruction of Our City," 338.

18   *Sefer Podhajce*, 328.

19   Haber, "The Campaign of Annihilation," 354. Similarly, many Jews in the death camps including Bełżec, Treblinka, and Sobibór, resisted in the one small way they could: by throwing their valuables like watches into latrines to keep them out of Nazi hands. Gross and Grudzinska Gross, *Golden Harvest*, 25–26.

Endnotes | 261

20 Shourz, "A Path Full of Obstacles," 297.

21 Leon Thorne writes of a "suicide epidemic" in the Drohobycz Ghetto in December 1942. He tells the horrific story of discovering a woman and her eleven-year-old son dead, and the couple who shared a room with the family wailing. When he tried to comfort them, the woman exclaims, "They used the cyanide we bought for ourselves! It was *our* poison!" *It Will Yet Be Heard*, 105.

22 "Podhajce," in *Pinkas Hakehillot Polin* [Encyclopedia of Jewish communities, Poland], https://www.jewishgen.org/yizkor/pinkas_poland/pol2_00506.html#:~:text=%E2%80%9CRohatyn%E2%80%9D%20%2D%20Encyclopedia%20of,MM.YYYYReturn. Henia Schourz also writes about Silber, whom she calls the "living spirit behind the idea of organizing resistance activity, of preparing defense cells in the forests with food supplies and kitchens with the help of the Subotniks (Christians who observed the Sabbat on Saturday). . . ." *Sefer Podhajce*, 297.

23 "Podhajce."

24 *Sefer Podhajce*, 467, lists among those killed by the Nazis: Moshe [Moses] Ornshtein, his wife Heiche, their daughter Sara, and their sons Yehoshua and David. "Ornshtein" is a transliteration of the Polish "Ornsztajn." In a table (*Sefer Podhajce*, 507) labeled "Podhajce Yizkor Names," with page numbers corresponding to the original Yiddish *yizkor* book, are entries for "Moshe Orenstein" and "Suzia (Sara) Orenstein." "Suzia" is probably short for "Susanna" (Zuzanna) in Polish or "Susan" in English. There is also a reference to a Mordechai Orenstein. The table is a bit confusing because it also has entries for "Moshe Ornstein"—a slightly different English spelling of the surname—and for "Munia Ornstein," which is very close to what my father wrote. Of course, the vast majority of Jews in Podhajce perished in the Shoah.

25 See *Sefer Podhajce*, 3.

26 Henia Shourz notes that after leaving "liberated" Podhajce following the war (her quotation marks), she and her family spent a few months in Wrocław, where they met several people from Podhjace, "such as Hirsch Kimmel and his family." Shourz, "A Path Full of Obstacles," 332. As noted earlier, "Hirsch" (or Hersh) was the middle name of my grandfather Leon (born Leib Hersh). At some point, he changed the spelling of our last name to Kimel, with only one "m." So many Jewish returnees settled in lower Silesia that Wrocław rivaled Łódz as a Jewish population center and, like Łódz, became a center of Jewish theater in Poland. Redlich, *Life in Transit*, 58.

27 Snyder, *Bloodlands*, 342.

28 Modeled on Bełżec, the Germans established a death factory in Sobibór, just northeast of Lublin, which became operational in April 1942. Ibid., 260–261.

29 Ibid., 342–343. As a part of the former Soviet Union, Ukraine also has never come to grips with the role of Ukrainians in the Holocaust.

30 Fulbrook, *Reckonings*, 422. Snyder also points out that in none of the Communist Soviet bloc countries "would the robbery of Jews be challenged, and in none of them would the murder of Jews enter history as a distinct subject." Snyder, *Black Earth*, 287. Heller writes that "The Polish government, like the Soviet one to whom it owed its existence, decreed that Jews must not be cited as particular victims of the Nazis, in writings about that period or in monuments to it." Heller, *Edge of Destruction*, 301. She also notes that "[a]lso silenced in Communist Poland was the story of those exceptional Poles who risked their lives to help Jews." Ibid.

31 Gross, *Fear*, xiv.

Part 2

1   The population number of 85,000 is based on Gold, *The Life of Jews in Poland*, 1. Historian Lukasz Krzyzanowski, himself a Radomer, similarly puts the number at 90,000. Krzyzanowski, *Ghost Citizens*, 11 (citations omitted). According to Gold, a rabbi born and raised in Radom who later served as the director and rabbi at the Harvard-Radcliff Hillel for over forty years, less than a third of the 85,000 inhabitants of Radom were Jewish and less than a third of the city's Jews were Orthodox. By contrast, about sixty percent of Podhajce was Jewish. It seems that most of them would be considered Orthodox, by which I mean fairly observant.

2   My grandmother may have been named Frania or Franja originally instead of Franciszka.

3   For a rare prewar video of Radom, taken in 1936, see "Jewish Life in Radom, 1936," United States Holocaust Memorial Museum, RG number: RG-60.7190, film ID: 4505, collections.ushmm.org/search/catalog/irn722697.

Chapter 23

1   The information about Lutka comes from Steinman, *Lost World*, 73. Lutka's family and my mother's family lived in the same building.

2   Ibid., 215.

3   For example, the Germans "commanded Jews to empty the latrines and pour the filth-feces, one on another—then form a circle and sing and dance." Weisbard, "The German Army Arrives," 278. The Nazis took great sadistic pleasure in humiliating their defenseless Jewish victims at every opportunity during the Holocaust. Writing the Foreword for *Remembering Rohatyn*, Holocaust scholar Michael Berenbaum said, "The Nazis loved to play God. It was not quite satisfying enough to kill the Jews, but one had to defile them and demoralize them." *Remembering Rohatyn*, xx.

4   Weisbard, "The German Army Arrives," 279.

5   Snyder, *Bloodlands*, 126–127 and "Einsatzgruppen operate in Poland," WW2History. com, http://ww2history.com/key_moments/Holocaust/Einsatzgruppen_operate_in_ Poland.

6   Levine, *Fugitives of the Forest*, 10.

7   Snyder, *Bloodlands*, 127.

8   Ibid. Jews were not the only ones fleeing east. After his army barracks in Oświęciem were destroyed by the *Luftwaffe*, Second Lieutenant Jan Karski and some remnants of the Polish army headed toward Tarnopol, where they surrendered to the Red Army. Karski, *Story of a Secret State*, 6–14.

9   Benjamin Lutkin, "Luts'k," *The YIVO Encyclopedia of Jews in Eastern Europe*, https:// encyclopedia.yivo.org/article/1375.

10   Ibid. Snyder doesn't cite a source, but he writes the Jewish population around 1942 was about 10,000 and constituted half of the city's population. Snyder, *Bloodlands*, 222.

11   Snyder, *Black Earth*, 219.

12   What actually happened is unclear. After the war, Lutka apparently told her sister-in-law that my mother's family disappeared in Łuck, and that Lutka assumed they had been deported to Siberia by the NKVD. Steinman, *Lost World*, 215. While Łuck was still under Soviet control, Lutka found work in a lab, as she had completed a degree in bacteriology in Warsaw before the war. Ibid., 216.

13   Bauer, *The Death of the Shtetl*, 276.

14 Snyder, *Bloodlands*, 195. Snyder also writes (ibid., 196):

> Violence against Jews served to bring the Germans and elements of the local non-Jewish population closer together. Anger was directed, as the Germans wished, towards the Jews, rather than against collaborators with the Soviet regime as such. . . . Violence against Jews also allowed local Estonians, Latvians, Lithuanians, Ukrainians, Belarusians, and Poles who had themselves cooperated with the Soviet regime to escape any such taint. The idea that only Jews served communists was convenient not just for the occupiers but for some of the occupied as well.

15 Ibid., 222–223.

Chapter 24

1 Asher Gurfinkel, "History of the Community: The Town," in *Sefer Ludwipol*, 5.
2 "The Jewish Community of Sosnove," ANU-Museum of the Jewish People, https://dbs.anumuseum.org.il/skn/he/c6/e263770. According to the museum's numbers, only about 150 out of 2150 people in Ludwipol weren't Jewish. That a shtetl would be that overwhelmingly Jewish seems quite unusual and may not be accurate.
3 Gurfinkel, "History of the Community," 7.
4 Ibid., 6.
5 Yona Raver Blostein, "The Sights of Ludvipol," trans. Yocheved Klausner, in *Sefer Ludwipol*, 8.
6 Hakman, "There Once Was a Shtetl Ludvipol," 167.
7 Baruch Gutman, "Days of Murder," in *Sefer Ludvipol*, 79–85, https://www.jewishgen.org/yizkor/ludvipol/lud078.html#Page79.
8 Ibid.
9 "Ludwipol," Yad Vashem, https://collections.yadvashem.org/en/untold-stories/community/14622598-Ludwipol.
10 See Mordechai Volman, "Life in the Ghetto—and Its Destruction," in *Sefer Ludvipol*, 89 (Hebrew). Volman, however, says that some Judenrat members helped Nazis find hiding Jews and suggests that they could have run away but did not.
11 Yehuda Raver, "In the Valley of Death," in *Sefer Ludvipol*, 100–101 (Hebrew).
12 Ibid., 103.
13 Ibid., 102.
14 Ibid., 103. According to Martin Dean, ghetto inmates in Volhynia also received some salt. Martin Dean, "German Ghettoization in Occupied Ukraine: Regional Patterns and Sources," paper presented at the conference "The Holocaust in Ukraine: New Sources and Perspectives," Center for Advanced Holocaust Studies, United States Holocaust Memorial Museum, 2013, https://www.ushmm.org/m/pdfs/20130500-holocaust-in-ukraine.pdf, 67.
15 Gutman, "Days of Murder," 79–85.
16 Ibid.
17 Volman, "Life in the Ghetto," 91; and Raver, "In the Valley of Death," 102.
18 Thorne, *It Will Yet Be Heard*, 29. Indeed, Thorne tells, at length, how he risked his life to smuggle a fur coat into the Drohobycz Ghetto to effect a prearranged sale of the fur to a non-Jewish Polish woman. Ibid., 199–210.

Chapter 25

1 It is possible the man was Israel Mendelovich, who climbed out of the mass grave and fled to the forest. Yosef Gitterman, "My Experiences," in *Sefer Ludvipol*, 207 (Yiddish).

2 Mordechai Volman, a Ludwipol survivor, refers to Ukrainians who went to rob the houses of Jews and found people hiding. See Volman, "Life in the Ghetto," 92.

3 "Murder Story of Ludwipol Jews at the Military Barracks in Ludwipol," trans. from *Sefer Ludwipol* for Yad Vashem, https://collections.yadvashem.org/en/untold-stories/killing-site/14628007-Military-Barracks-in-Ludwipol.

4 Ibid.

5 Ibid.

6 See, for example, Patrick Desbois, "The Witnesses of Ukraine or Evidence from the Ground: The Research of Yahad-In Unum," paper presented at the conference "The Holocaust in Ukraine: New Sources and Perspectives," Center for Advanced Holocaust Studies, United States Holocaust Memorial Museum, 2013, https://www.ushmm.org/m/pdfs/20130500-holocaust-in-ukraine.pdf, 91. ("Almost everywhere, Hitler's squads surrounded cities and towns and rounded up Jewish men, women, and children. They were first forced to undress and then slaughtered before being buried in mass graves.") Sometimes, they were ordered to lie down naked in a mass grave, head to toe, in the Nazis' "can of sardines" method, and then were shot from above. See ibid., 98. The Germans and Ukrainians perfected this method in slaughtering Jews outside of Kyiv, in the infamous Babyn Yar massacre (formerly called Babi Yar), over two days in late September 1941. Snyder, *Black Earth*, 175–176.

  Hillel Zeidman of Skalat relates an incident in which two people refused to strip before being murdered, in *Skalat Yizkor Book*: "Berle, the Rabbi's son, refused to strip naked, and remained wrapped in his Tallit [prayer shawl]. The Ukrainians and Germans struck him with murderous blows, but he did not give in, and finally they killed him with a gunshot, while he remained dressed. This also was the fate of a young woman, Margaliot, who refused to strip her garments." See also Abraham Weissbrod, "Berel the Rabbi's Son, and the Brave Teacher from Skalat," in *Skalat Yizkor Book*, 68–69, https://www.jewish-gen.org/yizkor/skalat/ska064.html#Page68. Abraham Aviel, from the village of Radun, Belarus, escaped from a column of Jews being marched to mass graves to be shot. He recounts that a Jewish girl refused to undress at the mass grave. The Germans hit her and then shot her. Gilbert, *The Holocaust*, 459 (citation omitted). Similarly, on August 21, 1942, in Kielce, school children were ordered to strip. When they balked, the Nazis ordered their teacher to strip as an example. When she too refused, the Germans and their accomplices "began to pummel the children cruelly and undress them by force," after which they shot the children followed by the teacher. Bender, *Enemy Land*, 166 (citation omitted).

7 Dean, "German Ghettoization," 68.

8 I discuss this further in my Co-Author's Note on the Use of *Yizkor* Books and Rohatyn Memoirs.

9 Volman's testimony in "Murder Story of Ludwipol Jews." In his account, "In the Valley of Death," Raver says that people were ordered to lie down naked in the mass grave and then shot, but my mother heard that Natan was shot standing. According to Yad Vashem, the Nazis massacred about 1,000 Jews that day. As we saw in Galicia, the Nazis liked massacring Jews in nearby ghettos on the same dates. The Volhynian shtetls of Sarny and Rokitno—each less than sixty miles from Ludwipol—were both liquidated on August 26–27, 1942. Bauer, *The Death of the Shtetl*, 67. The Germans may have done this to prevent advance news of imminent mass murder from spreading between towns.

Chapter 26

1 Levine, *Fugitives of the Forest*, xvi. Levine notes, however, that these statistics are only general estimates. Ibid., xxi. Bauer similarly estimates that about 25,000 Jews of the Kresy (Northeastern Poland, east Galicia and Volhynia) survived, and that about 3,000–4,000 Jews (like my mother, Babcia, Regina, and Motek) survived in family camps in the forest (though my family members weren't in the forest the entire time). *The Death of the Shtetl*, 166.

2 Levine, *Fugitives of the Forest*, 2.

3 Gutman, "Days of Murder," 79–85. Yossef Shemesh also writes, "In the woods were the Russian partisans, and all the survivors were gathering there." Yossef Shemesh, "On the Way to the Forest," in *Sefer Ludwipol*, 118–124 (Hebrew). Although Russian partisans were generally hostile to Jewish fugitives in forests, neither Gutman nor Shemesh suggests this.

4 Glotzer, *I Survived*, 26.

5 Levine, *Fugitives*, 139. See also Bauer, *The Death of the Shtetl*, 72.

6 See, for example, Amitz, "With the Kovpak Men," 90 ("Our raids increased the hatred of the peasants towards us, with additional intensity"). Browning similarly suggests that some Poles directed the Germans to Jewish hiding places in the woods because the Jews stole food from the peasants' fields in a desperate attempt to stay alive. Browning, *Ordinary Men*, 126. Jews hiding in the Dulcza forest in the Kraków District also sometimes stole poultry from the peasants. Grabowski, *Hunt for the Jews*, 187. My mother didn't mention this being done where she was, and I haven't seen references to it elsewhere.

7 Levine, *Fugitives*, 139–140. See also Gilbert, *The Holocaust*, 695. According to Yehuda Raver, people turning in Jews were promised three kilograms of salt. "In the Valley of Death," 130.

8 Ringelblum, *Polish-Jewish Relations*, 137.

9 Aharon Appelfeld, *The Story of a Life*, trans. Aloma Halter (New York: Schocken Books, 2004), 64. The hunt appears to have taken place somewhere in the Ukraine, but Appelfeld doesn't indicate whether the pursuing peasants were Polish or Ukrainian.

10 Snyder, *Black Earth*, 204–205.

11 Gross and Grudzinska Gross, *Golden Harvest*, 54.

12 Ibid., 59–62.

13 Ibid., 62 (citation omitted).

14 Gross, *Fear*, 180.

15 Gitterman, "My Experiences," 209–210.

16 Ibid. 210.

17 Ibid., 213.

18 Snyder, *Black Earth*, 306.

19 Grabowski, *Hunt for the Jews*, 117. Grabowski was focusing on Dąmbrowa County in the General Government's Kraków district. If anything, the danger of being denounced, seized or outright killed must have been greater in territory that had been occupied by the Red Army, such as where my mother, grandmother and Regina were hiding.

20 Browning, *Ordinary Men*, 133–134 (citation omitted).

21 Grabowski, *Hunt for the Jews*, 251.

22 Levine, *Fugitives*, 142–143.

23 See Gross and Grudzinska Gross, *Golden Harvest*, 111 ("To this day the parish priest remains the highest moral authority in Polish villages. And yet the documents from the epoch show no reaction by the Catholic priests to the crimes of genocide that were happening in exactly the places in which they were fulfilling their pastoral duties"). Ringelblum

The Pessimist's Son

praises the "rare act . . . of nobility" of a parish priest in the village of Kampinos who saved the lives of many Jews who were imprisoned in a labor camp by preaching fiery sermons in their defense every Sunday, leading peasants to help them. Ringelblum, *Polish-Jewish Relations*, 209 and n. 25. For more on the absence of the Catholic Church more generally, see Gross and Grudzinska Gross, *Golden Harvest*, 109–116.

24 See, for example, Levine, *Fugitives*, 250–251.

25 My mother didn't remember what tools the Jews in the forest used to build their shelters. She assumed they went into fields at night and stole shovels, handsaws, and other tools, which the peasants didn't lock up. Raver, "In the Valley of Death," 139, writes that a forester they knew lent them saws and axes to build a bunker, and suggests it was for money but notes that it was difficult for Christians to aid Jews because of their great fear of the Germans. As mentioned above, Gitterman writes that a villager actually built a forest bunker for Gitterman and others.

26 Raver writes of meeting a man named Goldman in the forests. "In the Valley of Death," 144. It could be the same person, but it is a very common Jewish name.

Chapter 27

1 See Raver, "In the Valley of Death," 147.

2 Ibid.

3 See Volman, "Life in the Ghetto," 91.

4 Ibid.

5 See Raver, "In the Valley of Death," 148. Gutman, "Days of Murder," writes that, in the village of "Metshulenka," the Russian administration set up offices, which oversaw the entire region. I assume this is the same place.

6 See Raver, "In the Valley of Death," 148.

7 Ibid.

8 Ibid., 149.

9 Glotzer, *I Survived*, 32.

10 *Remembering Rohatyn*, 334.

11 "Sosnove, Ukraine," Geder Avos Jewish Heritage Group website, https://www.gedera-vos.org/portfolio/sosnove-ukraine/.

Chapter 28

1 See "Lodz," *Holocaust Encyclopedia*, https://encyclopedia.ushmm.org/content/en/article/lodz.

2 Ringelblum, *Notes*, 47.

3 In August 1944, the Germans sent Rumkowski to Auschwitz, where *Sonderkommando* prisoners murdered him as revenge for his actions in Łódź. According to Bartov, Rumkowski may have been killed before he reached the death camp. *Borderlands*, 53. This is similar to the fate of Moshe Merin, the head of the Sosnowiec Ghetto Judenrat. (Merin also effectively controlled the Będzin Judenrat, which was chaired by his brother, Chaim, and many other Judenrats in Upper Silesia.) In February 1943, Merin informed on at least two young leaders of the Sosnowiec Ghetto underground, presumably because of

Merin's position that he could save the most Jews by sacrificing others and by maintaining order in the ghetto to please his Nazi overlords. The two young leaders were killed by the Gestapo. Merin himself was deported to Auschwitz in June that year. Gilbert, *The Holocaust*, 452–453. Henryk Schonker calls Merin a "traitor to the Jewish people" and says Merin was lynched and "nearly torn to pieces" by his fellow prisoners. *The Touch of an Angel*, 54.

Often, however, members of different Jewish councils refused to provide lists of people to be "deported," and were themselves killed by the Germans. Trunk, *Judenrat*, 439–443. Sometimes, Judenrat members killed themselves rather than turn over other people. Ibid., 443–445. For example, Adam Czerniakow, the head of the Warsaw Ghetto's Judenrat, committed suicide on being told the Judenrat had to select 2,000 more people daily to be sent to their deaths. Fulbrook, *Reckonings*, 83 (citation omitted).

4   *German Crimes in Poland*, vol. 1, 141.
5   Fulbrook, *Reckonings*, 75.
6   Redlich, *Life in Transit*, ix. Warsaw had been largely destroyed by the Germans.
7   Some of this information comes from chapter 31 of Steinman, *Lost World*.
8   "Jewish Survivors Registered in Łódź, Poland, Origin-Zionist Federation," Relatives Information Service, March 15, 1946?, https://atom.lib.uct.ac.za/uploads/r/university-of-cape-town-libraries-special-collections/7/b/7/7b7aa083ed89f6191553d0a0f735a008eddb6bf084537f89fae6218958d1a0cd/mss_sahgf_survivor_listings_050.pdf, 15. It lists my grandmother as Frania and misspells Najnudel.
9   At Potsdam in late July 1945, the United States and United Kingdom accepted Stalin's proposed borders for Poland, meaning the USSR would keep the territory in eastern Poland it had annexed, and Poland's western border would be the Oder-Neisse line. (See map, "Poland Territorial Losses and Gains 1945".) In May, the Polish Communist government had decided that all Germans on Polish territory were to be removed. Many Germans in the western territories (known in Poland as the "recovered territories") were expelled or encouraged to leave. Snyder describes this as ethnic cleansing directed by Stalin. *Bloodlands*, 320–325. As noted earlier, Poles and Jews were also ethnically cleansed from the parts of Poland that the Soviet Union had annexed. See ibid., 352. From 1944 through July 1946, Jews like my mother's family were repatriated from Soviet territory, with half of the transports disembarking in Lower Silesia (part of the recovered territories). Redlich, *Life in Transit*, 53. This region included Wrocław and nearby Legnica.
10 Germany apparently had a military training facility in Liegnitz during the war. See Fulbrook, *A Small Town Near Auschwitz*, 282–283. Later, the Soviets would have a military base in Legnica.
11 Some of this is based on Steinman, *Lost World*, 233.
12 Personal communication with Saba's daughter, Honey Miller (September 6, 2022).
13 Browning, *Remembering Survival*, 89.
14 See also *Yad Vashem Encyclopedia of the Ghettos*, 560. (On October 6, 1942, German, Polish, and Lithuanian policemen rounded up 2,800 Jews in the Ostrowiec Ghetto and shot several hundred dead.)
15 Grabowski and Engelking, *Night without End*, 48.
16 Antoine Mercier, ed., *Convoi No. 6 [Destination: Auschwitz, 17 Juillet 1942]* (Paris: Le Cherche Midi, 2005), 237. His work as a doctor in Auschwitz-Birkenau is also noted by Yishaye Eiger, "Radom Martyrs and Rebels," in *Sefer Radom*, 346–350. As a doctor, he was given larger food rations, which helped him survive. Personal communication from his daughter, Hélène Sebbon.
17 Snyder, *Black Earth*, 248. When the Polish state was destroyed by the joint German-Soviet invasion, Polish Jews living in France flocked to the Soviet embassy in Paris seeking papers from Germany's ally so they would have some state protection from the Nazis.

268 | The Pessimist's Son

Unfortunately, when Germany invaded the USSR in June 1941, those papers became worthless. Ibid. By the end of 1942, the French had deported 42,500 Jews to Auschwitz. Friedlander, *The Years of Extermination*, 683 (citation omitted).

18 Françoise S. Ouzan, *How Young Holocaust Survivors Rebuilt their Lives: France, the United States and Israel* (Bloomington: Indiana University Press, 2018), 67 (regarding the number of deportees who returned).

Chapter 29

1 Lower, *The Ravine*, 117.

2 Ibid, 128.

3 Gross, *Golden Harvest*, 71. See also Lower, *The Ravine*, 128.

4 Gilbert, *The Holocaust*, 607–608.

5 Lenga and Lenga, *The Watchmakers*, 195–196. The Nazis' sadistic, inhuman treatment of Jews was foreshadowed by some of the conduct of Petliura's army. For example, in February 1919 in the Podilian town of Proskuriv, a soldier similarly threw a one-month-old Jewish baby into the air and stabbed her with his bayonet. Veidlinger, *Civilized Europe*, 148. (In 1954, the Soviets renamed the town as Khmelnytskyi, omitting mention of the tens of thousands of Jews that Khmelnytskyi was responsible for killing. Hanebrink, *Specter*, 46.)

6 For a detailed summary of the desecration and destruction of synagogues in ghettos, see German Crimes in Poland, vol. 1, 140–141.

7 See *Sefer Radom*, 299.

8 Ibid., and "Radom," Holocaust Historical Society, https://www.holocausthistoricalsociety.org.uk/contents/ghettosj-r/radom.html.

9 See *Sefer Radom*; and Browning, *Remembering Survival*, 37 (the latter discussing Wierzbnik, a town south of Radom). See also Fulbrook, *Reckonings*, 73 ("This was not productive labor but . . . a means of public degradation," referring to the Germans seizing Jews in Łódź). This was the same kind of ritual humiliation Austrian Nazis subjected Austrian Jews to the day after the *Anschluss*—Austria's merger into Germany on March 11, 1938—when Austrian Jews were forced to kneel and clean streets with brushes in front of jeering Viennese crowds. Snyder, *Black Earth*, 82.

10 Weisbard, "The German Army Arrives," 278.

11 Petrovsky-Shtern and Polonsky, *Polin: Studies in Polish Jewry*, vol. 26: *Jews and Ukrainians*, 37.

12 Anita Frishman Gabbay, trans., "Lack of Living Conditions, Forced Labour and Jewish Offices," in *Sefer Radom*, 281.

13 Personal communication with Mendel Goldstein, who has a copy of his father's account of his Holocaust experience (written in German).

14 Browning, *Remembering Survival*, 57–58.

15 Philip Goldstein's interview, June 2, 1992, US Holocaust Memorial Museum, 4, https://collections.ushmm.org/oh_findingaids/RG-50.233.0037_trs_en.pdf (hereafter Goldstein Testimony).

16 "Radom," Holocaust Historical Society. In an October 1940 entry, Emmanuel Ringelblum writes that the Jewish Council in Radom often did this and calls it "the best of the Councils." *Notes from the Warsaw Ghetto*, 67. Ringelblum's view, however, may have changed. A year later, he recounts the story of thirty-two Jews who had been assigned to transport horses from another town to Radom. Upon arrival, with the horses in good

condition, the Judenrat (with its president absent) gave the men a pass to go wherever they pleased, but then informed the Germans that there were out-of-town Jews in Radom for whom they were not responsible. The Germans arrested them, ordered them to dig a mass grave and shot them. Only two of the thirty-two managed to escape. Ibid., 227–228. The Podhajce Judenrat also sent food parcels to young men it had sent to work camps and tried to free people who became ill. "Podhajce," in *Pinkas Hakehillot Polin.*

17 Goldstein Testimony, 4. Workers from Radom taken to the labor camp at Cieszanów (like Philip) composed a lament in Yiddish:

> Work, brothers, work fast,
> If you don't, they'll lash your hide.
> Not many of us will manage to last—
> Before long, we'll all have died.

Dawidowicz, *War*, 272–273.

18 Krzyzanowski, *Ghost Citizens*, 24.

19 See "The Liquidation of the Glinice Ghetto: August 5, 1942," in *Sefer Radom*, 301.

20 Grabowski, "The Polish Police Collaboration in the Holocaust," 8. Thirty thousand Polish police members would take part in the murder of Jews. Snyder, *Black Earth*, 112. Snyder notes, however, that the Polish police answered to the German Order police, which answered to Himmler, and that Polish police could be shot for refusing orders to shoot civilians. Ibid. Even if so, they avidly persecuted and killed Jews. Bender takes a less charitable view of the Polish police than Snyder. She writes: "In their operations against the Jewish population, [the Polish police in the Kielce area] acted autonomously even though they were subordinate to the German authorities. . . ." *Enemy Land*, 253.

21 Krzyzanowski, *Ghost Citizens*, 25.

22 Goldstein Testimony, 3.

23 Ibid.

24 For a first-hand account of the transport from Radom to Auschwitz, see Yishaye Eiger, "Radom Martyrs and Rebels," in *Sefer Radom*. Philip arrived in Birkenau on May 1, 1942. Goldstein Testimony, 3–4.

25 On July 19, 1942, Himmler had ordered that by the end of December 1942 all Jews within the General Government, with a few exceptions, be killed. Arad, *The Operation Reinhard Death Camps*, 261.

26 "After the Evacuation," in *Sefer Radom*. See also Goldstein Testimony, 7. ("So about three or four months after I was shipped to Auschwitz and my brother executed, my family, that is my father, my mother, my sister and the entire extended family were shipped to and killed at Treblinka. Treblinka became the killing fields of the Jews from the ghettos of the towns and cities in the districts of Warsaw and Radom. . . .") According to the Holocaust Historical Society, the deportations were carried out by German and Ukrainian SS forces. *Pinkas Hakehillot Polin* also notes that Jewish police participated. Browning puts the number of Jews from the Radom Ghetto who were deported or shot on the spot at 24,000. *Remembering Survival*, 66. Nazi authorities in the Radom District had "developed what was perhaps the most efficient and destructive ghetto-clearing organization of the entire General Government." Ibid., 67. Browning also notes that, although Treblinka's killing capacity was stretched to its breaking point after deportations from Radom and Kielce, the Lublin SS and police leader, Odilo Globocnik, "impatiently decided to commence deportations from northern Lublin as well." *Ordinary Men*, 89.

27 "Radom," *Pinkas Hakehillot Polin*, https://www.jewishgen.org/yizkor/pinkas_poland/pol7_00530.html.

28 *Yad Vashem Encyclopedia of the Ghettos,* 632. According to Krzyzanowski (*Ghost Citizens,* 32),

> Nothing suggests that the attitude of the Christian inhabitants of Radom toward their fellow-citizen Jews at the time of the Holocaust stood out in any way from what was going on throughout the entire General Government. . . . Radom differed from large cities like Warsaw or Kraków in that it was more difficult to hide or "disappear" here for a long time. Therefore, one can speculate that fewer individuals, especially those from Radom itself, survived there on so-called Aryan papers. . . .

29 Steinman, *Lost World,* 238.

30 Snyder, *Bloodlands,* 272–273. Bender puts the number at about 357,000. *Enemy Land,* 189. For a harrowing account of the deportation of Jews in the Kielce Ghetto (which was in Radom district) to Treblinka, see *Enemy Land,* chapter 4. In the Kielce actions, the Nazis and their Ukrainian accomplices shot many ghetto residents because the Germans knew their railway freight cars wouldn't hold all the anticipated deportees (despite their being crammed in like cattle). See ibid., 166.

31 Browning, *Remembering Survival,* 100. The fifth anniversary of the liquidation of the Radom Ghetto, in August 1947, coincided with the criminal trial in Radom of Wilhelm Blum, the former deputy chief of the SS and police in Radom, who was personally responsible for the deportation of Radom Ghetto inmates to Treblinka. Some Jewish survivors living in Radom then and former Radom residents living elsewhere in Poland testified against him. Many survivors living outside Radom traveled there to attend the trial. Blum was sentenced to death. Krzyzanowski, *Ghost Citizens,* 191–195.

32 Browning, *Ordinary Men,* 95–96.

33 "The 'Action' of January 13," in *Sefer Radom,* 322.

34 "Radom," *Pinkas Hakehillot Polin*; and *Yad Vashem Encyclopedia of the Ghettos,* 633. Speaking of the small ghetto in Kielce and Radom District more generally, Bender calls this the "Palestine Aktion," but says that those who signed up and paid special fees were immediately arrested, marched to the Jewish cemetery, and murdered. *Enemy Land,* 200 (citation omitted).

35 See, for example, Rena Margulies Chernoff and Allan Chernoff, *The Tailors of Tomaszow: A Memoir of Polish Jews* (Lobbock: Texas Tech University Press, 2014), 173–174; and Lenga and Lenga, *The Watchmakers,* 171–173. Bauer notes that the Germans "pursued the same policies everywhere, with but minimal differences among them." *The Death of the Shtetl,* 90.

36 *Sefer Radom,* 322.

37 Gross and Grudzinska Gross, *Golden Harvest,* 34–35.

38 Ibid., 36.

39 Personal communication from Mendel Goldstein dated October 16, 2022 (citing a letter from Philip to his brother Chilek dated October 3, 1946).

40 *Yad Vashem Encyclopedia of the Ghettos,* 633.

41 The Red Army liberated Radom on January 16, 1945. By that point, of course, Jewish Radom had been thoroughly destroyed.

42 Fulbrook, *Reckonings,* 21. Philip credited his survival in part to his having developed immunity to typhus in early 1942 (Goldstein Testimony, 5), but he also must have been amazingly strong mentally.

Endnotes | 271

43 Goldstein Testimony, 6; and Snyder, *Black Earth*, 137. Snyder points out that the mass refusal by Jews of Soviet passports provides strong evidence that they didn't want Soviet rule. *Black Earth*, 137.

44 Personal communication with Mendel Goldstein. See also Snyder, *Bloodlands*, 128. ("With the registration of citizens came the military draft: some 150,000 young men . . . soon found themselves in the Red Army.")

45 Abe Zukerman, "Where No Birds Fly," in *Sefer Wierzbnik-Starachowice* [Wierzbnik-Starachowitz; a memorial book (Wierzbnik, Poland)], ed. Mark Schutzman, 242, transl. for JewishGen, https://www.jewishgen.org/yizkor/wierzbnik/wie240.html#Page242. For more on the horrors that Jews and others who were sent to the Soviet labor camps experienced as *zeks* (prisoners), see Julius Margolin, *Journey into the Land of the Zeks and Back: A Memoir of the Gulag* (Oxford: Oxford University Press, 2020).

46 Irena Grudzinska-Gross and Jan Gross, eds., *War Through Children's Eyes: The Soviet Occupation of Poland and the Deportations, 1939–1941* (Stanford: Hoover Institution Press, 2019), xxv. See also Margolin, *Journey*, 275.

47 Steinman, *Lost World*, 219–224.

48 Ibid., 222.

49 Ibid., 262.

Chapter 30

1 Goldstein Testimony, 24. Joseph Steinman, the husband of my mother's murdered Aunt Sabina, also was sent to Stuttgart after liberation. Steinman, *Lost World*, 240.

2 "The 'Radom Center in Stuttgart," in *Sefer Radom*, 381, https://www.jewishgen.org/yizkor/radom/rad381.html.

3 Yakov Vayngort, "Jewish Life in Radom after Liberation," in *Sefer Radom*, 372, repr. from the journal *In Freedom*, which was published in "Radom Center" in Stuttgart, 1946–1947, https://www.jewishgen.org/yizkor/radom/rad365.html#Page372. Krzyzanowski discusses the killings in chapter 2 of *Ghost Citizens*. In mid-February 1945, about 490 Jewish survivors were living in Radom, with 959 there in the first half of August 1945. Mass departures began in the summer of 1945 after an escalation of violence against Radom Jews. At the end of 1946, only 111 survivors were in Radom, barely a dozen of whom had been there since winter 1945. Krzyzanowski, *Ghost Citizens*, 59–60.

4 Vayngort, "Jewish Life in Radom after Liberation"; and Krzyzanowski, *Ghost Citizens*, 96–97. The notices "confirmed" that Jews were working against Poland on behalf of the NKVD and advised them to flee by August 15 or be "ruthlessly punished." *Ghost Citizens*, 96.

5 Jews who remained in Radom unsuccessfully sought protection from Polish authorities. Some even armed themselves. Krzyzanowski, *Ghost Citizens*, 129–134.

6 Gross, *Fear*, chapter 2 ("The Unwelcoming of Jewish Survivors"), 35–36. In addition, righteous gentiles who had sheltered Jews during the war often were the subjects of hostility from their rural neighbors. Grabowski tells the story of a farmer who was mocked in his village and shunned because he had hidden two Jewish men during the war. He invited them to his wedding after the war, in 1945, but felt it necessary to hire two armed guards to protect these two guests. Grabowski, *Hunt for the Jews*, 287–288. While not as bad as the situation in Poland, Romanians who had benefited at the expense of their Jewish neighbors who were expelled during the war, met the small number of returnees there with hostility. Hanebrink, *Specter*, 165 and 169. Jews returning to their homes in Lithuania and

Kyiv also met with violence. Porat, *Nakam*, 81–82. According to Bender, however, only in Poland did Jews continue to be murdered after the war. *Enemy Land*, 273.

7   Thorne, *It Will Yet Be Heard*, 181. While the focus usually is on fears that surviving Jews would seek to reclaim their homes and other property, Thorne writes that the townspeople's faces "reflected their terror that we had returned to bear witness to their crimes against our people." Ibid., 176. Of course, the two motives to "unwelcome" returning Jews are not mutually exclusive.

8   Ibid., 222–228; and Gross, *Fear*, 73–80.

9   Gross, *Fear*, 81–82.

10 Thorne, *It Will Yet Be Heard*, 236. The murder of four Jews in a Radom work cooperative the day before the Kraków pogrom also made international news. Krzyzanowski, *Ghost Citizens*, 95. Regarding the Polish press's attitudes toward Jews during the war, Ringelblum writes, in September 1943, "Why has the Polish anti-Semitic press not stopped its incitement even for a moment, and why does the Government press so rarely break its silence on the Jewish question, why does it take so weak a stand in defence of the Jew?" *Polish-Jewish Relations*, 9. In the Kraków *yizkor* book—*Memorial Journal in Honor of the Jews from Crakow, Perished 1939–1945* (New York: New Cracow Friendship Society, 1967), 26, translated for JewishGen, https://www.jewishgen.org/yizkor/Krakow2/kra021.html#Page25—Moshe Singer writes: "The Polish press was far from being sympathetic to the Jews. As a matter of fact, it went to great lengths in order to hide the truth from the Polish population of the Jewish heroism." (Moshe Singer is also the name of Saba Weinwurzel's husband, but he was from Radom, and I don't know whether he wrote for the Kraków *yizkor* book.)

11 Alas, this proved to be far from the case.

12 Ringelblum, *Polish-Jewish Relations*, 256–257 (emphasis added).

13 Viewing the treatment of Polish Jews through the lens of public opinion about Poland was not something new. As discussed earlier, after Polish soldiers and civilians brutally attacked Jews in Lwów over three days in November 1918, setting fire to and looting Jewish properties, raping Jewish women, desecrating cemeteries, and killing nearly 200 Jews and wounding 443 in the process, the US government called for an investigation. In a response that could have come from 1945, Poles complained that the international press was spreading false reports and that the real victim was *Poland*, which the Jews were discrediting to damage Poland's territorial integrity and to obtain a privileged status. Veidlinger, *Civilized Europe*, 84–88.

14 Dariusz Stola, "Jewish Emigration from Communist Poland: The Decline of Polish Jewry in the Aftermath of the Holocaust," *East European Jewish Affairs* 47, nos. 2–3 (May 2017): 172.

15 Gross and Grudzinska Gross, *Golden Harvest*, 105. They also call it a "staple phrase." Ibid., 117.

16 Ringelblum, *Polish-Jewish Relations*, 138.

17 For a more detailed discussion of the Kielce pogrom, see Gross, *Fear*, chapters 3 and 4. For a detailed description of the pogrom based on the accounts of various pogrom survivors, see Joanna Tokarska Bakir, *Cursed: A Social Portrait of the Kielce Pogrom*, trans. Ewa Wampuszyc (Ithaca, NY: Cornell University Press, 2023), chapter 1.

18 Bender, *Enemy Land*, 283 (citation omitted). See also Tokarska Bakir, *Cursed*, 36.

19 Gross, *Fear*, 142–149.

20 Krzyzanowski, *Ghost Citizens*, 115 (citation omitted). Not surprisingly, the Catholic Church regards Wyszyński quite differently, as a *foe* of antisemitism. See, for example, "Cardinal Wyszynski and the Jews—Opposition to Anti-Semitism under Two Totalitarian Regimes," The John Paul II Foundation, September 7, 2021, https://fjp2.com/cardinal-wyszynski-and-the-jews-opposition-to-anti-semitism-under-two-totalitarian-regimes/. Some lower-level Polish clergy also expressed antipathy towards Jews following Kielce.

For example, the priest of a prominent Radom church declared, "Jews are our enemy." Krzyzanowski, *Ghost Citizens*, 116.

21 Gross, *Fear*, 149–150. The first use of the blood libel in Poland took place in 1399 and involved the archbishop of Poznań. Heller, *Edge of Destruction*, 16.

22 See Krzyzanowski, *Ghost Citizens*, 125.

23 Steinman, *Lost World*, 260 and 272.

24 Ibid., 272 and 289.

25 Ibid., 290–291.

26 Goldstein Testimony, 24.

27 Margulies Chernoff and Chernoff, *The Tailors of Tomaszow*, 262–264. Margulies Chernoff left Poland before the Kielce pogrom.

Chapter 31

1 Margulies Chernoff, having survived Auschwitz, also was bullied in Polish public school. Margulies Chernoff and Chernoff, *The Tailors of Tomaszow*, 261.

2 For an account of antisemitic taunting before the war in a Polish public school in a town about sixty miles from Radom that was similar to what my mother experienced after the war, see ibid., 100. See also Heller, *Edge of Destruction*, 225–226 (discussing antisemitism in Polish public schools in the interwar period).

3 Gross notes that, after the war, "scores of Jewish children ended up in regular Polish state schools where, as a rule, they met with hostility." He adds: "If not too many Jewish children were directly affected by discrimination in schools, it is because so few had survived the war." Gross, *Fear*, 66.

4 Margulies Chernoff recounts how, back in public school in Tomaszów after the war, she sat in class when the Polish students stood to recite their Catholic prayers and did not participate when a nun taught the class religion. Margulies Chernoff and Chernoff, *The Tailors of Tomaszow*, 261.

5 Celia Heller writes:

> [Jewish a]dults born into very acculturated families did not give their children [Old Testament names or Polonized versions of Old Testament names]. They chose names that were used by Poles, which they considered esthetically superior to Jewish names, both the original and the Polonized renditions. Thus, . . . the distinctively Polish name *Mieczysław* . . . replaced the Polonized versions of Moses.

Heller, *Edge of Destruction*, 216–217 (italics in original).

6 Gold, *The Life of Jews*, 80. Glotzer, who didn't appear to come from a particularly religious family, writes that his uncle sat *shivah* for (that is, mourned as dead) one of the uncle's daughters when she converted to Catholicism and married a Catholic man in a church. *I Survived*, 5.

274 | The Pessimist's Son

Part 3

Chapter 32

1 Stola, "Jewish Emigration from Communist Poland," 178. The beginning of de-Staliniza-tion was "marked by strong anti-Jewish excesses. Jews were branded as Stalinists or their lackeys and incited to get out of Poland." Heller, *Edge of Destruction*, 298.
2 Because he had deducted two years from his age, documents from the university list his birth year as 1928, instead of 1926. Curiously, his father's name is listed as Henryk (which maybe was translated from Hersh). I don't know whether my father gave the school that name because Leon sounded Jewish or because his father was in America and the use of Henryk was part of an effort to conceal that fact.
3 Stola, "Jewish Emigration from Communist Poland," 176.
4 Ibid., 177.

Chapter 33

1 In the words of Jeremy Black, "Despite the best efforts of religious leaders and thinkers, and arguments about God's inscrutable purpose, and the testing of the devout, the notion of an omnipotent and benign, indeed interested and engaged, God also took a savage knock" as a result of the Shoah. *History and Memory*, 379. Another approach is to continue believing in God, but to question God's goodness. For example, in an unpublished version of his classic, *Night*, Elie Wiesel "expressed terrible anger against God. . . ." Porat, *Nakam*, 38.
2 Thorne, *It May Yet Be Heard*, 12.
3 Bauer, *Rethinking the Holocaust*, 186–188.
4 Lang provides a somewhat densely written but interesting analysis of various explanations of how God could have allowed the Holocaust, including the argument that God's ways are inscrutable. See Berel Lang, *Post-Holocaust: Interpretation, Misinterpretation, and the Claims of History* (Bloomington: Indiana University Press, 2005), chapter 3.
5 Nissan Dovid Dubov, "Belief After the Holocaust," Chabad.org, https://www.chabad.org/library/article_cdo/aid/108398/jewish/Belief-After-the-Holocaust.htm.
6 Bauer, *Rethinking the Holocaust*, 205–206.
7 Bauer, *The Death of the Shtetl*, 169.

Chapter 34

1 A. Ross Johnson, "After the Six-Day War: Political Crisis in Poland," Sources and Methods: A Blog of the History and Public Policy Program, Wilson Center, June 26, 2017, https://www.wilsoncenter.org/blog-post/after-the-six-day-war-political-crisis-poland; see also Dariusz Stola, "The Hate Campaign of March 1968: How Did It Become Anti-Jewish?," in *Polin: Studies in Polish Jewry*, vol. 21: 1968. *Forty Years After*, ed. Leszek W. Gluchowski and Antony Polonsky (Oxford: Littman, 2009) ("The hate campaign that began in

March 1968 included aggressive and omnipresent antisemitic propaganda—barely covered with the fig leaf of antiZionism—mass mobilization against 'the enemies of socialist Poland,' among whom the Zionists stood prominently; expulsion of Jews from the party, government posts, and other positions; the destruction or drastic restriction Jewish institutions and organizations; and discrimination against and harassment of individuals for being Jewish"); and Heller, *Edge of Destruction*, 299–301. It is depressing that, some fifty-six years later, another war forced on Israel has also led to manifestations of antisemitism and rabid antizionism at many college campuses and elsewhere in America.

2   It is telling that *Austria* was seen as safer for Jews than Poland.

3   Stola, "Jewish Emigration from Communist Poland," 180.

4   "Poland since 1939," *The YIVO Encyclopedia of Jews in Eastern Europe*, https://encyclopedia.yivo.org/article/18.

5   Research conducted in Poland after the fall of Communism regarding children of Holocaust survivors who had remained in Poland found that "in all cases [in the study] the survivor had married a non-Jewish person." Only six of the twenty children in the sample had been aware since early childhood of their Jewish heritage. Fulbrook, *Reckonings*, 472–473.

Chapter 35

1   One example of describing survivors as broken is found in the afterword to Thorne's book, in which his children write: "Our parents, like the other survivors, were shattered people. . . ." *It Will Yet Be Heard*, 293. In their story of their father's life in America, however, his children describe him as a "delightful man who was a marvelous raconteur and master of the telling anecdote. . . ." Ibid., 294.

2   Lower, *The Ravine*, 120 (emphasis added).

3   For a lengthy discussion suggesting some degree of trauma was generally inescapable, see Fulbrook, *Reckonings*, 461–476.

4   I am using the conventional term for children of survivors and "third generation" for grandchildren of survivors. I do not mean to imply, however, that I consider myself a "second-generation survivor." My parents were survivors; I was not.

5   Fulbrook, *Reckonings*, 464.

6   Ibid., 468.

7   Menachem Z. Rosensaft, ed., *God, Faith & Identity from the Ashes: Reflections of Children and Grandchildren of Holocaust Survivors* (Woodstock: Jewish Lights, 2015), xxiv. See also Ouzan, *Young Holocaust Survivors*, 33. ("Social psychologists and mental health professionals often marvel at the high rate of success in this cohort [of survivors], despite many documented cases of failures.")

8   Fulbrook, *Reckonings*, 470.

9   See Martin Kimel, "The Inheritance of Holocaust Trauma," *The Times of Israel*, April 5, 2021.

10   Fulbrook, *Reckonings*, 345–346.

11   Ibid.

Bibliography

Yizkor (Memorial) Books

Ayalon, N., ed. *Ludvipol (Wolyn); Sefer zikaron le-kehilat Ludvipol (Slisht Gadol)* [In memory of the Jewish community, Ludwipol (Sosnove, Ukraine)] (Hebrew and Yiddish). Tel Aviv: Irgun yots'e Ludvipol be-Yiśra'el uva-tefutsot [Ludvipol Relief Society of Israel], 1965. Translated into English as *Sefer Ludwipol* by Yocheved Klausner for JewishGen. https://www.jewishgen.org/yizkor/ludvipol/ludvipol.html.

"Murder Story of Ludwipol Jews at the Military Barracks in Ludwipol." Translation from *Sefer Ludvipol* for Yad Vashem. https://collections.yadvashem.org/en/untold-stories/killing-site/14628007-Military-Barracks-in-Ludwipol.

Bakalczuk-Felin, M., ed. *Yisker-bukh Chelm* [Commemoration book Chelm]. Johannesburg: Former Residents of Chelm, 1954. Translated for JewishGen. https://www.jewishgen.org/yizkor/chelm/chelm.html.

Bronshtain, Chaim, ed. *Skalat: Kovets zikaron lekehila sheharva bashoah* [Skalat: A memorial anthology for a community destroyed in the Holocaust (Ukraine)]. Tel Aviv: Bet ha-sefer 'al shem Ya'aḵov Ḵarol ye-'Irgun Yehude Sḵalaṭ be-Yiśra'el, 1971. Translated for JewishGen. https://www.jewishgen.org/yizkor/skalat/skalat.html.

Geshouri, Me'ir Shimon, ed. *Sefer Podhajce* [The memorial book of Podhajce (Pidhaytsi, Ukraine)]. Tel Aviv: Podhajce Society, 1972. Translated for JewishGen, 2013. https://www.jewishgen.org/yizkor/Podhajce/Podhajce.html/.

Kane, S. ed. *Sefer Bursztyn* [Book of Bursztyn]. Jerusalem: The Encyclopedia of the Jewish Diaspora, 1960. Translated by Rivka Chaya Schiller for Jewish Gen. https://www.jewishgen.org/yizkor/Burshtyn/Burshtyn.html#TOC301.

Memorial Journal in Honor of the Jews from Crakow, Perished 1939–1945. New York: New Cracow Friendship Society, 1967. Translated for JewishGen. https://www.jewishgen.org/yizkor/Krakow2/Krakow2.html.

Shtokfish, David, ed. *Sefer Przytyk* [Przytyk memorial book]. Tel Aviv: Przytyk Societies in Israel, France and the USA, 1973. Translated for JewishGen. https://www.jewishgen.org/yizkor/przytyk/przytyk.html.

Perlow, Y., and Alfred Lipson, eds. *Sefer Radom* [The book of Radom; the story of a Jewish community in Poland destroyed by the Nazis (Radom, Poland)]. Tel Aviv: n.p., 1961. Translated for JewishGen. https://www.jewishgen.org/yizkor/radom/radom.html.

Preshel, Haim, ed. *Mikulince; sefer yizkor* [Mikulince memorial book (Mikulintsy, Ukraine)]. N.p. [Israel]: Organization of Milulincean Survivors in Israel and the USA, 1985. Translated for JewishGen. https://www.jewishgen.org/yizkor/mikulintsy/mikulintsy.html.

Shwarzstein, Dora [Donia] Gold, ed. *Remembering Rohatyn and Its Environs.* N.p.: Meyer Shwarzstein, 2019.

Zukerman, Abe. "Where No Birds Fly." In *Sefer Wierzbnik-Starachowice* [Wierzbnik-Starachowitz; a memorial book (Wierzbnik, Poland)], edited by Mark Schutzman. Translated for JewishGen. https://www.jewishgen.org/yizkor/wierzbnik/wie240.html#Page242.

Memoirs, Diaries, and Other Primary Sources

Appelfeld, Aharon. *The Story of a Life.* Translated by Aloma Halter. New York: Schocken Books, 2004.

Chernoff, Rena Margulies, and Allan Chernoff. *The Tailors of Tomaszow: A Memoir of Polish Jews.* Lobbock: Texas Tech University Press, 2014.

Fein, Yochanan. *Boy with a Violin: A Story of Survival.* Translated by Penina Reichenberg. Bloomington: Indiana University Press, 2022.

Glotzer, Jack. *I Survived the German Holocaust against All Odds: A Unique and Unforgettable Story of a Struggle for Life.* Rohatyn Jewish Heritage, 2022. https://rohatynjewishheritage.org/en/memoir/glotzer/e00/.

Goldstein, Philip. US Holocaust Memorial Museum, interview with Philip Goldstein. June 2, 1992). https://collections.ushmm.org/oh_findingaids/RG-50.233.0037_trs_en.pdf.

Karski, Jan. *Story of a Secret State: My Report to the World.* Washington: Georgetown University Press, 2013.

Kessler, Edmund. *The Wartime Diary of Edmund Kessler, Lwow, Poland, 1942–1944.* Edited by Regina Kessler. Boston: Academic Studies Press, 2010.

Kimel, Alexander. USC Shoah Foundation testimony. 1996.

Kimel, Eva. USC Shoah Foundation testimony. 1996.

Lederman, Sylvia. *Sheva's Promise: Chronicle of Escape from a Nazi Ghetto.* Syracuse, NY: Syracuse University Press, 2013.

Lenga, Harry, and Scott Lenga. *The Watchmakers: A Story of Brotherhood, Survival, and Hope Amid the Holocaust.* New York: Citadel Press, 2022.

Margolin, Julius. *Journey into the Land of the Zeks and Back: A Memoir of the Gulag.* Translated by Stefani Hoffman. Oxford: Oxford University Press, 2020.

Milch, Leon Leib. Yad Vashem testimony. January 5, 1989. https://collections.yadvashem.org/en/documents/3559163.

Ringelblum, Emmanuel. *Notes from the Warsaw Ghetto: The Journal of Emmanuel Ringelblum.* Edited and translated by Jacob Sloan. Berkeley: ibooks inc., 2006.

Schonker, Henryk. *The Touch of an Angel*. Translated by Scotia Gilroy. Bloomington: Indiana University Press, 2020.

Steinman, Josefa. *Lost World*. 2nd edition, 2013, unpublished.

Thorne, Leon. *It Will Yet Be Heard: A Polish Rabbi's Witness of the Shoah and Survival*. Edited by Daniel Magilow and Emmanuel Thorne. New Brunswick: Rutgers University Press, 2019.

Secondary Sources

Arad, Yitzhak, *The Operation Reinhard Death Camps: Belzec, Sobibor, Treblinka*. Bloomington: Indiana University Press, 2018.

Bakir, Joanna Tokarska. *Cursed: A Social Portrait of the Kielce Pogrom*. Translated by Ewa Wampuszyc. Ithaca, NY: Cornell University Press, 2023.

Bartov, Omer. *Anatomy of a Genocide: The Life and Death of a Town Called Buczacz*. New York: Simon & Schuster Paperbacks, 2018.

———. *Erased: Vanishing Traces of Jewish Galicia in Present-Day Ukraine*. Princeton, NJ: Princeton University Press, 2007.

———. *Genocide, the Holocaust and Israel-Palestine: First-Person History in Times of Crisis*. London: Bloomsbury Academic, 2023.

———. *Tales from the Borderlands: Making and Unmaking the Galician Past*. New Haven, CT: Yale University Press, 2022.

Bauer, Yehuda. *The Death of the Shtetl*. New Haven, CT: Yale University Press, 2009.

———. *Rethinking the Holocaust*. New Haven, CT: Yale University Press, 2001.

Bechtel, Delphine. "The 1941 Pogroms as Represented in Western Ukrainian Historiography and Memorial Culture." Paper presented at the conference "The Holocaust in Ukraine: New Sources and Perspectives," Center for Advanced Holocaust Studies, United States Holocaust Memorial Museum, 2013. https://www.ushmm.org/m/pdfs/20130500-holocaust-in-ukraine.pdf.

Bender, Sara. *In Enemy Land: The Jews of Kielce and the Region, 1939–1946*. Boston: Academic Studies Press, 2018.

Black, Jeremy. *The Holocaust: History and Memory*. Bloomington: Indiana University Press, 2016.

Browning, Christopher R. *Ordinary Men: Reserve Police Battalion 101 and the Final Solution in Poland*. New York: Harper Perennial, 2017.

———. *Remembering Survival: Inside a Nazi Slave-Labor Camp*. New York: Norton, 2010.

Central Commission for the Investigation of German Crimes in Poland. *German Crimes in Poland*. New York: Howard Fertig, 1982.

Dawidowicz, Lucy S. *The War against the Jews, 1933–45*. New York: Rinehart and Winston, 1975.

Desbois, Patrick, "The Witnesses of Ukraine or Evidence from the Ground: The Research of Yahad-In Unum." Paper presented at the conference "The Holocaust in Ukraine: New Sources and Perspectives," Center for Advanced Holocaust Studies, United States Holocaust Memorial Museum, 2013. https://www.ushmm.org/m/pdfs/20130500-holocaust-in-ukraine.pdf.

Feierstein, Daniel. "The Jewish Resistance Movements in the Ghettos of Eastern Europe." In *Life in the Ghettos during the Holocaust*, edited by Eric J. Sterling, 191–219. Syracuse, NY: Syracuse University Press, 2005.

Friedlander, Saul. *The Years of Extermination: Nazi Germany and the Jews, 1939–1945*. New York: HarperCollins, 2007.

Fulbrook, Mary. *A Small Town Near Auschwitz: Ordinary Nazis and the Holocaust*. Oxford: Oxford University Press, 2012.

———. *Reckonings: Legacies of Nazi Persecution and the Quest for Justice*. Oxford: Oxford University Press, 2018.

Gilbert, Martin. *The Holocaust: The Human Tragedy*. New York: Rosetta Books, 2014.

Gold, Ben-Zion. *The Life of Jews in Poland before the Holocaust*. Lincoln: University of Nebraska Press, 2007.

Grabowski, Jan. "The Polish Police Collaboration in the Holocaust." In a Levine Annual Lecture, Center for Advanced Holocaust Studies, United States Holocaust Memorial Museum, November 17, 2016. https://www.ushmm.org/m/pdfs/20170502-Grabowski_OP.pdf.

———. *Hunt for the Jews: Betrayal and Murder in German-Occupied Poland*. Bloomington: Indiana University Press, 2013.

Grabowski, Jan, and Barbara Engelking, eds. *Night without End: The Fate of Jews in German-Occupied Poland*. Bloomington: Indiana University Press, 2022.

Gross, Jan T. *Fear: Anti-Semitism in Poland after Auschwitz*. New York: Random House, 2006.

———. *Neighbors: The Destruction of the Jewish Community in Jedwabne, Poland*. Princeton, NJ: Princeton University Press, 2001.

Gross, Jan Tomasz, with Irena Grudzinska Gross. *Golden Harvest: Events at the Periphery of the Holocaust*. Oxford: Oxford University Press, 2012.

Grudzinska-Gross, Irena, and Jan Gross, eds. *War through Children's Eyes: The Soviet Occupation of Poland and the Deportations, 1939–1941*. Stanford: Hoover Institution Press, 2019.

Gutman, Yisrael, and Shmuel Krakowski. *Unequal Victims: Poles and Jews during World War II*. New York: Holocaust Library, 1986.

The Hamburg Institute for Social Research. *The German Army and Genocide: Crimes Against War Prisoners, Jews, and Other Civilians in the East, 1939–1944*. New York: The New Press, 1999.

Hanebrink, Paul. *A Specter Haunting Europe: The Myth of Judeo-Bolshevism*. Cambridge, MA: Belknap Press, 2018.

Bibliography | 281

Heller, Celia S. *On the Edge of Destruction: Jews of Poland between the Two World Wars.* Detroit, MI: Wayne State University Press, 1994.

Hett, Benjamin Carter. *The Death of Democracy: Hitler's Rise to Power and the Downfall of the Weimar Republic.* New York: St. Martin's Griffin, 2018.

Huener, Jonathan. *Auschwitz, Poland, and the Politics of Commemoration, 1945–1979.* Athens, OH: Ohio University Press, 2003.

Katz, Steven T., ed. *The Shtetl: New Evaluations.* New York: NYU Press, 2007.

Kimel, Alexander. *Anatomy of Genocide.* Unpublished, available in the US Holocaust Memorial Museum.

Krzyzanowski, Lukasz. *Ghost Citizens: Jewish Return to a Postwar City.* Translated by Madeline G. Levine. Cambridge, MA: Harvard University Press, 2020.

Kugelmass, Jack, and Jonathan Boyarin, eds. *From a Ruined Garden: The Memorial Books of Polish Jewry.* Bloomington: Indiana University Press, 2nd edition, 1998.

Landau-Czajka, Anna. "The Jewish Question in Poland: Views Expressed in the Catholic Press between the Two World Wars." In *Polin: Studies in Polish Jewry,* vol. 11: *Focusing on Aspects and Experiences of Religion,* edited by Antony Polonsky, 263–278. Oxford: Littman, 1998.

Lang, Berel. *Post-Holocaust: Interpretation, Misinterpretation, and the Claims of History.* Bloomington: Indiana University Press, 2005.

Levine, Allan. *Fugitives of the Forest: The Heroic Story of Jewish Resistance and Survival During the Second World War.* Guilford: Lyons Press, 1998.

Lower, Wendy. *The Ravine: A Family, a Photograph, a Holocaust Massacre Revealed.* New York: Mariner Books, 2021.

———. "Anti-Jewish Violence in Western Ukraine, Summer 1941: Varied Histories and Explanations." Paper presented at the conference "The Holocaust in Ukraine: New Sources and Perspectives," Center for Advanced Holocaust Studies, United States Holocaust Memorial Museum, 2013. https://www.ushmm.org/m/pdfs/20130500-holocaust-in-ukraine.pdf.

———. "Facilitating Genocide: Nazi Ghettoization Practices in Occupied Ukraine, 1941–42." In *Life in the Ghettos during the Holocaust,* edited by Eric J. Sterling, 120–144. Syracuse, NY: Syracuse University Press, 2005.

Mercier, Antoine, ed. *Convoi No. 6 [Destination: Auschwitz, 17 Juillet 1942].* Paris: Le Cherche Midi, 2005.

Miron, Guy, and Shlomit Shulhani, eds. *The Yad Vashem Encyclopedia of the Ghettos during the Holocaust,* vol. 2. Jerusalem: Yad Vashem Publications, 2009.

Ouzan, Françoise S. *How Young Holocaust Survivors Rebuilt Their Lives: France, the United States and Israel.* Bloomington: Indiana University Press, 2018.

Patterson, David. "Death and Ghetto Death." In *Life in the Ghettos during the Holocaust,* edited by Eric J. Sterling, 160–176. Syracuse, NY: Syracuse University Press, 2005.

Petrovsky-Shtern, Yohanan, and Antony Polonsky, eds. *Polin: Studies in Polish Jewry,* vol. 26: *Jews and Ukrainians.* Oxford: Littman, 2014.

Podolsky, Anatoly. "Collaboration in Ukraine during the Holocaust: Aspects of Historiography and Research." Paper presented at the conference "The Holocaust in Ukraine: New Sources and Perspectives," Center for Advanced Holocaust Studies, United States Holocaust Memorial Museum, 2013. www.ushmm.org/m/pdfs/20130500-holocaust-in-ukraine.pdf.

Polonsky, Antony, and Joanna B. Michlic, eds. *The Neighbors Respond: The Controversy over the Jedwabne Massacre in Poland*. Princeton, NJ: Princeton University Press, 2004.

Porat, Dina. *Nakam: The Holocaust Survivors Who Sought Full-Scale Revenge*. Translated by Mark L. Levinson. Stanford: Stanford University Press, 2023.

Redlich, Shimon. *Life in Transit: Jews in Postwar Lodz, 1945–1950*. Boston: Academic Studies Press, 2010.

Ringelblum, Emmanuel. *Polish-Jewish Relations during the Second World War*. Translated by Dafna Allon, Danuta Dabrowska, and Dana Keren. Evanston, IL: Northwestern University Press, 1992.

Rochelson, Meri-Jane. *Eli's Story: A Twentieth-Century Jewish Life*. Detroit, MI: Wayne State University Press, 2018.

"Rohatyn." In *Pinkas Hakehillot Polin* [Encyclopedia of Jewish communities, Poland], vol. 2, 506–510. Jerusalem: Yad Vashem, n.d. https://www.jewishgen.org/yizkor/pinkas_poland/pol2_00506.html#:~:text=%E2%80%9CRohatyn%E2%80%9D%20%2D%20Encyclopedia%20of,MM.YYYYReturn.

"The Shoah in Rohatyn." Rohatyn Jewish Heritage. https://rohatynjewishheritage.org/en/history/timeline-shoah/.

Rosensaft, Menachem Z. ed. *God, Faith & Identity from the Ashes: Reflections of Children and Grandchildren of Holocaust Survivors*. Woodstock, VT: Jewish Lights, 2015.

Rudnicki, Szymon. "Economic Struggle or Antisemitism?" In *Polin: Studies in Polish Jewry*, vol. 30: *Jewish Education in Eastern Europe*, edited by Eliyana R. Adler and Antony Polonsky, 397–406. Oxford: Littman, 2018.

Samelson, William. "Piotrków Trybunalski: *My Ancestral Home*." In *Life in the Ghettos during the Holocaust*, edited by Eric J. Sterling, 1–16. Syracuse, NY: Syracuse University Press, 2005.

Snyder, Timothy. "Biographical Essay of Jan Karski." In Jan Karski, *Story of a Secret State: My Report to the World*, xxv–xxxi. Washington: Georgetown University Press, 2013.

———. *Black Earth: The Holocaust as Warning and History*. New York: Crown, 2015.

———. *Bloodlands: Europe Between Hitler and Stalin*. New York: Basic Books, 2010.

Stola, Dariusz. "Jewish Emigration from Communist Poland: The Decline of Polish Jewry in the Aftermath of the Holocaust." *East European Jewish Affairs* 47, nos. 2–3 (May 2017): 169–188.

Trentmann, Frank. *Out of the Darkness: The Germans 1942–2022*. New York: Knopf, 2024.

Trunk, Isaiah. *Judenrat: The Jewish Councils in Eastern Europe under Nazi Occupation*. Lincoln: University of Nebraska Press, 1996.

Unger, Michal, ed. *In Those Terrible Days: Writings from the Lodz Ghetto*. Translated by Naftali Greenwood. Jerusalem: Yad Vashem Publications, 2003.

Veidlinger, Jeffrey. *In the Midst of Civilized Europe: The Pogroms of 1918–1921 and the Onset of the Holocaust.* New York: Metropolitan Books, 2021.

Vital, David. *A People Apart: The Jews in Europe, 1789–1939.* Oxford: Oxford University Press, 1999.

"Luts'k." In *The YIVO Encyclopedia of Jews in Eastern Europe.* https://yivoencyclopedia.org/article.aspx/lutsk.

Zimmerman, Joshua D. *Jozef Pilsudski: Founding Father of Modern Poland.* Cambridge, MA: Harvard University Press, 2022.

Zubrzycki, Genevieve. *Resurrecting the Jew: Nationalism, Philosemitism, and Poland's Jewish Revival.* Princeton, NJ: Princeton University Press, 2022.

Index

A

Africa, 122
Allies, 41, 121
Alte Shul (Podhajce), 39
Amarant, Shlomo, 65–66, 69
Amidah, 33
Anielewicz, Mordechai, 197
Anschluss, 268
Anton, farmer, 122–23
Appelfeld, Aharon, 184
Arbeitsamt, 65
Archangelsk, 199
Arctic Circle, 172, 199
Armia Krajowa, 141, 256
Arnold (Arnoldek), classmate, 82–83
Auschwitz, 3, 5, 6, 12, 16, 48, 56, 84, 96–97, 102, 191–93, 195, 197–98, 218, 227, 231, 237, 240, 242, 248, 252–53, 255, 266–69, 273
Australia, 162, 224, 260
Austria, 28, 275
Austria-Hungary, 10, 237
Aviel, Abraham, 264

B

Babyn Yar (Babi Yar), 16, 264
Babylon, 26
Baltic Sea, 45, 206
Bandera, Stepan, 140–41, 190, 258
Banderites, 140–41, 152, 185, 187, 190, 258
Barron, Shmulek, 105-106, 119-120
Będzin, 171, 249, 255, 266
Belarus (Belorussia), 183, 249, 264
Belgium, 2, 116
Bełżec, 96–97, 102, 131, 150–51, 154, 252–54, 260–61
Bereza Kartuska camp, 43, 52
Berlin, 83, 149, 207, 227, 247, 253
Berliner, Meir, 253
Białystok, 42, 63–64, 102, 255
Bible, 123, 149
Blech, Cyla, 51, 63, 96, 247, 249
Blechs, 84, 249, 251, 256–57

Bloch, Willie, 70, 81, 83, 119, 149, 250
Blochs, 104
Blum, Leon, 240
Blum, Wilhelm, 270
Bochnia ghetto, 116
Bolsheviks, 55, 58–59, 141, 205, 241–43, 258
Bolshevism, 48, 243–44
Bolshowce, 85, 100
Boris, Judge, 148
Borki Wielki labor camp, 77, 251
Braite Shul (Podhajce), 39
Brandeis, Mr., 85, 87
Bremerhaven, 206
Bricha organization, 206
Brody, 255
Bronx, 217, 223, 226
Brzeżany, 44, 62, 104, 125, 258
Buchenwald, 193
Buczacz, 104, 115, 247–48, 250
Bukaczowce, 85, 100, 253
Burstiner Rebbe, 23
Bursztyn, 10, 12, 85, 87, 100, 251

C

Canada, 2, 13, 224
Catholic Church, 47–48, 56–57, 209–210, 222, 228, 241, 244–45, 248, 256, 265–66, 272–73
Catholicism, 48, 210, 273
Catholics, 2, 48, 222, 241
Caucasian republics, 200
Chełm, 73, 171, 250
Chełmno, 115, 191, 252
Chevra Kedisha, 108
Chmielnik, 249
Christianity, 37, 44
Christians, 247, 261, 266
Cieszanów labor camp, 196, 269
Communism, 44, 55, 190, 206, 242–44, 275
Communists, 43, 49–50, 54–55, 141, 173, 243–44, 247, 263
Cossacks, 35, 40, 59
Coughlin, Father Charles, 244

286 | The Pessimist's Son

Cuba, 113, 153
Czechoslovakia, 45, 169, 206, 226
Czerniakow, Adam, 267
Częstochowa, 206, 249

D

Dąbrowa Tarnowska County, 139, 265
Dachau, 198
Dmowski, Roman, 48, 241
Donbas, 147, 150, 152
Drohobycz, 62, 115, 203, 258, 261, 263
Dulcza forest, 265

E

Egypt, 69
Eiger, Yishaye, 267, 269
Einsatzgruppen, 62, 64, 77, 80, 84, 171, 246, 248–49, 251, 262
El Alammein, 135
Endecja, 47–48, 241–42
Engelberg, Mieczysław, 161, 190–92, 210, 273
England, 44, 116, 127
Erde, Moses, 52
Estonia, 259
Ethiopia, 44

F

Fascism, 3, 43, 44, 84, 154
Feldberg, Leah, 54, 260
Feldman, Yaakov, 253
Fidler, Mark, 73
Fink, Lonek, 52
Finks, 51
Finland, 246
Flossenburg labor camp, 198
Ford, Henry, 243
France, 2, 44, 116, 158, 193, 224, 240, 255, 267–68
Frank, Hans, 66, 72, 248–50

G

Galicia, 25, 61–62, 141, 175, 238–39, 243, 246–47, 249, 258, 264–65
Gestapo, 64, 67, 84, 101, 111, 115, 127, 130, 151, 248, 253, 260, 267
Gitterman, Yosef, 185, 264–66
Glinice District, 196, 269
Globocnik, Odilo, 252, 269

Glotzer, Jack, 11, 140, 183, 189, 247, 249, 251, 253, 258–59, 265–66, 273
Gnila Lipa river, 69
Goebbels, Joseph, 135, 138, 191
Gogol, Nikolai, 239
Goldstein, Azriel, 198
Goldstein, Henri, 158, 193, 198, 255
Goldstein, Moshe, 197,
Goldstein, Philip, 5, 164, 172, 196–99, 203, 206–7, 268–70
Goldstein, Yechiel (Chilek), 9, 54, 164, 172, 196–97, 199–200, 206–7, 270
Gomułka, Władyłsaw, 213, 215
Gomułka Aliyah, 5, 213
Goralniks, 113, 221, 254
Gurfinkel, Asher, 175, 263

H

Haber, Shoshana, 150–51, 260
Hakman, Batya, 242, 263
Haley, Alex, 2
Hanukkah, 40
Hashomer Hatzair movement, 197
Hasidism, 218, 238
Haskalah, 238
Hecht, Ania, 87, 103–4, 107, 110, 149, 253
Hecht, Aviva, baby, 108, 110, 149
Hecht, Chaja, 94–95, 104, 107–9, 111.
Hecht, Shmuel (Shmulek), 84–85, 87–88, 94, 103–9, 111, 119–20, 128
Hermann, 111, 115
Heydrich, Reinhard, 246, 249
Himmler, Heinrich, 64, 77, 246, 251, 255, 269
Hitler, Adolf, 2, 40–41, 43, 45, 49, 55, 58, 77, 113, 122, 141, 169, 205, 225, 240–43, 250–51, 259, 264
Hlond, Cardinal August, 244
Hochberg, Fruma, 73
Holland, 116
Holon, 214
Hudish, Dr., 107–8, 149
Hungary, 114, 116, 226, 246

I

Isonzo river, 136, 257
Israel, 2, 5, 10, 13, 56, 123, 149, 160–61, 175, 206, 213–15, 217, 222, 224, 227, 275
Israel, The People of, 37–38, 66,

Index | 287

Italy, 44, 84, 136, 246, 257
Ivano-Frankivsk (Stanisławów), 245

J
Jabłonna, 56
Janowska labor camp, 77, 116, 251, 254
Jaruzelski, Wojciech, 226
Jedwabne, , 64, 244, 248
John Paul II (Karol Wojtyła), Pope, 48, 206, 241, 243, 272
Judaism, 3, 12–13, 35, 38, 218, 227, 259
Judeo-Bolshevism (Judeo-Communism), 55–56, 213, 241
Jupiter, 26, 149, 235, 253
Jupiter, Mottel Mechel, 149, 235, 253

K
Kaddish, 82–83, 101, 109
Kahan, Lazar, 73, 250
Kampinos, 266
Karski, Jan, 55, 243, 262
Katowice, 252
Katyn, 52, 138, 242, 258
Kaunas (Kovno), 115, 253, 259
Kessler, Edmund, 246–47, 251, 258
Khmelnytskyi, Bogdan, 35, 40–41, 59, 258, 268
Khmelnytskyi, (Proskuriv), 59, 246, 268
Kiddush Hashem, 40, 218, 259
Kielce, 47, 153, 204–7, 239–40, 264, 269–70, 272–73
Koenigsberg, Cesia, 134
Koenigsberg, Janina, 134
Koenigsberg, Mr. and Mrs., 133-135, 138-140
Koenigsberg, Ursula, 134
Kolbe, Father Maximillian, 44, 48
Kolomyja, 62, 107, 115, 125, 254
Konev, Marshal Ivan, 138
Korkush (Korkushes), 187
Kovpak, Sydir, 124, 185, 256, 265
Kraków (Crakow), 78, 204–5, 227–28, 265, 270, 272
Kazimierz District, 227, 258
Krasnik, 196
Kresy, 265
Kruk, Herman, 253
Kubina, Teodor, 206
Kursk, 135

Kyiv, 90, 201, 250, 264, 272
Kyrgyzstan, 200

L
Lativia, 259
Latvians, 55, 64, 192, 252, 263
Lederman, Sylvia, 11, 115, 247, 254
Legnica, 153, 159–60, 163, 192, 209–210, 213, 217, 222, 227–28, 267
Lehrer, Chaim, 36, 72, 149
Lehrer (Fogel), Regina, 235, 245
Lehrer, Roncia, 30, 149, 176, 235, 260
Lehrer, Zysio, 57, 235, 245
Levatshes, 184
Lithuania, 115, 172, 183, 253, 259, 271
Lithuanians, 55, 64, 192, 252, 263
Łódź, 115, 190–93, 196, 201, 209, 214, 237, 250, 252–53, 266–68
Lohnert, Heinz, 178–79
London, 55
LOPP, 46
Łopuszna, 125, 133, 140, 149, 184, 259
Lubavitcher Hasidic movement, 218
Lublin, 97, 196, 206, 252–53, 261, 269
Łuck, 172–73, 175, 201, 262
Ludwipol (Sosnove), 5, 11–12, 150, 175–77, 179, 183–84, 187, 189–90, 195, 214, 242, 260, 263–65
Lustig, Chana, 89, 99–100, 121, 149
Lustigs, 84–85, 120
Lwów (Lviv), 10, 24, 47, 62, 77, 113, 115–16, 175, 196, 199, 247, 251, 258, 272

M
Madagascar, 45, 240
Majdanek, 16
Manhattan, 217, 223
Marx, Karl, 55
Mechele the *Stolar*, 114, 222
Meir, Reb, 44, 50, 125, 149
Meir Shapse, 32, 44
Meir the *Balagule*, 113, 121–22,
Mendelovich, Israel, 264
Merin, Moshe, 266–67
Messing, Genia, 247
Mikulince, 12, 71, 73, 152, 245, 250
Milch, Adolph Abraham, 156, 162, 235, 238, 245, 250, 260

Milch (Lehrer), Ethel, 30, 57, 71, 73, 152, 156, 245, 260
Milch, Leon-Leib, 245
Milch (Lehrer), Roncia, 30, 149, 176, 260
Minsk, 55
Mochulyanka, 184, 189
Molotov-Ribbentrop line, 97, 154, 242
Morgenthau, Henry, 47–48
Munich, 206

N
Nachum, Reb, 93, 114, 260
Najnudel, Eliezer (Lejzor, Lazer), 169
Najnudel, Motek, 183, 186, 189, 205, 265
Najnudel, Natan, 12, 156, 169, 171, 175, 179, 181, 192, 201, 235, 264
Najnundel (Goldstein), Fala, 2, 156, 161, 169–70, 175, 179, 183, 185–86, 190–93, 201, 205, 210, 214, 217, 222, 226–27, 265
Najnundel, Sabina, 171, 197, 235, 271
Narutowicz, Gabriel, 241
New Jersey, 1, 206
NKVD, 53, 59, 61–62, 124, 140, 148–49, 173, 189–90, 242–43, 246, 256, 262, 271
Noah, 149
Nuremberg trials, 250
Nusen the *Melamed*, 25–26

O
Odesa, 201
Old Testament, 273
Operation Barbarossa, 62, 124, 141, 246
Operation Reinhard, 96, 197, 252–53, 269
Orel, 135
Orenstein, Moshe and family, 29, 93–94, 152, 252, 261
Osh, 200
Ostrowiec (Ostrowiec Świętokrzyski), 64, 67, 169, 192–93, 203–4, 206, 249, 256, 267
Oświęciem, 248, 262
OUN (Organization of Ukranian Nationalists), 140–41

P
Paderewski, Ignacy, 244
Palestine, 116, 198, 200–201, 206, 241
Paris, 25, 59, 193, 227, 267
Parnussy, 29

Parnuvke, 131
Passover, 39, 197, 229
Petliura, Symon, 58–59, 247, 258–59, 268
Piłsudski, Marshal Josef, 43, 47, 56, 238–41, 244
Pinsk, 55, 244
Pirkei Avot, 36
Płaszów, 78
Potsdam, 267
Poznań, 196, 273
Przemyśl, 122, 171
Przemyślany, 63, 125
Przytyk, 43, 239–40
Purim, 40, 50
Pushteig, Nachum, 150–51, 260
Putin, Vladimir, 237

R
Raber (Raver), Yehuda, 150, 180–81, 189, 242, 260, 263–66
Radom, 5, 11–12, 73, 115–16, 169–72, 175–76, 192–93, 195–99, 201, 203, 206, 209, 238–40, 243, 249–50, 254, 256, 262, 267–73
Radun, 264
Radziłów, 64
Rasch, Otto, 77, 251
Red Army, 3, 47, 49, 54, 56–57, 59, 97, 124, 128, 140, 176, 189, 191, 199, 242, 259, 262, 265, 270–71
Reder, Rudolf, 96
Ringelblum, Emmanuel, 42, 56, 205, 239–40, 242, 245, 250, 253, 256, 259, 265–66, 268, 272
Rokossovsky, Marshal Konstantin, 138
Roma, 191, 206, 236
Romania, 122, 240, 244, 246
Romanians, 271
Romanov dynasty, 58
Roosevelt, Franklin D., 122
Rosen, Naftali, 85, 87–89, 121–22, 252
Rosenberg, Alfred, 240
Rosh Hashanah, 39, 209, 217, 253
Roth, Visha, 67
Rubler, Elke, 100, 120, 149, 235
Rubler (Jupiter), Libby, 100, 149, 235
Rumkowski, Chaim, 191, 266
Russia, 28, 45, 49–51, 61, 140, 148, 172, 183, 237, 248
Russian Duma, 47

Russian Empire, 58, 172
Rzeszów, 204

S

Sabbath, 25, 30–31, 38
Sambor, 62, 67
Samson, 123
Sarny, 256, 264
Schneerson, Rabbi Menachem, 218
Schodnica, 203
Schourz, Henia, 34, 260–61
Schwartzbard, Sholom, 59, 62
Schwarz family, 67
Schweizer, Nusia, 250
Sefer Ostrovtsah, 67, 193, 203, 249
Semelke, 27
Sevastopol, 257
Shabbatai Tzvi, 57
Shabse Zwinkes, 57
Shapse, Meir, 32
Shemesh, Yossef, 180, 265
Shlein, Khaim, 180
Shloyme the *Balagule*, 32–33
Shourz, Henia, 151–52, 238, 260–61
Shtokfish, David, 240
Siberia, 6, 51–52, 54, 57, 139–40, 172, 190, 199, 221, 239, 262
Sikorska (Najnundel), Regina, 2, 57, 159, 161, 171–72, 177, 179, 183, 185, 190, 192, 201, 205, 213, 222, 228, 235, 245–46, 265
Silesia, 198, 213, 252, 261, 266–67
Simchat Torah, 40
Sinai War, 214
Singer, Isaac Bashevis, 218, 272
Sinti, 191
Six-Day War, 16, 222, 274
Skalat labor camp, 75-77, 124, 185, 251, 256, 264
Składkowski, Sławoj, 44, 47
Slovenia, 257
Słucz river, 176, 179, 184
Sobibór, 42, 96, 102, 154, 253, 260–61
Sosnowiec, 255, 266
Spain, 246
Spinoza, Baruch, 87
SS, 63–64, 67, 77, 96–97, 115, 171, 181, 191, 195–98, 248–49, 269–70
Stalin, Joseph, 49–53, 61, 122, 138, 140, 153, 210, 213, 242, 259, 267

Stalingrad, 104, 122, 253–54
Stalinists, 274
Stara Huta, 190
Starachowice, 97, 253
Stein, Edith, 48
Stein, Salek, 84
Steinman, Buchek, 236
Steinman, Lutka, 171, 173, 201, 262
Steinman, Mietek, 201, 206
Steinman (Najnundel), Sabina, 235
Sterzer, Abraham, 84, 101, 131, 247, 251, 253–54, 260
Stockholm, 153
Stryj, 62
Strzelnica labor camp, 116
Stuttgart, 199, 203, 206, 271
   DP camp, 203, 206
Styr, river, 172
Subotniks, 261
Suez Crisis, 214
Sukkoth, 40
Sweden, 153
Sydney, 162
Szczecin, 206-7

T

Talmud, 26, 93, 175
Tarnopol, 62–63, 67, 97, 101, 104, 127, 138, 152–53, 247, 249–50, 259, 262
Teaneck, 1, 217, 222
Teicher, Shlomo, 77, 251
Tel Aviv, 214, 238, 240, 242, 249, 251
Thorne, Rabbi Leon, 67, 77, 102, 203–5, 218, 224, 249, 251, 253–54, 261, 263, 272, 274–75
Tish'a B'av, 40
Tobruk, 135
Tomaszów, 273
Torah, 31–32, 36–40, 46, 101, 114, 239, 248, 257
Tory, Avraham, 253
Totalitarian, 272
Trawniki, 97, 252
Treblinka, 42, 96, 102, 154, 193, 197–98, 253, 260, 269–70
Treiber, David, 113
Trief, Oscar ("Sunio"), 9, 152, 157, 229
Truskawiec, 30
Tunis the Matchmaker, 27
Turkish Ottoman Army, 35

290 | The Pessimist's Son

Turzysk, 255
Tyrol mountains, 136

U
United Kingdom, 80, 255, 267
United States of America (USA), 2, 5, 13, 17–18, 77, 116, 127, 153, 206, 213, 215, 217, 222–26, 228, 239–40, 243–44, 246, 250, 255, 262–64, 267–68, 274–75
Uzbekistan, 200

V
Vayngort, Yakov, 203, 271
Vienna, 111, 206, 222
Vilna (Vilnius, Wilno), 55, 253
Vinnytsia, 90
Vitebsk, 135
Vlaska, Janina, 201
Volhynia, 172, 175, 184, 246–47, 255–56, 263, 265
Volman, Mordechai, 181, 263–64, 266

W
Waffen-SS, 246, 258
Wannsee Conference, 80
Warsaw, 16, 42, 56, 67, 102, 121, 127, 169–70, 191–92, 197, 214, 227–28, 239–40, 242–43, 250, 253, 255–56, 262, 267–70
Warthegau, 252
Wehrmacht, 81, 90, 140–41, 198, 248–49
Weinwurzel (Najnudel), Chaja, 192–93, 201, 203, 206
Weinwurzel (Singer), Saba, 192, 267, 272
Weinwurzel (Menk), Sarah, 192, 206
Weinwurzel, Shmuel (Shmulek), 192, 206, 229
Weisbraun, Meir, 66, 89, 127
Weiss, Leon, 24, 152,

Wieliczka, 78, 115, 228
Wierzbnik, 199, 268, 271
Wiesel, Elie, 274
Wilczek, Jeremiah, 253
Wilson, Thomas Woodrow, 47
Wisniowczyk, 47
Wohl, Tsvi, 67, 249, 251
World War I, 28, 45, 65, 135, 243, 257
Wrocław (Breslau), 12, 153–54, 205, 210, 226, 228, 261, 267
Wyszyński, Cardinal Stefan, 206, 272

X
Xenia, neighbor, 109–110, 149

Y
Yad Vashem, 56, 149, 245, 253,
Yom Kippur, 39–40, 50, 93–94, 97, 150, 252–53
Yugoslavia, 116

Z
Zahajce, 151
Zamość, 169
Zaolzie, 45
Zawada, 169, 171–72, 177
Żegota, 56, 245
Zeidman, Hillel, 77, 264
Zelkowicz, Josef, 250
Zhukov, Marshal Georgy, 138
Zilber (Silber), Israel, 152
Zionism, 175, 238
Zionists, 275
Złoczów, 246
ZOB, 255
Zomo, 227
Zukerman, Abe, 199, 271

About the Authors

Alexander Kimel was born in Podhajce, Poland (now Pidhaitsi, Ukraine), in 1926. After the war, he earned a Bachelor's and Master's degrees in electrical engineering at the Wrocław Polytechnic University in Poland. In the United States, he started and ran a consulting engineering firm. Poems from his award-winning website on the Holocaust have been used in schools, universities, and exhibits, widely reprinted, and recited on YouTube. He also contributed a chapter to Eric J. Sterling, ed., *Life in the Ghettos During the Holocaust* (Syracuse University Press, 2005). He was married for over fifty years to his beloved wife, Eva. He died in 2018.

Martin Kimel, the son of Alexander and Eva Kimel, is a graduate of the University of Pennsylvania and Stanford Law School. He is a securities lawyer in Washington, D.C., and lives in Maryland. He has written on the Holocaust and other topics for the *Washington Post*, the *Los Angeles Times*, the *Baltimore Sun*, the *Wall Street Journal*, the *Times of Israel*, the *Forward*, the *Chicago Tribune*, and many other publications.

www.ingramcontent.com/pod-product-compliance
Lightning Source LLC
Jackson TN
JSHW010159210525
84795JS00011B/32